The end of anthropology?

First published in 2011
Paperback edition published in 2013
**Sean Kingston Publishing**
www.seankingston.co.uk
Canon Pyon

British Library Cataloguing in Publication Data
A catalogue record for this book is available from the British Library.

The moral rights of the authors have been asserted.

Printed by Lightning Source

ISBN 978-1-907774-28-7

# THE END OF ANTHROPOLOGY?

EDITED BY HOLGER JEBENS & KARL-HEINZ KOHL

SK Publishing

**Sean Kingston Publishing**
www.seankingston.co.uk
Canon Pyon

# Contents

# INTRODUCTION[*]

## Karl-Heinz Kohl

My first encounter with peoples who at the time were regarded as the classical 'object' of anthropological studies dates back more than thirty years. It was in 1975 when my later wife and I landed on the airstrip of Wamena, the major settlement of the Baliem valley in the part of the highlands of New Guinea under Indonesian control. When we disembarked from our airplane, an old and rusty DC 3 from the time of the Second World War, we saw ourselves surrounded by a group of Dani men their hair greased with pig fat and strings of white cowry shells about around their necks, and wearing nothing but long yellow gourds to hide their genitals. They stared at us no less curiously than we were about them. The contrast could not have been sharper: modern Western technology on the one hand, and almost completely naked human beings on the other. A few years earlier, not more than a hundred miles from the Baliem valley, the Eipomek a population of approximately 600 people who lived in their valley without having had any contact with so-called white civilisation had been 'discovered' by a missionary air patrol. One week previously in Jayapura, the one-time capital of the former colony of Dutch New Guinea, we had met a German cameraman who was a member of a research team of more than thirty geographers, botanists, medical scientists, human ethologists, linguists, and, of course, also a number of anthropologists, who had settled down among the Eipomek to study them and their natural habitat with all their scientific toolkits, a horrible sight when looked at from the vantage point of our present-day ethical concerns. However, this may have been one of the last research endeavours of its kind. Today, at least, there is no spot on the globe where a population may still be found living in such complete isolation from all the influences of global culture as the Eipomek did at that time.

Since then the autochthonous populations of the West New Guinea highlands have been subject to considerable changes. The Indonesian government, which has only been occupying this part of the former Dutch East Indies since 1963, has done its best to 'civilise' them. Schools have been built in the remotest corners of their territories to teach them the language of their new nation. The *transmigrasi*

---

[*]     The contributions by John Comaroff, Andr Gingrich and Ulf Hannerz, referred to in this intro-
        duction, were first published in *American Anthropologist* 112(4): 524–562 (2010). I wish to thank
        Katja Rieck for her editorial assistance in the preparation of this volume.

programme of the Indonesian government has enticed settlers from Java, Bali and Sumatra into the fertile fields of the New Guinea highlands. The resistance with which some Dani and other ethnic groups have opposed this kind of interior colonisation, especially after the neighbouring former Trust Territory of Papua and New Guinea had become an independent state, was suppressed with crude violence. The Javanese policemen persecuted those who still went naked in the larger settlements and put them into detention camps. Along the same policy lines, they did everything to abolish the big pig feasts and other traditional ceremonies that Indonesian government officials regarded as an obstacle to economic progress. Nevertheless, if I had the opportunity to revisit the Baliem valley today, the first visual impression might well be much the same as it was when I first went there. Of course, Wamena is now a flourishing town with more than 12,000 inhabitants, government houses, restaurants and hotels. But the Dani men who welcome the foreigners at the large airport that has replaced the old small landing strip still look much the same having freed themselves from trousers and T-shirts to dress again in their yellow penis gourds and traditional body ornaments. And now the policemen no longer intervene. The tourist industry has become an important source of income to the Baliem valley's inhabitants, to both the 'natives' and the newcomers from Java. Tourists want to see the exotic, and the government officials have to abide by their wishes. I doubt that even the new anti-pornography law, which was passed by the Indonesian parliament in October 2008 and aims to suppress the 'indecent' habit of 'going naked' in some of the country's remote regions, will be able to force the 'natives' back into pants and shirts. Commercial interests are stronger than Muslim lawmakers in the Indonesian capital, some 2,500 miles away from West New Guinea. For revitalising old customs, tourism seems to be the best possible ally. Yet to revitalise something suggests that it must have died previously. While the visible surface may be the same, in being reinstated, the traditional dress has altered its meaning. The nakedness of these alleged primitives has become an attraction for tourists. Contemporary Dani have become citations, disguising themselves as what they supposedly once were.

Talk of the decline of the classical object of anthropological studies is nothing new. Holger Jebens has put together an impressive list of quotations from leading representatives of the discipline, such as Bronislaw Malinowski, Margaret Mead and Claude Lévi-Strauss, who were haunted by the notion that the last 'primitive peoples' were dying out right in front of their eyes. This nightmare is in fact older than academic anthropology itself. A similar statement can be found in the work of one of its most important predecessors, the Jesuit Pater Joseph François Lafitau, who between 1712 and 1717 spent almost five years among the Mohawk in the former French colony of Nouvelle France. As he wrote in the introduction to his "Mœurs des sauvages amériquains, comparées aux mœurs des premiers temps" (1724), through their contact with Europeans they had lost so many of their old habits and customs that he decided to describe them as they should have been from the time of their ancestors and as they were before all these changes took place (Lafitau 1724:25f.). When, therefore, more than a century and a half later, Adolf Bastian, the founding father of German anthropology, spoke of the 'conflagration of civilisation' which would wipe out the last 'primitive peoples' still existing on our planet, it was merely an echo of these and other complaints. As Jebens and Mark Münzel remark, anthropologists often tend to identify with the supposed fate of the object of their research.

Probably the first member of this 'tribe in decline' (Münzel) who used the title "The end of anthropology?" to express his fears about the future of the discipline was Peter Worsley. In a paper he prepared for the Sociology and Anthropology Working Group of the Sixth World Congress of Sociology in 1966, he expressed his conviction that anthropologists had to cede their field of study to political scientists, economists and sociologists because the small-scale societies that had been the mainstay of classical ethnographic research were disappearing almost everywhere (Worsley 1970). Only as these societies' historians would anthropologists be able to survive. Underlying this pessimistic view was the notion that with the political independence of the former colonies anthropology had not only lost its *raison d'être*, it would also fade away with the rapid integration of small and economically backward local societies into flourishing new nations. Yet, Worsley, like many other anthropologists of his time, underestimated the agency of these societies and the resilience they have shown in the face of changing historical conditions. According to the holistic anthropological view at that time, these societies' 'traditional' cultures were adapted to their natural habitat to such a degree that intensification of contact with the outside world would make them tumble down like a house of cards. Tradition and modernity seemed to stand in an insurmountable opposition to one another. There was no alternative: becoming modernised would invariably mean that they had to abandon all their former means of production, social structures, values, norms, practices and beliefs. In fact, of course, the societies to which anthropology has traditionally dedicated itself were generally anything but fossilised isolates. They proved to be astonishingly flexible, retaining what they thought to be indispensable, and appropriating what they thought useful. In fact, as the example of the Dani of the Baliem valley shows, these same societies survived not only the age of decolonisation. Today, in much the same vein, they are facing and adapting to the challenges of globalisation, and they have proved no less adept at using modern means of communication than the researchers who study them, while at the same time retaining central aspects of their cultural traditions.

The current crisis in anthropology thus has little to do with its object of study, which has always been engaged in processes of change, but rather with the discipline itself. Following the so-called 'writing culture debate', anthropology's customary approaches and forms of representation have been subjected to a trenchant critique that destabilised the field's very foundations. What we have come to refer to as 'othering' today is viewed as the field's great fall from grace. With their critiques of their predecessors' authoritative styles, today's anthropologists have also undermined their own authority. The post-colonial debate has contributed further to anthropology's disempowerment. The view from outside has given way to the view from within, as the 'natives' now raise their own voices to express 'the native's point of view'. At the same time, cultural studies is outstripping anthropology, while sociology, political science and globalisation theory are encroaching upon its classical domains. Under such circumstances, what is the point of continuing with the anthropological project? Have we finally reached the end of anthropology? Has its world – as Clifford Geertz suggested in the title of one of his last essays – finally fallen to pieces (Geertz 2000)? Or is the dissolution of its classical fields of study opening up new domains, in which its classical methods can once again prove their worth?

These were some of the provocative questions asked in the letter we sent to a number of anthropologists to invite them to the 2008 Jensen Memorial Lectures at the Frankfurt Frobenius Institute, entitled "The end of anthropology?" All of them have, during the last three decades, contributed substantially to the development of anthropology in their homelands anthropologies, whether they have been teaching at Austrian, British, Dutch, French, German, Italian, North American, Norwegian, South African or Swedish universities. And most of them, too, are regarded today as internationally leading representatives of the discipline. Our letter met with a surprisingly good response. Only one of the anthropologists whom we asked to read a paper turned down our invitation. And as the contributions to this collection show, there was nobody who did not take our questions seriously as a point of departure for reflecting on the current state of the discipline.

Adam Kuper and Patricia Spyer provide their responses via a detour through their own on-going research. According to Kuper, classical anthropology was always based on a fiction: the notion of the 'primitive society' opposed to and defined by the self-image of 'progressive' industrial societies of the West. Yet, in fact, what has always been regarded as a distinguishing feature of small-scale societies, i.e., a kinship-based social organisation, played a no less important role in nineteenth-century British industrial society. Using the categories developed in one of anthropology's most prominent sub-fields, Kuper shows how widespread first cousin marriage was among the English upper- and middle-classes as a means of creating effective social and economic networks. Paradoxically, this social strategy used by the British royal family, the Rothschild dynasty, the Darwins and the Wedgwoods, began to wane in Europe just as evolutionist anthropologists were incorporating cousin marriage into the contemporary image of 'primitive society'. Although classical anthropology may have been based on 'figments of Western imagination' (Kuper), it provided us with concepts and tools that enable us to gain new insights if applied to our own society.

By taking some examples from her recent ethnographic fieldwork in the North Moluccas, Spyer shows how the long debate on 'othering' has missed its point.

Under the fragmented, globalising conditions of today's world, 'otherness' often rests hidden beneath the surface of the seemingly familiar. Instead of explaining it away, as anthropologists have usually done, they should 'take seriously that which one cannot accept'. Given such a stance, which consists of 'listening to' rather than aiming at an immediate understanding, subduing and taming of the Other, anthropologists possess a kind of openness that transforms each ethnographic encounter into a personal engagement and enables them to make truly new discoveries that often remain beyond the purview of other disciplines.

The relationship of anthropology to its neighbouring disciplines is a topic that is intensively discussed or at least touched on in almost all the contributions. What sociology, political science and development studies were to anthropology at beginning of the late 1960s, post-colonial studies, cultural studies and literary criticism have become to the discipline since the last decade of the twentieth century. Edward Said sparked the confrontation with his seminal work "Orientalism", which, although it was not directed against anthropology, strongly influenced the discipline and triggered a process of self-reflection that led to the writing culture debate of the 1980s and early 1990s. This was undoubtedly a very important movement that allowed its practitioners to free themselves from the naïve empiricism of their predecessors. When George Marcus, Dick Cushman, James Clifford and Michael Fischer published their attacks on 'ethnographic realism' and demanded new 'experimental forms of representation', anthropology's grand theories found themselves in a state of decline. Yet the hope for new theoretical paradigms that would help the discipline overcome this vacuum ultimately proved to be in vain. In anthropology and in its neighbouring disciplines too, postmodernism and deconstructivism replaced the old master-narratives. Referring to Jacques Derrida, Michel Foucault, Jean-François Lyotard or Edward Said in the introductory chapters of anthropological treatises became as fashionable as a generation earlier it had been to quote Karl Marx and Sigmund Freud. They were the new mandarins to whom anthropology, too, had to kowtow. The 'writing culture movement' lingered on for almost two decades. And it had disastrous side-effects. The discipline's self-criticism, justified though it may have been with regard to its past, paralysed the production of first-hand anthropological knowledge. Ethnographers became so intimidated by their own hidden prejudices that nothing seemed more difficult than writing down a simple ethnographic sentence. The critique from within was complemented by the critique from without, often from self-appointed spokespersons of the 'natives' as well as from representatives of the emerging post-colonial and subaltern studies. One early example is the fervent discussion on the 'invention of tradition' that broke out among Pacific historians and anthropologists in the late 1980s, which culminated in the fierce attack by the Hawaiian political activist Haunani-Kay Trask, who stated that, 'for Hawaii, anthropologists in general [...] are part of a colonising horde because they take away from us the power to define who and what we are, and how we should behave politically and culturally' (1991:162). But this was only a prelude to what was to come. In any event, the legitimacy of outsiders' anthropological investigations was seriously put into question.

Especially in the states that had grown out of former British settler colonies such as Australia, Canada, New Zealand and the United States, ethnic groups declared their reservations and territories to be off-limits to those professional anthropologists who were reluctant to share their hosts' views of their own cultural heritage. The native authorities granted permissions for research only to those ethnographers who committed themselves to handing over the products of their research before publishing their results. Professional associations adopted ethical codes that complied with these and other legitimate demands of the ethnographers' hosts. There is no reason to complain about this development, especially if one takes into account how thoughtlessly, not to say ruthlessly, anthropologists once behaved in respect of the interests of the people from whom they had gained their knowledge. Current research must bear the consequences of past sins. Working among the autochthonous minority populations of the former settler states therefore became complicated, indeed sometimes extremely difficult even for anthropologists who belonged to the majority society. Some of these ethnic groups produced their own well-educated anthropologists, who took on the task of maintaining the cultural legacies of their ancestors. But in the former so-called third-world countries, too, ethnographic research ceased to be a privilege of its 'white' practitioners, who today have to compete with local anthropologists as well trained in the discipline's methods and theories as themselves. But is anthropology 'at home' really the same as classical anthropology? Of course, native anthropologists have the big advantage of their command of the language and of sharing the cultural view of the people they study. On the other hand, they do not look at their own society as the classical ethnographer has always done, that is, as a 'professional stranger'. This means that they have yet to develop that alienating perspective, often connected to the painful effect of self-alienation, to which anthropology owes its most important insights. According to Vincent Crapanzano, it is exactly this 'straddling' position on the edge that risks being lost 'as anthropologists devote more and more attention to their own cultures' (Crapanzano).[1]

The shift to anthropology at home was accompanied by the emergence of new disciplines such as cultural, post-colonial and subaltern studies, to which the discipline had to cede many of its root concepts, fields and topics that had grown out of its own history (John Comaroff). Though strongly contested within the discipline itself because of its essentialising aspects, 'culture' is one of these concepts, perhaps even the most important one. Geertz provided the catchword in his metaphor 'culture as text', which literary critics took literally, thereby following

---

[1]     On cultural difference, critique and the 'in-betweenness' of the anthropologist, see also the contributions by Crapanzano, Godelier, and Jebens in the present collection.

the path he had opened up to them: if the works of anthropologists are nothing but constructions of texts about texts, then it should be the legitimate task of literary scholars to analyse them. They adopted the history of anthropology as their domain, focussing on the textual strategies and ambiguous exoticism hidden in the writings of its classical epoch. A blurring of the boundaries between the disciplines took place. Cultural studies combined anthropological approaches with literary theory, the politics of identity and the cultural critique of the Frankfurt school. Post-colonial and subaltern studies protested against 'hegemonic discourses' and gave their voice to the marginalised – something anthropologists felt they had always done, if, perhaps, usually in a rather paternalistic way. But in fact, as Crapanzano notes, post-colonial intellectuals find themselves in a dilemma very similar to that of anthropologists by virtue of the fact that they speak for the powerless in a language 'that is not even their own but that of the former coloniser – one that is philologically weighted by domination'. Indeed, there seems to be no big difference in the ways in which ethnicity, class, race, gender and all the other fashionable postmodern key concepts are currently being used in the writings of post-colonial writers, whether intellectuals, literary critics or anthropologists.

Bearing the consequences of the loss of their classical object of study, anthropologists began looking for new fields of research, especially within their own societies, which today they must share not only with cultural studies, but also with sociology, economics and religious studies. This has produced a confusing situation. As Comaroff remarks, 'we have no real subject matter of our own any longer'. Anthropology lost its brand because its subject matter 'diffused itself into anything, everything, anywhere and, hence, nobody or nothing or nowhere in particular'. But in Comaroff's view, retreating back into the study of the local, into literarily ambitious descriptions of foreign societies or even into the revitalisation of obsolete key concepts is no alternative. It is small comfort that sociology, too, finds itself in a state of crisis, although the way in which it is proposed to solve this has rather ambiguous effects on anthropology. Suffering from the decline of its classical theoretical and methodological approaches, sociologists have tried to import new ones from other disciplines. One of these newly adopted devices is the method of ethnographic fieldwork, formerly one of the distinguishing features, indeed even the central trademark of our discipline. Obviously, it is ironic that sociologists are adopting this approach at the same time as some anthropologists have come to distance themselves from 'participant observation' as too limited an approach and to replace it with 'multi-sited ethnography', which they assert to be much better suited to examining the impact of the world system, the capitalist market regime, the state and the mass media regarding the interplay between the global and the local.[2] In this case, too, we can observe a blurring of

---

[2]    On 'multi-sited ethnography', see also the contributions by Crapanzano, Godelier, and Jebens in the present collection.

the boundaries between the disciplines. Multi-sited ethnography as advocated by George Marcus (1995) is an explicitly multidisciplinary endeavour, embracing media studies, science and technology studies, and cultural, gender and subaltern studies as well.

The shift away from the classical principles of participant observation, however, may have other reasons too. As Signe Howell states, the reluctance to spend a considerable span of time in a faraway place with all the discomfort this entails, to learn a foreign language, to acquire an intimate knowledge of local practices, ideas and values and to renounce all the amenities of urban life corresponds to the loss of the 'general desire to explore the unknown' (Howell). Since Malinowski and Lévi-Strauss, we know that it was a critical stance towards the prevailing norms and values of their own society that moved anthropologists to engage in the ethnographic adventure. To endure the hardships of 'primitive life' seemed to be a possible antidote to what Sigmund Freud had referred to as "Civilisation and its discontents". Seen from such a point of view, ethnographic fieldwork as practice represented a kind of cultural critique. Yet this romantic bent, still highly esteemed by the generation that was part of the student and the hippie movement, has faded. Today's younger anthropologists feel better at home, especially since doing fieldwork outside the Western hemisphere has been stigmatised as politically incorrect by some postmodernists: 'the fifth column within our own ranks', as Howell calls them. According to their more pragmatic orientations, students tend to turn to limited research topics in their own country which can be explored in a calculable timeframe. The example Howell gives of the Norwegian Ph.D. students who study the life ways of immigrants without learning a single immigrant language is no exception. Crapanzano points to similar cases of parochialism in the writings of American anthropologists who master no other language but their own, even ignoring the studies of their colleagues in countries in which they themselves have done research.

Howell touches on another point that is rarely mentioned in reflections on the current state of scientific disciplines, which may be, at the same time, an excuse for the pragmatic behaviour she criticises, i.e., the external pressures and constraints that the universities and funding organisations impose on research. What Howell writes in this regard with reference to Norway and the United Kingdom applies to other European countries too. Funding is policy-oriented, research projects have to serve practical goals, multidisciplinary approaches are preferred and scientists should indicate the results of their investigations even before they begin their work. Therefore, it has become almost impossible today to obtain funds for that kind of single-handed, disinterested research in distant, unknown places which has played such an important role in the history of anthropology and has provided new insights into the nature of human society. The omnipresent audit-culture and its constant stream of evaluations shape the contemporary academy: the extended period of time it takes to conduct ethnographic fieldwork, to analyse the data collected and to publish them in the form of a monograph – Edward Evans-Pritchard once talked of an average time span of ten years (1971:76) – would not stand up to the critical examination of bureaucratic steering committees.

Andre Gingrich also stresses the extent to which the interior structures of the national university and funding organisations determine the production of anthropological knowledge, but he treats these and other questions from a more optimistic point of view. According to Gingrich, it would be better to speak of the end of national anthropologies than to predict the demise of the anthropological project as such. From the early twentieth century, anthropology developed different national traditions and schools, some of which remained strongly connected to colonialism, while others were put into the service of nationalist ideologies. Today, these particular national traditions are converging on an international level. As Gingrich shows, anthropology is in a state of transition 'into an emerging future of transnational and global research'. What some of its practitioners interpret as symptoms of crisis, causing anxiety and pain, are necessary steps to free anthropology from its colonial legacy and its political abuses by hegemonic powers. Feminist, postmodern and post-colonial critiques have not only created the conditions to overcome national meta-narratives, they have also provided the means to cope with the challenges of global transformations. In this regard, anthropology seems to be better equipped for the future than its neighbouring disciplines in the humanities and the social sciences. But there still exist some obstacles to a truly global and transnational research approach. One of the problems Gingrich mentions is the unequal distribution of research funding between the affluent countries of the Western hemisphere and the post-colonial states. Therefore, he advocates a funding policy that supports transnational partnerships and cooperation. Anything but sceptical of the mutual exchange of theoretical and methodological approaches between the disciplines, Gingrich takes it as a proof of anthropology's importance that not only ethnographic fieldwork but also many of its key concepts are being adopted today by other social sciences.

Can we really talk of a decline of anthropology if we take into consideration the enormous growth of the discipline since the end of the Second World War? Just half a century ago, there were almost no anthropological departments outside Europe, North America and the area of what became the British Commonwealth. Today, however, anthropology is present in almost all countries of the world, and the number of its practitioners and students is steadily increasing. At the same time, a considerable enlargement of its traditional fields of study can be observed. Ulf Hannerz takes the still ongoing success story of anthropology as the starting point of his argumentation. In his view, there is no reason to question the future of the discipline. Only a general change in the production of knowledge by a restructuring of the university system could threaten its existence. But then, all its neighbouring disciplines would be confronted with a similar fate too. If there is a problem, it consists in anthropology's public image. In an age in which neoliberal thinking is also invading the academy, with all its modalities of assessment, evaluations and rankings, anthropology has to compete with other disciplines which often possess better marketing strategies. Therefore, Hannerz argues, anthropology should free itself from its outdated image as an exotic or antiquarian endeavour and create a new, strong brand to show what anthropologists always have done and are continuing to do: study human diversity. This primary concern is connected with the important ethical task of deepening respect for the different ways in which human beings organise their lives and of recognising 'people's rights to be who they are and do as they choose, within some limits of social justice and concern for the corresponding rights for others' (Hannerz). The decline of cultural diversity has often been predicted, but all such prophecies have failed. As long as diversity prevails, the future as well as the legitimacy of the anthropological project cannot be put into question.

Maurice Godelier argues in the same vein by stressing that today anthropology has become more important than ever. For him, the deconstructive movement was only a brief episode in the recent history of the discipline that now lies far behind us. Ultimately, it was a failure because, for Godelier, it rested on false presuppositions. By criticising the discipline's classical monographs as 'narrative fictions', the exponents of the writing culture debate transferred the obscure theoretical positions of Jacques Derrida and Paul de Man onto ethnographic accounts. It may be true for a literary work that there is no 'reality' beyond the text to which it refers, but scientific texts are neither dramas nor novels. The Trobriand Islanders, Nuer and Tikopia really existed at the times that Malinowski, Evans-Pritchard and Raymond Firth visited them, and what these authors wrote about their social and economic practices was anything but pure 'hallucination', as later studies have proved. And these peoples still exist today, although their societies have undergone many changes, just as they had done before their first ethnographers came. It would therefore be a fallacy to assert that the discipline has lost its object merely because indigenous ways of living have changed and because their descendants can be found today, not only in their homelands but also as migrants in large Western metropolises. And it is yet another fallacy to suppose that anthropology has no other object but allegedly 'primitive' or 'pre-industrial' societies, since even in the past the discipline managed to go beyond the narrow scope that was defined initially by the ideology of evolutionism. Like Hannerz, Godelier emphasises that the study of cultural diversity remains anthropology's most important task, and, like Spyer, he also tries to rehabilitate the concept of otherness, the essentialist use of which has been contested with good reason by the exponents of postmodern anthropology, but which seems to be justified if applied in a relative and not an absolute sense. In order to use this concept as a heuristic device, the anthropologist has to acquire a consciousness of his own otherness as a professional researcher, which means acquiring an awareness of his cognitive ego that is different from both his social and his intimate ego. In the present-day world, in which 'a multitude of local societies' are reacting to the pressures of globalisation by trying 'to re-affirm or re-invent their cultural and political identities', no other discipline seems better equipped 'to understand and explain the existence of facts, attitudes and representations that have never been part of our own way of living and thinking' (Godelier).

The last contribution to this collection engages in a general reflection on the talk of the end as a literary device in the history of anthropology. Obviously, it is no accident that it has an especially strong tradition in the German branch of the discipline, in which, still very much in the spirit of its roots in the Romantic Age, the notion of the birth, becoming, growth and decay of cultures played such an important role. Mark Münzel draws parallels with the uses of metaphors such as 'the fiery destruction of traditions', 'the grave', 'the vanishing race' or 'the burning library', once so popular in anthropological discourse, in literary works of the same epoch. Narratives of the end are therefore not to be understood as simple descriptions of reality, but rather as literary parables that express the views and sentiments of their authors. Since these metaphors occur in both genres of discourse, they seem to refer to a certain pessimistic worldview that 'the anthropologist as an author' shares with the writers of fictitious texts. Ultimately, this means that the fascination which talk of the end evoked and still evokes among anthropologists has its roots in their own society. It is an expression of the discontentedness with civilisation just mentioned that moved many of its most prominent practitioners to embark on it as a career.

Yet the 'the end of anthropology' – the title we have chosen for this collection – refers not only to the demise of the discipline. As Crapanzano points out, the 'end' may also be understood to refer to 'the goal of anthropology'. Ultimately, none of the contributors to this collection would assert that anthropology has come or is coming to an end; there are even some doubts whether it is actually in a state of crisis. They would all, however, agree with Gingrich's analysis that it is currently passing through a 'process of transition' caused by external as well as internal factors. The contributors discuss some of the new directions the discipline will take in the future, but they also ask what will remain or what is worth retaining from the classical epoch of anthropology. As different as these perspectives may be, there seems to be at least one common denominator. Anthropology embodies a unique view of human affairs, a view that grew out of its past, glorious or inglorious as this may have been. Alienation – 'that distressing by-product of intelligence' (Susan Sontag 1970:189) – has always been an important impetus in the history of the discipline. The ethnographic encounter seemed to be a refuge from the pressures and constraints of the anthropologists' own societies. Feeling at home neither in their own societies nor in those studied, they acquired a distance that made the familiar unfamiliar, that allowed them to see things from a new angle, here just like there. This attitude, acquired by crossing the borders between different cultures, is the discipline's most important historical achievement. Kuper and Spyer show that this has not lost its significance, regardless of whether it is applied to one's own or to a foreign culture. Comaroff speaks of the necessity of a 'critical estrangement of the lived world, itself founded on a double gesture – on the deconstruction of its surfaces and the radical relativisation of its horizons'. And Crapanzano states clearly that 'the anthropological stance rests on real or artificial alterity and distance. It gives anthropology its particular angle on both the society under study and the anthropologist's'. As long as the differences, the study of which is anthropology's privileged task and 'brand' (Hannerz), continue to exist, this stance will linger on. Therefore, we can conclude that the 'end of anthropology', in the double sense of the term, lies in its past.

*REFERENCES*

EVANS-PRITCHARD, Edward E.
1971    *Social anthropology*. London: Routledge & Kegan Paul

GEERTZ, Clifford
2000    "The world in pieces: culture and politics at the end of the century", in: Clifford Geertz, *Available light: anthropological reflections on philosophical topics*, 218–230. Princeton and London: Princeton University Press

LAFITAU, Joseph-François
1724    *Mœurs des sauvages amériquains, comparées aux mœurs des premiers temps*. Volume 1. Paris: Saugrain & Charles Estienne Hochereau

MARCUS, George E.
1995    "Ethnography in/of the world system: the emergence of multi-sited ethnography", *Annual Review of Anthropology* 24:95–110

SONTAG, Susan
1970    "The anthropologist as hero", in: E.N. and T. Hayes (eds.), *Claude Lévi-Strauss: the anthropologist as hero*, 184–196. Cambridge, MA: Cambridge University Press

TRASK, Haunani-Kay
1991    "Natives and anthropologists: the colonial struggle", *The Contemporary Pacific* 3:159–167

WORSLEY, Peter
1970    "The end of anthropology?", *The Western Canadian Journal of Anthropology* 1(3):1–9

# 1

## THE CRISIS OF ANTHROPOLOGY*

### Holger Jebens

*I.*

If the present state of anthropology is to be judged according to what eminent practitioners of the discipline have to say about it, one cannot help having the impression that it is in serious crisis or even faces imminent decline.[1]

Bruce Kapferer thinks that anthropology has not only become 'watered down', it has also 'lost its sense or its ability to criticise on the basis of in-depth knowledge of other forms of existence' (Smedal and Kapferer 2000/2001). Marshall Sahlins sees the discipline as having arrived 'in the twilight of its career' (1995:14), while George Marcus refers to the 'most senior generation of anthropologists' claiming that they are 'clearly most pessimistic or worried [...], even with statements in sotto voce that anthropology is dying just as they produce their own last works' (1998a:231).

Similarly, the late Clifford Geertz believed that, should anthropology departments still exist fifty years in the future, they will not look like they do today and will not even keep their names (Handler 1991:612).

Indeed, the profession of anthropologist currently seems to be more difficult than ever. The 'object' of research is no longer what it used to be, and the method – so-called 'participant observation' or fieldwork – often seems to be no less discredited than the unchallenged self-confidence and the almost encyclopaedic claim to completeness with which the ancestors of the discipline were able to gather their data 'in the field' and present them in the form of monographs. At a time when 'grand narratives' seem to belong to the past and handed down certitudes are being shaken to the core, the search for a theoretical paradigm that enjoys unanimous support remains unsuccessful. It is against this background that, in the second

---

* This paper is based on the *Antrittsvorlesung* I delivered to the Fachbereich Philosophie und Geschichtswissenschaften, Johann Wolfgang Goethe University, Frankfurt am Main, on 18 July 2007. It is also a revised version of an article that appeared under the title "Zum Verhältnis von Krisentopos und Methodendiskussion in der Ethnologie" in the German journal *Zeitschrift für Ethnologie* 134:51–78 (2009). I have benefited from inspiring discussions with Eva Raabe and Michael Wiener.

[1] The 'crisis of anthropology' is, in the present collection, also referred to by Spyer.

edition of his introduction to anthropology, Karl-Heinz Kohl notes a long-term
'climate of perplexity and uncertainty'.[2]

Whether in the context of museums of anthropology, universities or mere
research institutions, the sense of a common identity seems to be vanishing as the
discipline is subjected to increasing splitting or disintegration. The emergence of
more and more sub-groups within the American Anthropological Association,
for example, was denounced by Eric Wolf in 1980 in an article published by the
"New York Times" entitled "They divide and subdivide and call it anthropology".[3]
This splitting or disintegration seems to blur the boundaries of anthropology with
neighbouring disciplines.[4] At the same time, Sydel Silverman voices an undertone of
irony when, in sketching the history of anthropology in the United States, she claims
that 'other academic disciplines were encroaching on anthropology's heritage of
concepts and methods' and that 'everyone in the social sciences and humanities, it
seemed, was doing fieldwork and calling it ethnography' (2005:329). However, the
widespread use of terms such as 'fieldwork', 'ethnography' or 'the ethnographic gaze'
can also be taken to indicate a certain resonance or even a 'boom' in the discipline
(cf. Gottowik 2005:39). According to Doris Bachmann-Medick, anthropology
has 'helped an inclusive "cultural turn" to establish itself in the humanities' and
developed 'important guiding principles which have led cultural analysis towards
appreciating cultural otherness or pluralism and examining cultural differences in
human behaviour' (2006:28). Thus, anthropology 'presses for the emergence of an
anthropological perspective that can and should be focused on one's own culture as
well' (Bachmann-Medick 2006:28–29). Yet, many anthropologists see themselves
as being marginalised, misrepresented and pushed into the role of a 'cultural Other'
by non-anthropologists.[5] They claim that, beyond a small circle of specialists, the
results of their research fail to receive sufficient attention (cf. Marcus 2002:194)
and are distorted or, as Harri Englund and James Leach have it, that 'ethnographic
analyses become illustrations consumed by metropolitan theorists' (2000:238).

Pessimism, anxiety and bleak predictions, however, are by no means new
phenomena in the discipline. The alleged crisis of present-day anthropology has its
predecessors. Here, I will demonstrate that the whole history of the discipline can
indeed be described as a history of dangers and threats.[6] In so doing, I differentiate

---

[2]   Kohl (2000:168; all translations from the German, H.J.)
[3]   In her overview, "Theory in anthropology since the sixties", Sherry Ortner refers to this article
      and agrees that '[t]he field appears to be a thing of shreds and patches of individuals and small
      coteries pursuing disjunctive investigations and talking mainly to themselves' (1984:126). Cf.
      George Stocking, who notes a 'centrifugal proliferation of "adjectival anthropologies"' (1983a:4)
      and Crapanzano, who, in the present collection, speaks of a 'pluralization' of anthropology.
[4]   Cf. Stagl (1974:307, 1993a:43), Kohl (2000:172).
[5]   Cf. Stagl (1974:97), Carucci and Dominy (2005:224, 226, 230–231).
[6]   Similarly, William Kelly (2006) mentions the possibility of 'narrativizing the discipline's
      development as a history of crisis-and-response', while Paula Rubel asks 'whether anthropology is

between three phases, the first of which begins in the 1830s, the second in the 1960s and the third in the 1990s.

Anthropologists who believe they are in a precarious situation identify themselves, I would argue, with the people with whom they work.[7] In the course of time, the latter have been said to be merely dying out, to be losing their discreteness due to an alleged 'westernisation', or – just like anthropologists – to be marginalised, misrepresented and pushed into the role of a 'cultural Other'. Moreover, out of their supposedly precarious situation, they have been particularly interested in 'indigenous crises', that is, in the ways in which people cope with such crises by religious means. However, perceptions of Other and Self influence each other not only in the history of the discipline, but also 'in the field', when social reality, by offering a certain resistance, can force anthropologists to face and modify their preconceived ideas and expectations.[8] In my view, it is precisely this experience which makes participant observation or fieldwork so valuable. From this perspective there would be ample reason to confront the denounced marginalisation and misrepresentation of the discipline with self-confidence.


*II.*


Even before anthropology established itself as an academic discipline, its practitioners were afraid that they would soon lose their object of research. As the historian George Stocking (1982:409) writes, at the beginning of the nineteenth century they believed that, 'the dynamic of European colonial expansion and industrial growth initiated a new phase of race and culture contact, which by the 1830s was already seen as threatening the very survival of all "uncivilised" peoples'. Their disappearance was held to be inevitable during the phase of evolutionism between, according to Stocking, 1860 and 1895,[9] and corresponding ideas continued to be widespread in subsequent decades.

Thus, the foreword of Bronislaw Malinowski's famous "Argonauts of the Western Pacific" published in 1922, begins with the following words:

---

condemned to be always in crisis' (2003:3). Anthropologists' ideas about the imminent decline of their discipline are also referred to by Crapanzano, Godelier, Kohl and Münzel in the present collection.

[7]   Münzel, in his contribution to the present collection, speaks rather of 'the anthropologist's identification with the end'.

[8]   This defamiliarization of the familiar is also referred to by Spyer in the present collection.

[9]   Referring to this phase, Stocking states that 'savages and civilized men were integrated in a single developmental framework, in which the disappearance of the former was accepted as an inevitable concomitant of the same cultural process that produced the positive knowledge of anthropology' (1982:410).

Ethnology is in the sadly ludicrous, not to say tragic, position, that at the very moment when it begins to put its workshop in order, to forge its proper tools, to start ready for work on its appointed task, the material of its study melts away with hopeless rapidity. Just now, when the methods and aims of scientific field ethnology have taken shape, when men fully trained for the work have begun to travel into savage countries and study their inhabitants – these die away under our very eyes (Malinowski 1922:xv).

The dreaded loss of its object of research appears as an early threat to the discipline, but it was also called upon time and again in order to portray anthropological research as necessary, or even as not to be delayed. Correspondingly, on the second page of his foreword, Malinowski concludes that, '[t]he need for energetic work is urgent, and the time is short' (1922:xvi). This strategy should prove quite successful, since Malinowski's "Argonauts of the Western Pacific", that is, his previous stay on the Trobriand Islands to the southwest of what is now Papua New Guinea, marks the beginning of an era that has been termed the 'classic phase' of anthropology (Stocking 1978:535) and the 'golden age of ethnographic data-gathering' (Stagl 1974:108) and that, according to most historical accounts, lasted from approximately 1920 to 1960. During these years, the number of publications, students and positions within the discipline increased with what almost seems to be paradisiacal rapidity when viewed from the present-day perspective (cf. Stagl 1974:110, 1985:306). Yet, towards the end of the 1950s, Claude Lévi-Strauss was still invoking the 'disappearance of the last "primitive" tribe' (1985:24), and, in light of the 'terrible rate at which groups of people sometimes die out within a few years', asked himself if 'anthropology is not very soon doomed to become a discipline without an object'.[10]

Malinowski was by no means the first anthropologist to come close to complying with the methodological requirements formulated in the introduction to "Argonauts of the Western Pacific". However, despite the work of 'predecessors' such as Johann Stanislaus Kubary, Frank Hamilton Cushing, Franz Boas, Alfred Reginald Radcliffe-Brown or the participants in the famous Torres Straits expedition of 1898/99 (William Halse Rivers, Charles Gabriel Seligman and Alfred Court Haddon), and due to his personal charisma and his distinctive talent for self-promotion, Malinowski managed to surpass the others in turning participant observation or fieldwork into anthropology's major symbol of identity, or, as Justin Stagl has it, a 'ritual of admission into the guild', as well as its 'main means of control'.[11]

---

[10]  Lévi-Strauss (1985:23). Lévi-Strauss then echoes Malinowski's appeal for 'energetic work' by claiming that 'one should accelerate one's research and make use of the last remaining years to gather information' (1985:23; cf. Kohl 1988:252).

[11]  Stagl (1974:107). For Clifford fieldwork 'has played – and continues to play – a central disciplining function' (1997:1992), Marcus calls it 'the core activity that continues to define the discipline's collective self-identity through every anthropologist's defining experience' (1998b:126), while Gupta and Ferguson claim that 'fieldwork is increasingly the single constituent element of the anthropological tradition used to mark and police the boundaries of the discipline' (1997:1).

During the 'classic phase', the method significantly propagated by Malinowski was regarded as a sort of initiation that turned still ignorant students into inaugurated or regular members of the academic community. Lévi-Strauss writes that an anthropologist

> needs experience on the ground. For him, this experience is not a career goal, not a supplement to his culture and not a technical apprenticeship. It is a decisive moment in his education; before he may have unrelated data which will never form a coherent whole; it is only afterwards that these data can be understood as an organic whole and suddenly they acquire a meaning that they lacked before (1967:400).

In Lévi-Strauss's view this can be compared to the fact that psychoanalysts have to go through a training analysis, and, referring to the anthropologist's fieldwork, he continues:

> as with the psychoanalyst the experiment can succeed or fail and no examination but only the judgement of experienced members of the guild, whose work confirms that they have victoriously sailed round this cape, can decide if and when the candidate for the anthropological profession working on the ground has undergone this inner revolution which will truly make him a new man (1967:400).

In retrospect, Edmund Leach writes that, during the 'classic phase', a whole generation of Malinowski's followers 'were brought up to believe that social anthropology began in the Trobriand islands in 1914' (1957:124), and, to put it perhaps a little more bluntly, fieldwork came to be regarded as a ritual re-enactment of Malinowski's stay in the Trobriand Islands as a kind of mythic event. According to a much-cited dictum of Charles G. Seligman's (to whom Malinowski had dedicated his "Argonauts of the Western Pacific"), '[f]ield research in anthropology is what the blood of the martyrs is to the Church'.[12]

The religious character of words such as 'ritual of admission', 'new man' and 'blood of the martyrs' may seem surprising, since, after all, they are being used with reference to a scientific method, yet this relates to an exaggeration for which Stagl has coined the phrase the 'ideology of fieldwork'.[13] Part of this ideology was what

[12]   Cf. Köpping (1980:21) and Stocking (1995:115). Köpping refers to C.G. Seligman: Department of Anthropology 1972–3. London: L.S.E. 1972, p. 4; Stocking refers to a letter Seligman wrote to Malinowski on 7 January 1912. In an earlier publication, Stocking also quotes as Seligman's words 'as the blood of the martyrs is to the Roman Catholic Church' (1983b.83–84) and refers to Raymond Firth: "A brief history (1913–1963)", Department of Anthropology [London School of Economics] programme of courses 1963–64:1–9, 1963, p. 2.

[13]   A chapter of his book "Kulturanthropologie und Gesellschaft" (1974) has the heading "Die Feldforschungsideologie", and in a later article entitled "Feldforschung als Ideologie" he understands ideology as 'an obscuration of reality in the service of life interests' (1985:298). Marcus uses the same term, albeit without referring to Stagl, when he mentions a 'reigning traditional ideology of fieldwork' (1998b:119).

Morris Freilich, in his edited volume "Marginal natives at work: anthropologists in the field" (1977b), calls 'field-work mystique', that is, the idea of 'field work as a "mystery" to be solved by doggedly following tradition and being of right character and personality' (Freilich 1977a:17). Correspondingly, most anthropologists maintained that their method could only be learned through personal trial and error, not by reading manuals or attending seminars. Thus the 'candidate for the anthropological profession' had to rely on informal conversations with already initiated practitioners of the discipline.

Not only in the context of informal conversations or teaching, but above all in the monographs published during the 'classical phase', anthropologists have tried to make their own persons or the actual conditions of the research situation invisible. Mary Louise Pratt speaks succinctly of a 'self-effacement called for in formal ethnographic description' (1986:33), while Martin Fuchs and Eberhard Berg refer to an 'elimination of the subject' (1999:64) or of the 'subjective moment' (1999:65; cf. Gottowik 1997:188–189). 'If and to the extent the eliminated side was publicly articulated at all', Fuchs and Berg continue, 'it could at first only be expressed outside the canon of scientific writing, i.e., in the form of novelistic processings of individual fieldwork histories, [...] autobiographies [...] or documentations kept in a personal tone'.[14]

For Stagl, the exaggeration or ideology of fieldwork helped the 'anthropological guild' to establish itself as an academic discipline (1993b:103) and to develop 'a hierarchical grading' as well as 'a well-designed system of leadership' (1985:303). At the same time, however, Stagl attributes Lévi-Strauss's 'fervent doxology' of fieldwork to a 'sense of being threatened' (1974:107), and he refers to a 'hymn-like self-praise' that, in his view, has to be interpreted as 'a symptom of decline' (1985:307).

*III.*

The second phase of my history of the discipline as a history of dangers and threats begins in the 1960s, that is, at a time when the process of globalisation was believed to be leading to a loss of cultural difference or to 'a growing uniformity of the world' (Szalay 1975:117). Sahlins writes that, according to the corresponding

---

[14]   Fuchs and Berg (1999:65–66). Fuchs and Berg refer to Eleonore Bowen [Laura Bohannan]: Rückkehr zum Lachen. Ein ethnologischer Roman. Berlin: Reimer 1984 (¹1954); Robert H. Lowie: Robert H. Lowie, ethnologist: a personal record. Berkeley: University of California Press 1959; Hortense Powdermaker: Stranger and friend: the way of an anthropologist. New York: W.W. Norton 1966; Claude Lévi-Strauss: Traurige Tropen. Frankfurt am Main: Suhrkamp 1978 (¹1955); Jean Malaurie: Die letzten Könige von Thule. Leben mit den Eskimos. Frankfurt am Main: Krüger 1977 (¹1956), Georges Balandier: Afrique ambigue. Paris: Plon 1957; and Michel Leiris: Phantom Afrika. Tagebuch einer Expedition von Dakar nach Djibouti 1931–1933. 2 vols. Frankfurt am Main: Syndikat 1980/1984 (¹1934)

theories, '[i]ndigenous people who were not destroyed would be suborned by the commodification of everything and everyone, their ways of life thus transformed into marginalised and impoverished versions of the one planetary culture' (2005:3).

In the so-called 'Third World', the 1960s were also a time of liberation and decolonisation movements. The historical conditions which had been conducive to the emergence of the discipline and their corresponding power relations thus finally belonged to the past. Anthropologists not only lost direct access to their traditional 'field', they were increasingly accused of assisting in and benefitting from moribund colonialism, thus acting against the interests of their own hosts and informants.[15] The latter began to reject the role ascribed to them and, rather than serving as objects of research, they wanted to speak for themselves.[16] The Trobriand islander John Kasaipwalova, for example, referred to Malinowski's work by saying that 'if we are going to depend on anthropological studies to define our history and our culture and our "future", then we are *lost*'.[17]

The inhabitants of 'savage countries' became the citizens of independent states, self-conscious actors who by no means remained 'untouched' by Western influences and who did not conform or no longer conformed to the image coined by Malinowski. To the extent that these actors were not 'dying away', but, due to the process of globalisation, had allegedly lost their cultural discreteness – which is what had made them interesting from an anthropological perspective to begin with – and to the extent that they refused to be subjected to further examination, it seemed that initial fears of anthropology soon ceasing to have an object of research or of its material melting away had actually become reality, albeit in a different sense than at first expected. In Miklós Szalay's view, the 'indigenous refusal' in particular led to a 'crisis of fieldwork'. And because of the major significance of the method, he held this crisis to amount to a 'crisis of anthropology' in general, arguing that 'calling fieldwork into question [...] implies an existential threat to the discipline'.[18] At any rate, the era called the 'classic phase' of anthropology or the 'golden age of

---

[15]     Hoebel and Currier speak of 'reckless charges' that included the allegation of 'moral insensivity, imperialistic subversion and exploitation of subjected peoples, and political oppressionism' (1982:xxi). Cf. Fuchs and Berg (1999:67), Gottowik (2005:32), Köpping (1980:27), Stocking (1982:415).

[16]     Szalay states that '[t]he object of research has become a subject that wants to dispose of and decide for itself' (1975:11). Lynch refers to anthropologists being called 'nursemaids to colonialism or handmaidens to the CIA', and claims that such 'accusations come from those in the Third World now conscious of themselves as a subject, not just an object, of study' (1982:80). According to Eric Wolf, '[t]he object has become a talking subject with a definite point of view' (Friedmann 1987:117). Cf. Bachmann-Medick (2006:145).

[17]     Fuchs and Berg (1999:68; italics in the original) quote Michael Young (ed.): The ethnography of Malinowski. The Trobriand islands 1915–18. London: Routledge & Kegan Paul 1979, p. 17.

[18]     See Szalay (1975:109, 111) and, following Szalay, Stagl (1974:107, 1985:305, 1993b:105). A 'crisis of fieldwork' is also referred to by Hauschild (1987:52).

ethnographic data-gathering' was irretrievably over. The future seemed bleak, and in 1970 Peter Worsley published an article, the title of which aptly expressed the prevailing sentiment: "The end of anthropology?"[19]

Anthropology has reacted to its supposedly precarious situation by what Szalay calls 'turning back on itself' (1975:11). This includes the attempt by anthropologists to assure themselves of their own history in the sense of doing an 'anthropology of anthropology'.[20] In addition, anthropologists have scrutinised their own method, i.e., its political, ethical and psychological dimensions, increasingly critically.

Since the 1960s, more and more autobiographical reports, epistemological reflections and practical instructions related to fieldwork have been published, some of them compiled in much-read edited volumes and rather disparagingly referred to by Clifford Geertz as 'confessional literature'.[21] Here, the problem is no longer the person the anthropologist works with 'dying away', succumbing to a 'growing uniformity of the world' or refusing to be subjected to further examination, but the anthropologist himself and the web of relations in which he participates. Accordingly what has been eliminated returns, the 'subjective moment' is made conscious, and 'self-effacement' no longer called for. Freilich emphatically welcomed this development:

> The mystique of fieldwork – the aura of magic, mystery and glamour which anthropologists once attached to life in the field – has gone. In its place we have an ever growing literature of what problems, pains and pleasures face the researcher in a foreign culture. [Footnote omitted] In less than a decade many of the problems caused by the 'mystique' have been solved (1977c:vi).

The loss of aura and mystery welcomed by Freilich – and incidentally regretted by Stagl (1985:306) – can certainly also be attributed to the posthumous publication of Malinowski's diaries (1967), since the oft-cited passages in which he expressed disinterest in the 'life of the natives' or understanding for 'colonial atrocities' (cf. Kohl 1979:27–28) indicated that he himself had only partly managed to comply with his own methodological requirements.[22]

---

[19]   Kapferer summarises this article as saying 'that anthropology was a thoroughly colonial discipline and that the end of colonialism was the end of anthropology, now was the time of sociology' (Smedal and Kapferer 2000/2001). This corresponds to what, according to Hoebel, Malinowski had already claimed in 1941, namely that 'the future of anthropologists is to commit suicide by becoming sociologists' (1982:3).

[20]   Cf. Casagrande (1982:70), Hallowell (1965), Jarvie (1975:263), Kirsch (1982:92), Stocking (1978:534, 1983a:3–4), Trouillot (1991:17, 22–23).

[21]   This phrase is mentioned by Kämpf (2005:133). Edited volumes on fieldwork include Casagrande (1960), Freilich (1977b), Golde (1986), Spindler (1970). Cf. also Stocking (1983a:9), Fuchs and Berg (1999:66) and Gottowik (2005:29).

[22]   Cf. Fuchs and Berg (1999:66).

Apart from the engagement with its history and method, the very invocation of terms such as 'crisis' and 'end' can already be taken to indicate anthropology's 'turning back on itself'. Szalay claims that, '[i]n a rather simplifying and cynical way one could say that in this case an academic discipline is examining itself because it does not really have any other object left' (1975:117).

Together with the insights of the 'interpretive turn', decisively influenced by Geertz, the increasing awareness of the anthropologist's subjectivity contributed to the fact that interest shifted from the process of doing research towards the process of writing, from the anthropologist and his relationship with the people with whom he works towards the texts he writes.[23] Correspondingly, the means came under scrutiny by which the authors of ethnographies attempted to produce authenticity and plausibility or to construct the figure of the 'cultural Other' to begin with, involving, as Fuchs and Berg have it, 'a "deconstruction" of the formal conditions and rhetorical conventions of scientific accounts' (1999:72). A major factor in the history of this 'turning to the text' has certainly been James Clifford and George Marcus's edited volume "Writing culture" (1986). Significantly, in his introductory chapter, Clifford refers to a 'complex interdisciplinary arena, approached here from the starting point of a crisis in anthropology' (1986:3).

Clifford, Marcus and others criticised the ethnographies published during the 'classic phase' of anthropology for having misrepresented and marginalised Malinowski's inhabitants of 'savage countries'. In this context, the term 'othering' enjoyed great popularity: increasing the distance between oneself and those who are pushed into the role of a 'cultural Other', or, in the words of Fuchs and Berg, constructing 'the Other by way of exclusion' (1999:35n.26).

*IV.*

In the 1990s, anthropology's self-reflexive gaze returned from the ethnographic text to the method, or, to be exact, to the kind of fieldwork that was shaped in accordance with the archetypical example of Malinowski's stay in the Trobriand Islands. Authors such as James Clifford, George Marcus, Akhil Gupta and James Ferguson argued that one could no longer work like this today, not because of politics or ethics, but for epistemological reasons – not because of a critique of colonialism or an 'indigenous refusal', but because 'Malinowski's model' would fail in the modern world, characterised as it is by de-territorialisation, compression and acceleration, where new technologies of transportation and communication reduce spatial distance, partly imagined and partly real, and where time seems to pass ever

---

[23]    Thus Bachmann-Medick speaks of a 'turning back of reflexivity on one's own texts' (2006:144).

more quickly.[24] To the extent that the members of a given culture are not or are no longer living in one and the same place, and to the extent that the boundaries between different cultures or between 'here' and 'there', between 'the West' and 'the Rest', prove to be permeable, the notion of a separate and well-defined 'field' that the anthropologist first enters and then leaves after gathering sufficient data is called into question.[25]

On the one hand, Clifford, Marcus, Gupta, Ferguson and others claim that theoretical innovations have not caused changes in what anthropologists actually do, while on the other hand, they refer to an increasing number of research projects that allegedly no longer conform to handed-down conventions.[26] In Clifford's view the multiplicity of sites that are examined ethnographically and the increasingly heterogeneous composition of the anthropological guild in particular have made established practices 'come under pressure' (1997:206).

Since the mid-1990s, Marcus has attempted, in a number of articles, to counter 'handed-down conventions' or 'Malinowski's model' with an 'alternative paradigm of ethnographic practice' (2002:191) for which he propagates the term 'multi-sited ethnography'.[27] Corresponding studies would arise

> from anthropology's participation in a number of interdisciplinary (in fact, antidisciplinary) arenas that have evolved since the 1980s, such as media studies, feminist studies, science and technology studies, various strands of cultural studies, and the theory, culture, and society group (Marcus 1998c:80).

Forming what Marcus calls a 'second wave', such works allegedly build on the 'writing culture critique', which had largely left fieldwork 'untouched'.[28] Yet, in one of his own contributions to the edited volume that gave this critique or debate its name, Marcus had already suggested a possible 'experimentation with multi-locale ethnographies' which 'would explore two or more locales and show their interconnections over time and simultaneously'.[29]

---

[24]  Cf. Gupta and Ferguson (1997:3), also Englund and Leach (2000:225, 238). The latter refer to Arjun Appadurai: Modernity at large: cultural dimensions of globalisation. Minneapolis: University of Minnesota Press 1996; Ulf Hannerz: Transnational connections: culture, people, places. London, New York: Routledge 1996; James Clifford: Routes: travel and translation in the late twentieth century. Cambridge: Harvard University Press 1997.

[25]  Cf. Bamford and Robbins (1997:4), Gupta and Ferguson (1997:35).

[26]  Cf., e.g., Gupta and Ferguson (1997:32, 39), Marcus (2006:116).

[27]  Marcus (1998a–d, 1999, 2002, 2006). On 'multi-sited ethnography', see also the contributions by Crapanzano, Godelier and Kohl in the present collection.

[28]  Marcus (2002:192). The term 'second wave' also appears in Marcus (1999:6).

[29]  Marcus (1986:171). Later, Marcus equates 'multi-locale' with 'multi-sited' when he refers to this suggestion and writes about 'the multi-sited (then "multi-locale") possibility' (1998d:26n.2).

'Multi-sited ethnography' aims at the ethnographic construction of the local, the life worlds of differently placed subjects, on the one hand, and of the global as articulated in the relationships between various scenes or sites on the other. Marcus speaks of 'obvious cases of multi-sited ethnography' where movements of peoples, objects and technologies through time and space or dispersed communities and networks are concerned. In 'non-obvious' cases, however, the 'discovery and discussion' of the relationship between the various scenes or sites would be left to 'ethnographic analysis' (1999:67).

For Marcus, anthropologists and the people with whom they work look at each other with the same curiosity and share the same anxiety vis-à-vis a 'third', that is, 'specific sites elsewhere that affect their interactions and make them complicit (in relation to the influence of that "third") in creating the bond that makes their fieldwork relationship effective' (1998b:122). At the same time, anthropology increasingly relies on 'the reflexive maps and indeed crypto-ethnography of its subjects' (Marcus 2002:196), so that the separation between the productions of anthropologists and the people with whom they work decreases, or, as Gupta and Ferguson write, '[g]enres seem destined to continue to blur' (1997:38).

According to Marcus, 'multi-sited ethnography' cannot be understood as a mere supplement to the old practice with additional sites, since 'fieldwork engagements and collaborations in new arenas of research are far deeper and more complex than envisioned by the traditional Malinowskian paradigm' (2006:116). Marcus admits that it is not possible to examine all the sites that are selected in the same way or with the same intensity (1998c:84, 1999:8). Yet, in his view, 'accounting for the differences in quality and intensity of fieldwork material becomes one of the key and insight-producing functions of ethnographic analysis' (2002:196). In addition, Marcus stresses that, with his 'alternative paradigm of ethnographic practice', anthropology would lose neither its approach to perceive as foreign what is familiar – 'defamiliarizaton' deriving from the knowledge of relationships and connections that extend old frames (1998d:21) – nor 'the function of translation from one cultural idiom or language to another' (1998c:84). 'Good fieldwork is good fieldwork overall', Marcus writes, 'and it involves the same standards that are invoked by the pioneering projects of the greats such as Malinowski, Evans-Pritchard, Firth, and their descendants' (1999:10).

Marcus's co-editor of the 1986 volume, James Clifford, refers to 'Malinowski's model' as the 'exotic exemplar', claiming that although it 'retains considerable authority', it 'has, in practice, been decentered'.[30] Consequently, 'traditional

---

[30]     Clifford (1997:192). Accordingly Marcus writes that 'a certain valorized conception of fieldwork and what it offers wherever it is conducted threatens to be qualified, displaced, or decentered in the conduct of multi-sited ethnography' (1998c:84), while Gupta and Ferguson suggest 'a re-formulation of the anthropological fieldwork tradition that would decenter and defetishize the concept of "the field"' (1997:4–5).

fieldwork' still holds a certain legitimacy, but it does so only in connection with some of the selected sites or within a broader range of 'acceptable routes and practices' (Clifford 1997:207), while the knowledge gained through 'intensive fieldwork' can, in Clifford's view, no longer claim a privileged position (1997:194, 218). For Gupta and Ferguson, the process in which the method propagated by Malinowski has lost its aura and mystery during the 1960s appears to be perpetuated:

> Participant observation continues to be a major part of positioned anthropological methodologies, but it is ceasing to be fetishized; talking to and living with the members of a community are increasingly taking their place alongside reading newspapers, analyzing government documents, observing the activities of governing elites, and tracking the internal logic of transnational development agencies and corporations (1997:37).

The 1990s' critique of fieldwork has led to the impression of the serious crisis or imminent decline mentioned at the beginning of this paper, because it was taken as an attempt to devaluate or abolish anthropology's old symbol of identity, or even to do away with the discipline altogether. Here Bruce Kapferer's notion of anthropology having been 'watered down' refers to the process of 'decentering' propagated by Clifford and others, the splitting or disintegration denounced by Eric Wolf appears to result from the increasing number of different anthropologists, anthropological projects and sites examined ethnographically, as well as 'acceptable routes and practices', and the blurring of the boundaries between anthropology and neighbouring disciplines corresponds to the blurring of the genres or to the fact that different cultures are now more difficult to separate than ever.


V.


To learn that one's own discipline is in serious crisis or faces imminent decline can certainly be regarded as a 'disturbing experience', to use a term that Mario Erdheim (2008) has recently rendered useful in a comparison of the theories of Leo Frobenius and Sigmund Freud. I have tried here to cope with this experience by putting present-day prophecies of doom into a temporal perspective and by describing the history of the discipline from the 1830s through the 1960s to the 1990s as a history of dangers and threats.

Apparently the 'melting away' of anthropology's 'material of study', once predicted by Malinowski, corresponds to the allegedly imminent decline of the discipline. First the inhabitants of 'savage countries' disappear, then their Western visitors follow suit: the process remains the same, only the affected party is replaced. In my view, however, the idea of sharing the destiny of one's hosts and informants has to be interpreted as an identification which also manifests itself in the claim of many anthropologists – largely unchallenged up until the so-called 'writing culture debate' – to be able to speak for the people with whom they work or to act as their advocates.

This identification becomes even more obvious when practitioners of the discipline claim that they too are strangers, strangers not only 'in the field' but also at home, because a certain alienation from their own society is often regarded as a decisive factor in their career choice, which then, reinforced through the experience of fieldwork, enables them to view this society critically.[31] Dennison Nash writes that '[t]he typical anthropologist, by socialisation, training and the practice of his profession, becomes a stranger who can never go home, i.e. never find a point of rest in any society', and he suggests that we 'conceive the anthropological community as a place where strangers meet'.[32]

Anthropologists have also referred to themselves using the term 'marginal man', which Robert Park (1996) coined in 1928 for Christian converts in Asia and Africa, that is, for people who, in Park's view, lived in the borderland of two cultures, in two worlds without really belonging to either of them.[33] Accordingly, Stagl states that, because of their relatively recent professionalisation and their particular character, anthropology and related disciplines only play a marginal role within academia (1974:97), adding that 'a not yet established and not yet really respectable discipline attracts all kinds of weirdos, awkward customers and dreamers' (1974:98). At any rate, and as already mentioned, many present-day anthropologists see themselves as being marginalised, misrepresented and pushed into the role of a 'cultural Other' by non-anthropologists, just as, according to the protagonists of the 'writing culture debate', the inhabitants of 'savage countries' have been subjected to 'othering' during the 'classic phase' of anthropology. Even after their hosts and informants have failed either to 'die away' or to lose their cultural discreteness, anthropologists apparently continue to identify with them.

---

[31]    Cf. Stocking (1978:531) and Kohl, according to whom Malinowski stated a wish to flee from civili-
        sation (1979:41); Evans-Pritchard demanded from the anthropologist the ability to 'abandon
        himself without reserve', which, in Kohl's view, presupposes a broken relationship with his own
        society (1979:43); and Lévi-Strauss assumed that, in the life history of every anthropologist,
        there are certain factors that show that he was not or only poorly adjusted to the society into
        which he was born (1979:59). For Gottowik '[t]he alienation from the Self is [...] not only an
        initiating motive of the [anthropologist's] journey but particularly its immediate result' (2005:26).
        On cultural difference, critique and the 'in-betweenness' of the anthropologist, see also the
        contributions by Crapanzano, Godelier and Kohl in the present collection.

[32]    Nash (1963:164). Stagl expressed a similar view by stating that '[t]he ethnographer is at home
        everywhere without really being at home anywhere' (1974:66). Cf. Meintel (1973).

[33]    Cf. Stonequist, for whom '[t]he marginal man is the key-personality in the contacts of cultures'
        (1961:221); Freilich, who states that '[t]he anthropologist has been a marginal man for most of
        anthropology's history' (1977a:2); and Bargatzky's attempt to give 'an impression of the object and
        the possibility of a marginal man research' (1981:161–162).

Stanley Diamond curtly defines anthropology as 'the study of men in crisis by men in crisis',[34] and indeed anthropologists have long been particularly interested in 'indigenous crises', which result from, for example, the contradiction between individual needs and social conventions or from individual persons or whole groups changing their status, and which people attempt to manage with the help of rituals in general or initiation rituals in particular.[35] The anthropological literature has focused especially on certain religious phenomena that already have the term 'crisis' in their name: I am, of course, referring to so-called 'crisis cults', collective phenomena found in Africa, Asia, the Pacific, as well as in North, South and Central America which – unlike, for example, initiation rituals – emerge in the course of contacts between different cultures and which, under various headings, have been said to be motivated not only religiously, but also politically, economically and psychologically.[36]

There are, however, differences. Thomas Hauschild points out that crises 'can be described under the aspect of both structure and the dissolution of structure' (1993:470) and that 'the ambivalences of harmonising and revolutionary understandings of the term […] closely parallel each other' (1993:468). For Hauschild, anthropologists and scholars of religious studies who examine crisis cults 'even misunderstand crises, which by no means return to their point of departure as reconstituting and expressing stable basic attitudes or elementary structures' (1993:468). In my view, however, crises in the history of the discipline tend rather to be regarded as various stages following upon each other within the framework of a teleological development.[37]

On the other hand, the sentiments of pessimism, anxiety, perplexity and uncertainty, outlined in the first part of this paper, do not particularly provide reasons for an overly accentuated belief in progress. According to Bruce Knauft, the history of the discipline does not move on linearly but in the form of 'cycles of the long term', with a continuous alternation between theoretical innovations and their upbraiding 'for neglecting the details of socio-cultural life'.[38] Other authors

---

[34]  Diamond (1974:93). Cf. Smedal (Smedal and Kapferer 2000/2001) and Streck, who also cites Aidan Southall as saying that '[i]t is not that anthropology is in crisis, but that anthropology is crisis' (1997:13). Streck refers to J.W. Burton: "An interview with Aidan Southall", Current Anthropology 33(1):67–83, 1992, p. 81.

[35]  Cf., e.g., Bolte (2001), Grohs (1993), Kalinock (2001) and Streck (1987).

[36]  Cf. La Barre who stated: 'A "crisis cult" means any group reaction to crisis, chronic or acute, that is cultic. "Crisis" is a deeply felt frustration or basic problem with which routine methods, secular or sacred, cannot cope' (1971:11).

[37]  The word 'stages' in the subtitle of Fuchs and Berg's account of the 'history of the problem of ethnographic representation' (1999:8), for example ("Reflexionsstufen ethnographischer Repräsentation"), doubtlessly connotes ascent or advancement.

[38]  Knauft (1996:37). Moreover, Knauft states that 'there will always be an ebb and flow between more centripetal moments, which strive for relatively greater coherence, and more centrifugal ones, which expand our horizons in a more diffuse and fragmentary way' (1996:38).

speak of different paradigms, agendas or even turns that may succeed each other with increasing rapidity, but that often lack a thorough assessment of the theories just declared to be outdated.[39] 'As each successive approach carries the axe to its predecessors', Eric Wolf writes, 'anthropology comes to resemble a project in intellectual deforestation' (1990:588).

I would argue that the history of the discipline shows a mutual influence between perceptions of Other and Self when anthropologists believe that they too face the alleged destiny of the people with whom they work and when, out of their supposedly precarious situation, they prove to be particularly interested in 'indigenous crises'. The same mutual influence has already been noted to become manifest 'in the field', when, confronted with a somehow resistant social reality, one has to face and modify one's preconceived ideas and expectations, which in turn results in the development of a changed view. This very experience tends to be obfuscated by the critics who gained prominence during the 1990s, but it constitutes the specific value of fieldwork and differentiates 'talking to and living with the members of a community' from other 'acceptable routes and practices'. In view of the 'decentering' – or 'watering down' – propagated by Clifford, Marcus, Gupta and Ferguson, it is therefore necessary to stress that fieldwork is not the same as 'reading newspapers, analyzing government documents, observing the activities of governing elites, and tracking the internal logic of transnational development agencies and corporations'.

Accordingly, the much-denounced 'ideology of fieldwork' does appear to be justified to a certain extent, although the critique of its exaggeration, mystification and fetishisation is as appropriate now as the statement in the 1990s that the contemporary world has become quite different from what it was in Malinowski's times.

After anthropology's 'turning back on itself', after its engagement with its own history, method and texts, I think it would be worthwhile to shift one's gaze onto the Other again, not as, in Knauft's words, a 'retreat into neo-empiricism' or a 'tendency to take reactionary refuge by simply presenting more and more specifics' (1996:36), but in order to reclaim the ability lost, according to Kapferer, to 'criticise on the basis of in-depth knowledge of other forms of existence'.

Fieldwork can doubtlessly be made productive for self-reflexive concerns, for example, when one undertakes to examine indigenous ideas or constructions of 'being white' or of 'whiteness' that have emerged in various parts of the world in the course of contacts with Western colonial officials, traders, missionaries or anthropologists.[40] Although the latter have increasingly experienced situations in

---

[39]   Cf. Bachmann-Medick (2006), Kelly (2006) and D'Andrade (1995:4). Similarly Thomas Kirsch speaks of 'faddism' (1982:104) while Knauft sees the danger of a 'top-forty anthropology' for which 'today's new fad is tomorrow's rubbish' (1996:2).

[40]   Cf., in this collection, Crapanzano's reference to what he calls 'an informant's counter-ethnography'.

which their hosts and informants tell them about more or less famous colleagues who have previously worked in the same region or with the same ethnic group, and although such references may express culturally specific notions of 'tradition', the present or change in general, the indigenous view of 'anthropological predecessors' has, in my view, not yet received sufficient attention in the literature – much less, at least, than the way particular anthropological terms such as 'cargo cult' are understood and used by the people to whom they were applied in the first place.[41]

To assure oneself of one's own history also means discussing one's own identity, not the least vis-à-vis neighbouring disciplines. Without wanting to undo the splitting or disintegration denounced by Eric Wolf, it should be permitted to ask if, when speaking about 'fieldwork', 'ethnography' or just 'the ethnographic view', anthropologists and other scholars are really referring to the same long-term process of transformation that also affects the subject of research. The answer will not always be in the affirmative. Thus, neither the appropriation of such terms by other disciplines nor the 'anthropologisation of the cultural sciences' recently propagated by Därmann (2007) can be taken as proof of the specific value of fieldwork, although this specific value would be reason enough to confront the denounced marginalisation and misrepresentation of anthropology with self-confidence.

Whatever form the 'study of men in crisis by men in crisis' may take in particular, having begun my account with a reference to pessimism and anxiety, I would like to conclude with a perhaps more hopeful speculation. The fact alone that in 1970 Peter Worsley declared the end of anthropology and that in 1922 Malinowski spoke about its 'sadly ludicrous, not to say tragic, position' gives reason for the assumption that the successors of present-day 'weirdos, awkward customers and dreamers' will still be deploring the imminent decline of their discipline. At this moment, however, neither the currently widespread prophecies of doom have come true, nor has Malinowski's fear that the material of study 'is melting away with hopeless rapidity'.

---

[41]   For assessments of the indigenous view of 'anthropological predecessors', see Larcom (1982, 1983), Kühling (1998), MacDonald (2000), as well as my own work (Jebens 2004a, 2007, 2010) which, in taking up contributions by Hermann (1992) and Lindstrom (1993), also deals with the 'indigenous usage' of the term 'cargo cult' (Jebens 2004b, 2007, 2010).

## REFERENCES

BACHMANN-MEDICK, Doris
2006    *Cultural turns.* Neuorientierungen in den Kulturwissenschaften. Hamburg: Rowohlt.

BOLTE, Petra
2001    "Übergangsriten", in: Hubert Cancik, Burkhard Gladigow, and Karl-Heinz Kohl (eds.), *Handbuch religionswissenschaftlicher Grundbegriffe.* Volume 5: Säkularisierung – Zwischenwesen, 270–272. Stuttgart, Berlin, Köln: Kohlhammer

CARUCCI, Laurence M. and Michèle D. DOMINY
2005    "Anthropology in the 'savage slot': reflections on the epistemology of knowledge", in: Michèle D. Dominy and Laurence M. Carucci (eds.), *Critical ethnography in the Pacific: transformations in Pacific moral orders,* 223–233. Anthropological Forum 15(3)

CASAGRANDE, Joseph B.
1982    "Crisis in anthropology?", in: E[dward]. Adamson Hoebel, Richard L. Currier, and Susan Kaiser (eds.), *Crisis in anthropology: views from Spring Hill,* 1980, 65–78. New York, London: Garland

CASAGRANDE, Joseph B. (ed.)
1960    *In the company of man: twenty portraits by anthropologists.* New York: Harper & Brothers

CLIFFORD, James
1986    "Introduction: partial truths", in: James Clifford and George E. Marcus (eds.), *Writing culture: the poetics and politics of ethnography,* 1–26. Berkeley, Los Angeles, London: University of California Press
1997    "Spatial practices: fieldwork, travel, and the disciplining of anthropology", in: Akhil Gupta and James Ferguson (eds.), *Anthropological locations: boundaries of a field science,* 185–222. Berkeley: University of California Press

CLIFFORD, James and George E. MARCUS (eds.)
1986    *Writing culture: the poetics and politics of ethnography.* Berkeley, Los Angeles, London: University of California Press

D'ANDRADE, Roy
1995    *The development of cognitive anthropology.* Cambridge: Cambridge University Press

DÄRMANN, Iris
2007    "Statt einer Einleitung. Plädoyer für eine Ethnologisierung der Kulturwissenschaft(en)", in: Iris Därmann and Christoph Jamme (eds.), *Kulturwissenschaften.* Konzepte, Theorien, Autoren, 7–33. München: Wilhelm Fink

DIAMOND, Stanley
1974    *In search of the primitive: a critique of civilization.* New Brunswick: Transaction
        Books

ENGLUND, Harri and James LEACH
2000    "Ethnography and the meta-narratives of modernity", *Current Anthropology*
        41(2):225–248

ERDHEIM, Mario
2008    "Theorien als Verarbeitung beunruhigender Erfahrungen. Frobenius und Freud",
        *Paideuma* 54:27–39

FREILICH, Morris
1977a   "Field work: an introduction", in: Morris Freilich (ed.), *Marginal natives at work:
        anthropologists in the field*, 1–37. New York: Schenkman (¹1970)
1977c   "Preface", in: Morris Freilich (ed.), *Marginal natives at work: anthropologists in the
        field*, v–vi. New York: Schenkman (¹1970)

FREILICH, Morris (ed.)
1977b   *Marginal natives at work: anthropologists in the field*, 1–37. New York: Schenkman
        (¹1970)

FRIEDMAN, Jonathan
1987    "An interview with Eric Wolf", *Current Anthropology* 28(1):107–118

FUCHS, Martin, and Eberhard BERG
1999    "Phänomenologie der Differenz. Reflexionsstufen ethnographischer Repräsenta-
        tion", in: Eberhard Berg and Martin Fuchs (eds.), *Kultur, soziale Praxis, Text*. Die
        Krise der ethnographischen Repräsentation, 11–108. Frankfurt am Main: Suhrkamp

GOLDE, Peggy (ed.)
1986    *Women in the field: anthropological experiences.* Second edition, expanded and
        updated. Berkeley, Los Angeles, London: University of California Press (¹1970)

GOTTOWIK, Volker
1997    *Konstruktionen des Anderen.* Clifford Geertz und die Krise der ethnographischen
        Repräsentation. Berlin: Reimer
2005    "Der Ethnologe als Fremder. Zur Genealogie einer rhetorischen Figur", *Zeitschrift
        für Ethnologie* 130(1):23–44

GROHS, Elisabeth
1993    "Initiation", in: Hubert Cancik, Burkhard Gladigow, and Karl-Heinz Kohl (eds.),
        *Handbuch religionswissenschaftlicher Grundbegriffe.* Volume 3: Gesetz–Kult, 238–
        249. Stuttgart, Berlin, Köln: Kohlhammer

GUPTA, Akhil and James FERGUSON
1997    "Discipline and practice: 'the field' as site, method and location in anthropology",
        in: Akhil Gupta and James Ferguson (eds.), *Anthropological locations: boundaries of
        a field science*, 1–46. Berkeley: University of Chicago Press

HALLOWELL, Irving A.
1965    "The history of anthropology as an anthropological problem", *Journal of the History
        of the Behavioral Sciences* 1:24–38

HANDLER, Richard
1991    "An interview with Clifford Geertz', *Current Anthropology* 32(5):603–613

HAUSCHILD, Thomas
1987    "Feldforschung", in: Bernhard Streck (ed.), *Wörterbuch der Ethnologie*, 50–53.
        Köln: DuMont
1993    "Krise", in: Hubert Cancik, Burkhard Gladigow, and Karl-Heinz Kohl (eds.),
        *Handbuch religionswissenschaftlicher Grundbegriffe*. Volume 3: Gesetz–Kult, 461–
        473. Stuttgart, Berlin, Köln: Kohlhammer

HERMANN, Elfriede
1992    "The Yali movement in retrospect: rewriting history, redefining 'cargo cult'", in:
        Andrew Lattas (ed.), *Alienating mirrors: Christianity, cargo cults and colonialism in
        Melanesia*, 55–71. Oceania 63(1)

HOEBEL, E[dward]. Adamson
1982    "Ancient times", in E[dward]. Adamson Hoebel, Richard L. Currier, and Susan
        Kaiser (eds.), *Crisis in anthropology: views from Spring Hill, 1980*, 3–11. New York,
        London: Garland

HOEBEL, E[dward]. Adamson, and Richard L. CURRIER
1982    "The Spring Hill conference – genesis and concept", in E[dward]. Adamson
        Hoebel, Richard L. Currier, and Susan Kaiser (eds.), *Crisis in anthropology: views
        from Spring Hill, 1980*, xiii–xxi. New York, London: Garland

JARVIE, I[an]. C.
1975    "Epistle to the anthropologists", *American Anthropologist* 77(2):253–266

JEBENS, Holger
2004a   "'Vali did that too': on western and indigenous cargo discourses in West New
        Britain (Papua New Guinea)", *Anthropological Forum* 14(2):117–139
2004b   "Talking about cargo cults in Koimumu (West New Britain Province, Papua
        New Guinea)", in: Holger Jebens (ed.), *Cargo, cult, and culture critique*, 157–169.
        Honolulu: University of Hawai'i Press
2007    Kago *und* kastom. Zum Verhältnis von kultureller Fremd- und Selbstwahrnehmung
        in West New Britain (Papua-Neuguinea). Stuttgart: Kohlhammer
        (Religionsethnologische Studien des Frobenius-Institutes 3.)
2010    *After the cult: perceptions of other and self in West New Britain (Papua New Guinea)*.
        Oxford: Berghahn

KÄMPF, Heike
2005    "Der Sinn fürs Scheitern. Ethnologische Bekenntnisliteratur zwischen Selbsterfor-
        schung und Selbstverlust", *Paideuma* 51:133–151

KALINOCK, Sabine
2001    "Arnold van Gennep: Les Rites de passage", in: Christian F. Feest and Karl-Heinz
        Kohl (eds.), *Hauptwerke der Ethnologie*, 128–132. Stuttgart: Kröner

KELLY, William W.
2006    "Formulating disciplinary history (session 1)", http://classes.yale.edu/anth500a/
        session_notes/01-notes.htm (accessed 28 August 2006)

KIRSCH, A. Thomas
1982    "Anthropology: past, present, future – toward an anthropology of anthropology",
        in: E[dward]. Adamson Hoebel, Richard L. Currier, and Susan Kaiser (eds.), *Crisis
        in anthropology: views from Spring Hill, 1980*, 91–108. New York, London: Garland

KNAUFT, Bruce M.
1996    *Genealogies for the present in cultural anthropology*. New York, London: Routledge

KÖPPING, Klaus-Peter
1980    "Ist die Ethnologie auf dem Wege zur Mündigkeit? Einige erkenntnistheoretische
        Anmerkungen zur teilnehmenden Beobachtung", *Paideuma* 26:21–40

KOHL, Karl-Heinz
1979    *Exotik als Beruf*. Zum Begriff der ethnographischen Erfahrung bei B. Malinowski,
        E.E. Evans-Pritchard und C. Lévi-Strauss. Wiesbaden: B. Heymann (Studien und
        Materialien der anthropologischen Forschung IV.1.)
1988    "Ein verlorener Gegenstand? Zur Widerstandsfähigkeit autochthoner Religionen
        gegenüber dem Vordringen der Weltreligionen", in: Hartmut Zinser (ed.),
        *Religionswissenschaft*. Eine Einführung, 252–273. Berlin: Reimer
2000²   *Ethnologie: die Wissenschaft vom kulturell Fremden*. Eine Einführung. 2., erw.
        Auflage. München: C.H. Beck

KÜHLING, Susanne
1998    *The name of the gift: ethics of exchange on Dobu island*. Canberra: ANU (Ph.D. diss,
        Australian National University)

LA BARRE, Weston
1974    "Materials for a history of studies of crisis cults: a bibliographic essay", *Current
        Anthropology* 12(1):3–44

LARCOM, Joan
1982    "The invention of convention", in: Roger M. Keesing and Robert Tonkinson (eds.),
        *Reinventing traditional culture: the politics of kastom in Island Melanesia*, 330–337.
        Mankind 13(4)

1983      "Following Deacon: the problem of ethnographic reanalysis, 1926–1981", in: George W. Stocking Jr. (ed.), *Observers observed: essays on ethnographic fieldwork*, 175–195. London: University of Wisconsin Press (History of Anthropology 1.)

LEACH, E[dmund].R.
1957      "The epistemological background to Malinowski's empiricism", in: Raymond Firth (ed.), *Man and culture: an evaluation of the work of Bronislaw Malinowski*, 119–137. London: Routledge & Kegan Paul

LÉVI-STRAUSS, Claude
1967      *Strukturale Anthropologie*. Band 1. Frankfurt am Main: Suhrkamp
1985      "Die Zukunft der Ethnologie (1959–1960)", in: Claude Lévi-Strauss, *Eingelöste Versprechen*. Wortmeldungen aus dreißig Jahren, 23–41. München: Fink

LINDSTROM, Lamont
1993      *Cargo cult: strange stories of desire from Melanesia and beyond*. Honolulu: University of Hawai'i Press

LYNCH, Owen M.
1982      "Kuhn and crisis in anthropology", in E[dward]. Adamson Hoebel, Richard L. Currier, and Susan Kaiser (eds.), *Crisis in anthropology: views from Spring Hill, 1980*, 79–90. New York, London: Garland

MACDONALD, Judith
2000      "The Tikopia and 'what Raymond said'", in: Sjoerd R. Jaarsma and Marta A. Rohatynskyj (eds.), *Ethnographic artifacts: challenges to a reflexive anthropology*, 107–123. Honolulu: University of Hawai'i Press

MALINOWSKI, Bronislaw
1922      *Argonauts of the Western Pacific: an account of native enterprise and adventure in the archipelagoes of Melanesian New Guinea*. London: George Routledge & Sons, New York: E.P. Dutton
1967      *A diary in the strict sense of the term*. London: Routledge & Kegan Paul

MARCUS, George E.
1986      "Contemporary problems of anthropology in the modern world system", in: James Clifford and George E. Marcus (eds.), *Writing culture: the poetics and politics of ethnography*, 165–193. Berkeley, Los Angeles, London: University of California Press
1998a     "Sticking with ethnography through thick and thin (1997)", in: George E. Marcus, *Ethnography through thick and thin*, 231–253. Princeton: Princeton University Press
1998b     "The uses of complicity in the changing mise-en-scène of anthropological fieldwork (1997)", in: George E. Marcus, *Ethnography through thick and thin*, 105–131. Princeton: Princeton University Press

1998c    "Ethnography in/of the world system: the emergence of multi-sited ethnography
         (1995)", in: George E. Marcus, *Ethnography through thick and thin*, 79–104.
         Princeton: Princeton University Press
1998d    "Introduction: anthropology on the move", in: George E. Marcus, *Ethnography
         through thick and thin*, 3–29. Princeton: Princeton University Press
1999     "What is at stake – and is not – in the idea and practice of multi-sited ethnography",
         *Canberra Anthropology* 22(2):6–14
2002     "Beyond Malinowski and after *Writing Culture*: on the future of Cultural
         Anthropology and the predicament of ethnography", *The Australian Journal of
         Anthropology* 13(2):191–199
2006     "Where have all the tales of fieldwork gone?", *Ethnos* 71(1):113–122

MEINTEL, Deirdre A.
1973     "Strangers, homecomers and ordinary men", *Anthropological Quarterly* 46(1):47–
         58

NASH, Dennison
1973     "The ethnologist as stranger: an essay in the sociology of knowledge", *Southwestern
         Journal of Anthropology* 19(2):149–167

ORTNER, Sherry B.
1984     "Theory in anthropology since the sixties", *Comparative Studies in Society and
         History* 26(1):126–166

PARK, Robert E.
1996     "Human migration and the marginal man 1928", in: Werner Sollors (ed.): *Theories
         of ethnicity: a classical reader*, 156–167. Houndmills, London: Macmillan Press
         ([1]1928, The American Journal of Sociology 33(6):881–893)

PRATT, Mary Louise
1986     "Fieldwork in common places", in: James Clifford and George E. Marcus (eds.),
         *Writing culture: the poetics and politics of ethnography*, 27–50. Berkeley, Los Angeles,
         London: University of California Press

RUBEL, Paula G.
2003     "Travelling cultures and partial fictions: anthropological metaphors for the new
         millennium?", *Zeitschrift für Ethnologie* 128:3–24

SAHLINS, Marshall
1995     *How 'natives' think: about Captain Cook, for example*. Chicago: University of
         Chicago Press
2005     "Preface", in: Martha Kaplan (ed.), *Outside gods: history making in the Pacific*, 3–6.
         Ethnohistory 52(1)

SILVERMAN, Sydel
2005     "The United States", in: Frederick Barth, Andre Gingrich, Robert Parkin, and
         Sydel Silverman, *One discipline, four ways: British, German, French and American
         anthropology*, 257–347. Chicago, London: University of Chicago Press

SMEDAL, Olaf H and Bruce KAPFERER
2000/1 "Bruce Kapferer: an interview", http://www.anthrobase.com/Txt/S/Smedal_
         Kapferer_01.htm (accessed 28 August 2006)

SPINDLER, George D. (ed.)
1970     *Being an anthropologist: fieldwork in eleven cultures*. New York: Holt, Rinehart &
         Winston

STAGL, Justin
1974     *Kulturanthropologie und Gesellschaft*. Wege zu einer Wissenschaft. München: List
1985     "Feldforschung als Ideologie", in: Hans Fischer (ed.), *Feldforschungen*. Berichte zur
         Einführung in Probleme und Methoden, 289–310. Berlin: Reimer
1993a    "Szientistische, hermeneutische und phänomenologische Grundlagen der
         Ethnolgie", in: Wolfdietrich Schmied-Kowarzik and Justin Stagl (eds.), *Grundfragen
         der Ethnologie*. Beiträge zur gegenwärtigen Theorie-Diskussion. Zweite,
         überarbeitete und erweiterte Auflage, 15–49. Berlin: Reimer ([1]1981)
1993b    "Malinowskis Paradigma", in: Wolfdietrich Schmied-Kowarzik and Justin Stagl
         (eds.), *Grundfragen der Ethnologie*. Beiträge zur gegenwärtigen Theorie-Diskussion.
         Zweite, überarbeitete und erweiterte Auflage, 93–105. Berlin: Reimer ([1]1981)

STOCKING, George W., Jr.
1978     "Die Geschichtlichkeit der Wilden und die Geschichte der Ethnologie", in: Wolf
         Lepenies (ed.), *Die Wissenschaften und ihre Geschichte*, 520–535. Geschichte und
         Gesellschaft. Zeitschrift für Historische Sozialwissenschaften 4(4)
1982     "Anthropology in crisis? A view from between the generations", in E[dward].
         Adamson Hoebel, Richard L. Currier, and Susan Kaiser (eds.), *Crisis in anthropology:
         views from Spring Hill, 1980*, 407–419. New York, London: Garland
1983a    "History of anthropology: whence/whither", in: George W. Stocking Jr. (ed.),
         *Observers observed: essays on ethnographic fieldwork*, 3–12. Madison: University of
         Wisconsin Press (History of Anthropology 1.)
1983b    "The ethnographer's magic: fieldwork in British anthropology from Tylor to
         Malinowski", in: George W. Stocking Jr. (ed.), *Observers observed: essays on
         ethnographic fieldwork*, 70–120. Madison: University of Wisconsin Press (History
         of Anthropology 1.)
1995     *After Tylor: British social anthropology 1888–1951*. Madison: The University of
         Wisconsin Press

STONEQUIST, Everett V.
1961     *The marginal man: a study in personality and culture conflict*. New York: Russell &
         Russell ([1]1937)

STRECK, Bernhard
1987    "Initiation", in: Bernhard Streck (ed.), *Wörterbuch der Ethnologie*, 92–95. Köln: DuMont Buchverlag
1997    *Fröhliche Wissenschaft Ethnologie. Eine Einführung.* Wuppertal: Hammer


SZALAY, Miklós
1975    "Die Krise der Feldforschung: gegenwärtige Trends in der Ethnologie", *Archiv für Volkskunde* 29:109–120

TROUILLOT, Michel-Rolph
1991    "Anthropology and the savage slot: the poetics and politics of otherness", in Richard G. Fox (ed.), *Recapturing anthropology*, 17–44. Santa Fe: School of American Research Press

WOLF, Eric R[obert].
1980    "They divide and subdivide and call it anthropology", *New York Times*, Ideas and Trends Section November 30:E9
1990    "Distinguished lecture: facing power – old insights, new questions", *American Anthropologist* 93(3):586–596

WORSLEY, Peter
1970    "The end of anthropology?", *The Western Canadian Journal of Anthropology* 1(3):1–9

# 2

## THE ORIGINAL SIN OF ANTHROPOLOGY[*]

### Adam Kuper

The original sin of anthropology was to take for granted that there were two diametrically opposed types of human society: the civilised and the primitive. Anthropology defined itself initially as the science of primitive society. This was a very bad mistake. The term 'primitive society' implies a historical point of reference. It presumably defines a type of society ancestral to more advanced forms, on the analogy of an evolutionary history of natural species. However, it is simply impossible to reconstitute prehistoric social forms, let alone to classify them and to align them in a time series. There are no fossils of social organisation.

We do know that Upper Paleolithic societies were small-scale populations of hunters and gatherers, but there is no way in which the archaeological evidence can establish whether these societies were organised into family groups, or practiced monogamy or polygamy, or worshipped totems, or divided their work between men and women, or were ruled by chiefs. A popular alternative is to treat living populations of hunters and gatherers or nomads as stand-ins for the vanished and unknowable Upper Paleolithic societies. However, there are significant differences in the social institutions and religious beliefs of the Kalahari Bushmen, Amazonian Indians, Alaskan Inuit or Australian aborigines. Even if they did have some common features, these may not have been shared by Upper Paleolithic peoples. After all, thousands of years of history have intervened, a history that has treated modern hunter-gatherers harshly, driving them into inhospitable refuges, obliging them to adapt to disruptive neighbours. When they were studied in the nineteenth and twentieth centuries their lives had been decisively changed by encounters with farmers, pastoralists, traders and missionaries.

Not to put too fine a point upon it, the idea of primitive society is an illusion. Primitive societies – indeed, primitive people – are figments of the Western imagination. This does not mean that notions of the primitive serve no purpose. Like the alternative worlds of science fiction, ideas of primitive society help us to think about our own societies. The primitive, the barbarian, the savage are our opposite numbers. They are what we are not. They are good to think.

---

[*] This lecture, delivered at the University of Frankfurt, was also the basis of my Huxley Memorial Lecture for the Royal Anthropological Institute in December 2007.

Consider the case of Charles Darwin, who famously wrote: 'The astonishment which I felt on first seeing a party of Fuegians on a wild and broken shore will never be forgotten by me, for the reflection at once rushed into my mind – such were our ancestors' (C.R. Darwin 1874:919–920). What did Darwin see, and what did he make of it?

In a letter to his sister Caroline written in March 1833, Darwin described the visit he had made with HMS Beagle a few weeks earlier to Tierra del Fuego, an archipelago off the southern tip of South America:

> We here saw the native Fuegian; an untamed savage is I really think one of the most extraordinary spectacles in the world. – the difference between a domesticated & wild animal is far more strikingly marked in man. – in the naked barbarian, with his body coated with paint, whose very gestures, whether they may be peacible [sic] or hostile are unintelligible, with difficulty we see a fellow-creature (C.R. Darwin 1833).

He recorded more detailed observations in his diary. The homes of the wild Fuegians were rudimentary; they slept 'on the wet ground, coiled up like animals'; their food was miserable and scarce; they were at war with their neighbours over means of subsistence. 'Captain FitzRoy could never ascertain that the Fuegians have any distinct belief in a future life'. Their skills 'like the instinct of animals' were not 'improved by experience'. 'Although essentially the same creature, how little must the mind of one of these beings resemble that of an educated man'. And yet they sustained a viable way of life.

> There can be no reason for supposing the race of Fuegians are decreasing, we may therefore be sure that he enjoys a sufficient share of happiness (whatever its kind may be) to render life worth having. Nature, by making habit omnipotent, has fitted the Fuegian to the climate and productions of his country (Keynes 1988:222–224).

Before his encounter with 'untamed' Fuegians on that 'wild and broken shore', Darwin had become acquainted with another kind. The captain of the Beagle, Robert FitzRoy, had visited Tierra del Fuego on a previous voyage, in 1830. There he kidnapped three young men and a girl of about twelve, and took them back with him to England. FitzRoy decided that they were to be educated 'in English, and the plainer truths of Christianity, as the first objective; and the use of common tools, a slight acquaintance with husbandry, gardening and mechanism, as the second' (Hazelwood 2000:67). These were the elements of civilisation: language, religion and technology. One of the party (FitzRoy's favourite) died from a smallpox vaccination. The rest were duly instructed in civilisation by the rector of Walthamstow in London, and three years later they were returned home on the Beagle. FitzRoy intended them to serve as intermediaries for a missionary, who was also on board.[1]

---

[1]     For a full account of the encounter between Darwin and the Fuegians, see Hazelwood (2000).

In the course of the interminable voyage, Darwin was struck by the intelligence of York Minster, the older of the two men, and of the girl, Fuegia Basket. He noted that they picked up some Spanish during the ship's stopovers. His particular friend, Jemmy Button, the favourite of the sailors, was perhaps less clever, but he was very kind-hearted. When Darwin was sea-sick, Jemmy would 'come to me and say in a plaintive voice, "Poor, poor fellow!"', although he was clearly amused at the thought that the sea could trouble a grown man (C.R. Darwin 1839:260).

The Beagle dropped the Fuegians off near their old campsite. Their re-entry was not easy. Jemmy, in particular, struggled. He had apparently forgotten the Yamana language. Darwin noted, 'It was laughable, but almost pitiable, to hear him speak to his wild brother in English, and then ask him in Spanish ("no sabe?") whether he did not understand him' (C.R. Darwin 1839:220). And he scribbled in the margin of the diary entry: 'Man violently crying along side'. Then he wrote down his reflections:

> It was quite melancholy leaving our Fuegians amongst their barbarous countrymen; there was one comfort; they appeared to have no personal fears. – But, in contradiction of what has often been stated, 3 years has been sufficient to change savages, into, as far as habits go, complete & voluntary Europaeans [sic]. – York, who was a full grown man & with a strong violent mind, will I am certain in every respect live as far as his means go, like an Englishman.

Nevertheless, Darwin was concerned.

> I am afraid whatever other ends their excursion to England produces, it will not be conducive to their happiness. – They have far too much sense not to see the vast superiority of civilized over uncivilized habits; & yet I am afraid to the latter they must return (Keynes 1988:141–142).

Six weeks later the Beagle returned to Tierra del Fuego. Jemmy soon appeared – 'but how altered!', FitzRoy noted.

> I could hardly restrain my feelings, and I was not, by any means, the only one so touched by his squalid miserable appearance. He was naked, like his companions, except a bit of skin about his loins; his hair was long and matted, just like theirs; he was wretchedly thin, and his eyes were affected by smoke. We hurried him below, clothed him immediately, and in half an hour he was sitting with me at dinner in my cabin, using his knife and fork properly, and in every way behaving as correctly as if he had never left us. He spoke as much English as ever, and, to our astonishment, his companions, his wife, his brothers and their wives, mixed broken English words in their talking with him (FitzRoy 1839:324).

Yet Jemmy assured the captain that he was 'hearty, sir, never better'. He was contented, he said, and had no desire to alter his present way of life. Darwin accepted this. 'I hope & have little doubt [Jemmy] will be as happy as if he had never left his country', he wrote in his diary, 'which is much more than I formerly thought' (Keynes 1988:221). For his part, FitzRoy was confident that civilisation had left its imprint. He described the farewell signal fire that Jemmy lit as the Beagle sailed away, and commented that Jemmy's family 'were become considerably more humanized than any savages we had seen in Tierra del Fuego'. One day a shipwrecked seaman might be saved by Jemmy's children, 'prompted, as they can hardly fail to be, by the traditions they will have heard of men of other lands; and by an idea, however faint of their duty to God as well as their neighbor' (FitzRoy 1839:327).

Jemmy Button and his friends had in effect been the 'object' of an experiment, moving from savagery to civilisation within three years, and, apparently, back again in a matter of weeks. Watching in surprise as the experiment played itself out, Darwin was moved to ask why the Fuegians had not become more civilised on their own initiative. He ventured a sociological explanation. The Fuegians bartered freely and shared everything – 'even a piece of cloth given to one is torn into shreds and distributed; and no one individual becomes richer than another' (C.R. Darwin 1839:281). He recognised that this insistence on exchange was rooted in an assumption of equality. And it was precisely this insistence on equality, he thought, that held the Fuegians back.

When Darwin speculated on the association of equality and backwardness – and by implication on the necessary connection between civilisation and hierarchy – he was making a characteristic move. The primitive is the mirror image of whatever is thought to be quintessentially civilised. Savages are good to think with. Edward Said identified a discourse of Orientalism, which fashioned a stereotype of a feminised, sexually tempting, perhaps defiling Other that legitimated domination (1978). Said's thesis is maddeningly over-generalised and imprecise, but it has proved to be endlessly suggestive, since it is obviously true that colonialism required the rulers to stereotype – and dehumanise – their subjects. However, I am concerned here with something else, with the way in which the idea of the primitive is used to reflect upon ourselves.

Edward Tylor remarked in the first textbook of anthropology, his "Primitive culture", published in 1871, that

> [t]he educated world of Europe and America practically settles a standard by simply placing its own nations at one end of the social series and savage tribes at the other, arranging the rest of mankind between these limits according as they correspond more closely to savage or to cultured life (1871:26).

It is impossible to say whether or not Tylor was being ironic, but in any case the anthropologists were certainly claiming to be the experts on savagery and so, by implication, on civilisation itself. And yet there are no primitive societies! There are no primitive peoples! Darwin himself commented, 'I was incessantly struck, whilst living with the Fuegians on board the "Beagle", with the many little traits of character, showing how similar their minds were to ours' (C.R. Darwin 1874:276). In short, the civilised condition is defined as the opposite of an imaginary primitive state, and so it is equally imaginary. To compare civilised and primitive is to compare two imaginary conditions.

And yet to the early British anthropologists these conditions – the civilised and the primitive – seemed to be very real, indeed quite self-evident. Anthropologists studied primitive societies, and their central question was how civilisation had triumphed over savagery, how science and morality had emerged from the dark ages of superstition and promiscuity. Darwin kept an avuncular eye on the debates of the anthropologists, often referring back to his experience of the Fuegians. He had studied theology at Cambridge and had originally planned to become a clergyman, but by the 1860s he had little interest in religion. On the other hand, he was fascinated by what the anthropologists had to say about the regulation of sexual behaviour. Reproduction was, of course, the core issue in evolutionary theory. But Darwin also had very personal reasons for wanting to understand who should and who should not marry in a civilised society.

On board the Beagle, and more urgently on his return to England after five years voyaging, Darwin had pondered marriage – although not to anyone in particular. In July 1838 he took a sheet of paper, wrote 'This is the Question', and divided the page into two columns. 'M a r r y' he wrote at the head of one, 'N o t M a r r y' at the head of the other. He then laid out a balance sheet of arguments for and against marriage:

> Constant companion, (& friend in old age) who will feel interested in one, – object to be beloved & played with. – better than a dog anyhow. – Home, & someone to take care of house – Charms of music & female chit-chat. – These things good for one's health. – b u t   t e r r i b l e   l o s s   o f   t i m e '.

Companionship was the clincher. 'One cannot live this solitary life, with groggy old age, friendless & cold, & childless staring one in one's face, already beginning to wrinkle. – Never mind, trust to chance – keep a sharp look out – There is many a happy slave –'. And he concluded: 'Marry – Mary – Marry. Q.E.D' (Burkhardt and Smith 1986:444–445).

That question was settled then. Now another very important question had to be faced. Whom should he marry? Darwin soon settled on a daughter of his favourite uncle, his mother's brother, Jos Wedgwood. Only one of Jos's daughters was unmarried and about the right age. This was the youngest Wedgwood daughter, Emma, who was a year older than Charles. Emma was not only his first cousin. She was also his sister-in-law. Her oldest brother had married Charles's sister, Caroline, in 1837. Other romances had been rumoured between the young Wedgwoods and Darwins. Charles's elder brother Erasmus had shown an interest in Emma herself,

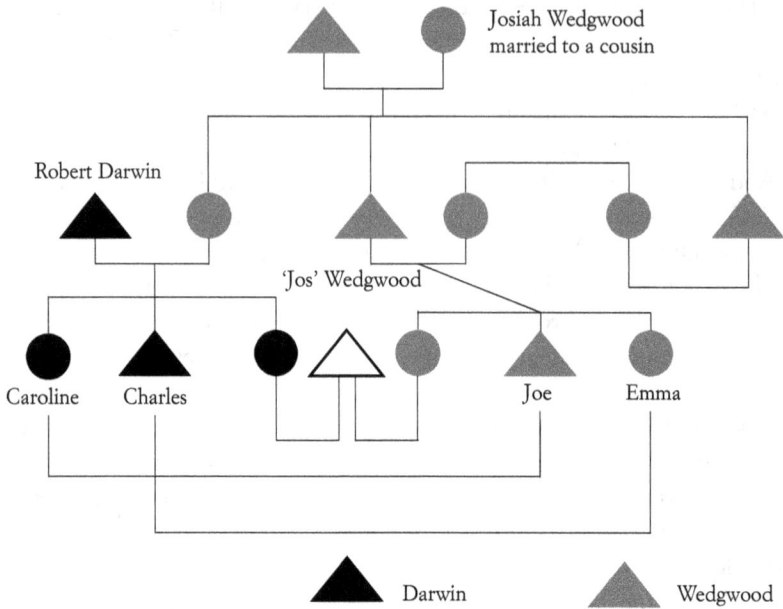

and perhaps also in her two older sisters (Browne 1996:392). And three of Emma's brothers had been very attentive to Darwin's sister Susan.

When Darwin wrote to Charles Lyell to announce his engagement, he emphasized the family links.

> The lady is my cousin, Miss Emma Wedgwood [...] and [she is also the sister] of the elder brother who married my sister, so we are connected by manifold ties, besides on my part by the most sincere love and hearty gratitude to her for accepting such a one as myself (E. Darwin 1915:1).

The engagement did not come as a surprise to either family. Emma's father – Charles's uncle – wept with joy when Charles asked his permission for the marriage. Charles's father was equally delighted. He was as happy, he wrote to Uncle Jos, as when young Jos married Caroline (Browne 1996:392). It was a match, Emma remarked, 'that every soul has been making for us, so we could not have helped it if we had not liked it ourselves' (Browne 1996:392). In fact, the Wedgwoods had a long-standing preference for marriages between first cousins, and in this they were typical of the rising educated upper-middle class in England.

And yet medical research was beginning to suggest that close-kin marriage had bad consequences for the health of the children. Charles Darwin was obsessively concerned with his own ill-health. Whenever one of his children fell ill, he was inclined to see the same symptoms in himself and to worry that it was the consequence of a hereditary weakness, or perhaps the price of his marriage with a cousin (Browne 2002:277, 279).

Darwin's researches insistently raised questions about breeding and fertility. Between 1868 and 1877 he published three monographs on cross-fertilisation in animals and plants (C.R. Darwin 1868, 1876, 1877) and claimed that

> the existence of a great law of nature is almost proved; namely, that the crossing of animals and plants which are not closely related to each other is highly beneficial or even necessary, and that interbreeding [i.e., inbreeding] prolonged during many generations is highly injurious.[2]

Darwin thought this was probably true of human beings. It was obviously very important to find out.

His neighbour and ally, the anthropologist John Lubbock, was a member of parliament. In the summer of 1870 Darwin asked him to propose that the census include a question on cousin marriage. He even drafted an argument for Lubbock to put to the House:

> In England and many parts of Europe the marriages of cousins are objected to from their supposed injurious consequences; but this belief rests on no direct evidence. It is therefore manifestly desirable that the belief should either be proved false, or should be confirmed, so that in this latter case the marriages of cousins might be discouraged.[3]

Darwin's son, George, reported that Lubbock's proposition was rejected, 'amidst the scornful laughter of the House, on the ground that the idle curiosity of philosophers was not to be satisfied' (G.H. Darwin 1875a:153). Darwin now asked George to compare the incidence of close-kin marriage in the general population with that among the parents of patients in mental asylums. If it turned out that marriages between close relatives produced a disproportionate number of 'diseased' children, this would 'settle the question as to the injuriousness of such marriages' (G.H. Darwin 1875a:153).

The first step was to find out how common it was in England for first cousins to marry. Apparently nobody knew the answer. George Darwin was given estimates that ranged from ten per cent to one in a thousand. 'Every observer', he concluded, 'is biased by the frequency or rarity of such marriages amongst his immediate surroundings' (G.H. Darwin 1857a:178). Clearly he had to discover the facts for

2     C.R. Darwin (1868:144). In the revised edition he dropped the qualification 'highly' before 'injurious' (C.R. Darwin 1875:126).

3     Letter Charles R. Darwin to John Lubbock, 17 July 1870. Darwin Correspondence Project; Cambridge University Library. Reproduced in F. Darwin (1887:129).

himself. George decided to attempt a scientific survey. It was to be one of the very first statistical studies of a social problem. After an ingenious and complex investigation, he concluded that 4.5 per cent of marriages in the aristocracy were with first cousins; 3.5 per cent in the landed gentry and the upper middle classes; 2.25 per cent in the rural population; and among all classes in London, 1.15 per cent. Summing up, George told his father 'that cousin marriages are at least 3 times as frequent in our rank as in the lower!' (G.H. Darwin 1874)

The next step was to gather statistics from mental asylums. His father wrote on his behalf to the heads of the leading institutions. Several provided detailed responses. These showed no significant difference between the incidence of cousin marriage in the general population and among the parents of patients in mental asylums. Other studies suggested that the offspring of cousin marriages were also more likely to suffer from blindness, deafness and infertility, but George Darwin found the evidence unpersuasive. In fact, first cousin marriages were, if anything, more fertile than others. He suggested that a man was more likely to marry a cousin if he had many to choose from. First cousin marriage would accordingly be more common among people who came from large – and therefore fertile – families (G.H. Darwin 1874:168–172). Only one small piece of evidence gave George pause. He noted that, among men who had rowed for Oxford or Cambridge, men who were obviously the fittest of the fit, sons of first cousin parents appeared slightly less frequently than might have been expected (2.4 per cent as opposed to 3–3.5 per cent among their peers) (G.H. Darwin 1875b:344–348).

Charles Darwin endorsed his son's conclusions, which were reassuring not only to himself but to the many English people whose family trees featured marriages between cousins. Englishmen could also rest more easily when they considered that Queen Victoria was married to a first cousin, and that several of her descendants had also married cousins.[4]

The question of cousin marriage shaded into a broader debate about incest. There was no crime of incest in England in the nineteenth century. A number of people thought that there should be a law, but the English were uncertain about what did, and what should, constitute incest. Incest was defined as sexual intercourse between people who were forbidden by the church to marry, but the doctrines of the church, mired in centuries of case law and theological argument, were often opaque to ordinary people. It was not always clear why a particular marriage was allowed or prohibited. Henry VIII had changed the laws of England in 1540 to allow the marriage of first cousins, and this reform was followed by most of Europe's protestant states. However, the old, baffling, Catholic rules on the marriage of relatives-in-law were retained. Marriage with a deceased wife's sister was illegal in England until 1907.

---

[4]     Landowners in the House of Lords did not require this reassurance: they knew that the inbreeding of good stock was sound policy.

Then in 1908 Parliament passed a law to make incest a crime in England. The statute only criminalised sexual relationships between members of the immediate family. And in the following year James George Frazer pointed out that 'among many savages the sexual prohibitions are far more numerous, the horror excited by breaches of them far deeper, and the punishment inflicted on the offenders far sterner than with us' (1909:47). In short, parliament had done the civilised thing.

As the experts on primitive society, Victorian anthropologists were necessarily experts on kinship and marriage, because they took it for granted that the first societies were essentially kinship groups. Henry Maine set out a general law: 'The history of political ideas begins, in fact, with the assumption that kinship in blood is the sole possible ground of community in political functions' (1861:124). As Maine saw it, the original primitive society must have been simply the family writ large. He had in mind something like the household of the patriarch Abraham, including several wives, sons and their wives and children, and servants and hangers-on. Other anthropologists imagined a promiscuous horde of kin, without families, without marriage, without even a taboo on incest. McLennan speculated that the most successful bands were made up of marauding warriors. They killed their daughters in order to be able to move more freely. And they captured women from other bands to be their wives. But at least they avoided incest. Edward Tylor, a Quaker, revolted against this violent scenario. The whole purpose of exogamy was to prevent war by setting up diplomatic alliances between groups. Henry Maine (who was married to his father's brother's daughter) thought that the prohibition of incest was a public health measure. People who had the brains to make fire and to domesticate animals would eventually have recognised that 'children of unsound constitutions were born of nearly related parents' (Maine 1883:228). The fastidious James George Frazer wondered whether finer feelings had not simply prevailed.

Darwin dismissed these speculations. 'The licentiousness of many savages is no doubt astonishing', he conceded. Yet even the lowest savages were not genuinely promiscuous (1874:896). Among the apes, adult males tended to be jealous. Primitive men had probably been equally reluctant to share their females. And incest was abhorred even among 'savages such as those of Australia and South America' with 'no fine moral feelings to confuse, and who are not likely to reflect on distant evils to their progeny'. Darwin thought that primitive men simply found foreign women alluring, 'in the same manner as […] male deerhounds are inclined towards strange females, while the females prefer dogs with whom they have associated' (1875:104–105). But whatever the original reason for the incest taboo, Darwin was sure that out-breeding groups would be more successful than their rivals. He concluded that avoidance of incest had spread by natural selection (1875:124).

There was, however, a difficulty with the argument from natural selection. E.B. Tylor pointed out that primitive peoples did not ban all marriages between close relatives. Quite often some first cousins were forbidden, while others were actually preferred as marriage partners. The marriageable cousins were usually the children of a brother and a sister: 'cross-cousins', Tylor called them. And he traced cross-cousin marriage back to very ancient days. The original society was imagined as a single undifferentiated band, in which promiscuity reigned. Then the band split into two. Men in one section had to marry women in the other. The children of two brothers belonged to the same section. So did the children of two sisters. However, the children of a brother and a sister – cross-cousins – belonged to different sections. Therefore they could marry one another. Tylor noted that this arrangement broke down as soon as the society became more complex and included more than two sections. However, he suggested that people would have got into the habit of marrying their cross-cousins. The custom would outlive the dual form of exogamy (Tylor 1889).

James George Frazer demonstrated in his usual encyclopaedic fashion that marriage with the mother's brother's daughter was particularly widely distributed. It was found in South India, and elsewhere in Asia, among the Chin and Kachin of Burma and the Gilyaks of Siberia. There were also traces of the custom in America, Africa, Indonesia, New Guinea and Australia (Frazer 1918: Chapter 4). But Frazer had his own ideas about how cousin marriage had come about. In Australia – and Australia represented for the Victorians the degree zero of social evolution – an Aboriginal man had to barter a sister or a daughter in exchange for a wife, for he had nothing else to offer (Frazer 1918:198). If two men were satisfied with the exchange of their sisters, then their sons might exchange sisters in turn. Their wives would be their double cross-cousins – mother's brother's daughters who were at the same time father's sister's daughters. And so the first form of marriage, sister exchange, led to cross-cousin marriage.

There was nothing much to choose between the scenarios dreamt up by Tylor and by Frazer. However, if either one of them was correct, then the institution of the incest taboo almost immediately led to marriage between cross-cousins. And cross-cousin marriage was still common in primitive societies. Did this mean that cousin marriage was primitive, its persistence in Victorian society a throw-back? The Catholic Church prohibited marriage between cousins, up to third cousins. Protestants, however, allowed first-cousin marriage. Which rule was more civilised?

This was a ticklish question for the Victorians. The American anthropologist, Lewis Henry Morgan, became the leading theorist on kin marriage. He wrote with relish about various imaginary types of group marriage, but he did not deal with marriage between cousins, despite the fact that several of his correspondents sent him reports of cousin marriage in Australia, North America and southern India.[5] His

---

[5]   Morgan's informant on the Tamil, the Reverend Ezekiel Scudder, pointed out to him that the same term was used for uncle and for husband's father, and suggested that this was appropriate because a person 'is expected to marry an uncle's daughter or son, and thus the two relationships are combined in one' (Trautmann 1987:242–243).

most recent biographer, Thomas Trautmann, suggests that Morgan failed to discuss these instances of cousin marriage for a very personal reason. He was married to his mother's brother's daughter. Consequently he was reluctant to label the practice as primitive (Trautmann 1987:243–245).

If only Morgan had been an Englishman! The Queen herself was married to her mother's brother's son. The Archbishop of Canterbury, Edward White Benson, was married to the daughter of his mother's brother's daughter. Darwin, the greatest naturalist of the age, was married to his mother's brother's daughter. The Darwinians had officially pronounced that cousin marriage was safe. However, opinion turned against cousin marriage in the United States from the 1860s. Before the Civil War there had been no laws against first-cousin marriage in any state in the Union. By the end of the nineteenth century, cousin marriages were prohibited in four states. Others soon followed (Ottenheimer 1996:37, 52–57).

A pioneering critic of cousin marriage was Morgan's friend and mentor, the Reverend McIlvaine (to whom Morgan dedicated his masterpiece, "Ancient society"). In 1866, in a speech to the Pundit Club, a society of intellectuals in Rochester, New York, McIlvaine announced that the practice of cousin marriage had been responsible for the 'degradation and inferiority' of the Tamil and the American Indian peoples. This was because 'the blood, instead of dispersing itself more and more widely, is constantly returning upon itself' (Trautmann 1987:244). Morgan must have been mortified. No wonder he preferred not to think about cousin marriage.

In Britain the reaction against cousin marriage only came much later. In the 1870s, when George Darwin made his study, approximately one marriage in twenty-five was between first cousins in the upper-middle class. The incidence was much higher in some clans, like the Darwin-Wedgwoods. By the 1920s, however, cousin marriage was being routinely condemned by the eugenicists, including another son of Charles Darwin, Leonard – who was himself married to a first cousin once removed – and by the 1930s, in England, only one marriage in 6,000 was with a first cousin.[6]

Yet while cousin marriage became uncommon in England, the anthropologists were increasingly obsessed with it. Cross-cousin marriage became a defining feature of primitive society. Immediately before the First World War, A.R. Radcliffe-Brown set out to demonstrate that among the Australian aborigines a person had to marry a cross-cousin. There were two Australian systems: in one, a man married a first cross-cousin, in the other, he married a second cross-cousin. Each type of marriage generated an appropriate classification of relatives into two

---

[6]   Medical Research Council (1935/36:139–140, 1936/37:157–158, 1938/39:81). By the middle of the twentieth century such unions accounted for only 0.004 per cent of the marriages of a middle-class London sample (Firth, Hubert, and Forge 1970:191–193).

[7]   Radcliffe-Brown later elaborated the model, adding new types and sub-types, and his ideas have been the object of much expert commentary. See especially Barnes (1967) and Scheffler (1978).

sets, roughly speaking 'in-laws' and others.[7] Radcliffe-Brown speculated that the Australian system fitted into

> a single general type of kinship organisation (the Dravidian-Australian type) found over a large area of South India and Ceylon [...] and perhaps over the whole of Australia, and in certain parts of Melanesia [...] possibly dating back to the first peopling of Australia and Melanesia. (1927:345)

A generation later, one of the greatest anthropologists of the twentieth century, Claude Lévi-Strauss, published a hugely ambitious study, "Les structures élémentaires de la parenté" (1949), which argued in effect that all the pre-modern societies of the world were organised on the basis of cross-cousin marriage. Or rather, as Marcel Mauss had said, their fundamental rule was reciprocity, their fundamental institution exchange. The most significant exchange was the exchange of women in marriage. This was, in fact, the basis of society itself. And the 'elementary' form taken by the exchange of women was the marriage of cross-cousins.

There are many things to say about Lévi-Strauss's theory – many, many things have been said, of course – but I want to draw attention to two features in particular. First, like the Victorians, and notwithstanding his repeated denials and qualifications, Lévi-Strauss's model assumes that social structures progress from a primitive to a civilised form. His 'elementary' structures are all associated with primitive societies, in which reciprocity rules. There are two types of reciprocity. The simplest form, restricted exchange, is associated with Australia, which, as ever, represents the closest approach to pure savagery. Generalised exchange is more advanced than restricted exchange, and it is found particularly in Asia, as Frazer had pointed out. (Asia was obviously a step up from Australia.) All the elementary systems were contrasted with complex systems – such as our own – which replaced the economy of gift exchange with a market economy. As Marshall Sahlins put it, 'money is to the West what kinship is to the Rest' (1976:216). Civilised and primitive are polar opposites. Second, Lévi-Strauss is really only interested in formal, ideal and (he believed) static structures. This was a characteristic feature of structuralism. Ultra-orthodox alliance theorists were even more idealist than the master. Much to the irritation of Lévi-Strauss, Rodney Needham argued that the "Elementary structures of kinship" was really only about categories and rules – or if it was not, it should have been (e.g., Needham 1971).

To be sure, there are examples of more realistic accounts of cousin marriage in the classical anthropological literature, beginning with Bronislaw Malinowski's notes on cross-cousin marriage in the Trobriand Islands. Most Trobriand adults chose their own marriage partners. Chiefs, however, often arranged infant betrothals for their sons. The Trobrianders were matrilineal. The chief was succeeded by his sister's son. His own son had no place in the new dispensation – unless he was married into the new chief's family. Therefore, as an infant he was betrothed to his father's sister's daughter, making him the brother-in-law of the next chief (Malinowski 1929:80–88).

Isaac Schapera, a student of Malinowski, used a statistical survey to analyse the pattern of kin marriage among the Tswana of Botswana. The Tswana favoured marriage with any cousin, but above all with a mother's brother's daughter. That was the ideology, and there were various proverbs and sayings to back it up. And indeed, marriage with a mother's brother's daughter was fairly common among ordinary Tswana. Nobles, however, preferred marriage with a father's brother daughter. In both cases, the reason was very similar. Men tried to reinforce relationships with powerful kin. For a commoner, these were often mother's brothers. For a noble, the best-placed relatives would be father's brothers.[8]

Marriage with a father's brother's daughter was also favoured in the Arab world, but it had no place in Lévi-Strauss's theory. The children of two brothers belonged to the same patrilineage. Marriage should be an exchange between men of different groups. So it was ridiculous – a scandal, Lévi-Strauss said – for a man to marry his father's brother's daughter (Lévi-Strauss 1959:13–14). Pierre Bourdieu pointed out, in his chapter on Berber marriage in the "Outline of a theory of practice", that this was a false problem. Lineages do not operate as corporate entities in the marriage market. Analysis should begin rather with individuals operating strategically, playing, more or less skilfully, the hands that they are dealt. Status comes into it, in the Berber case, and gender. Men might want their children to make dynastic marriages. Women have other priorities, and statistically, Bourdieu suggests, women usually win out. In any case, the formal rules do not determine how the game is played. People act selfishly on the whole, but they can usually find some socially acceptable justification for their actions. The marriage itself might be defined in various ways, the genealogies offering different options, kinship terms themselves being open to manipulation.

And there the argument petered out in anthropology. Debates on kinship and marriage had dominated the anthropology journals for a century. They ran into the sand at a very particular moment – Peter Laslett, the pioneer of family history in Britain, described it as 'the time of the Grand Climacteric in the family life of Western societies', when 'consensual unions began to be widespread, abortions to be exceedingly common, contraception to be universal and numbers of births to fall' (1989:843). Conservatives deplored these developments, but they were welcomed by others, particularly feminist theorists.

And in 1968 – a vintage year for revolutionary pronouncements – David Schneider made the even more audacious suggestion that, far from being the defining feature of primitive society, kinship was uniquely civilised. Americans happened to believe that certain relationships are biologically given, and that they are peculiarly

---

8       See Kuper (1987: Chapter 6).

important. This was their ideology. It was shared by many Europeans. However, there is no reason to think that any other peoples have developed the same set of ideas.[9] By implication, there was nothing natural about kinship. Perhaps the new reproductive technologies would render biology redundant and anachronistic, and erode what was left of the mythology of kinship in the West.

Anthropologists abandoned the study of kinship systems because they imagined that kinship was coming to an end and that it had, perhaps, always been just an ideological illusion. For much the same reasons, the field was now claimed by social historians. If kinship was vanishing, if gender relationships were in the process of transformation, if procreation was being handed over from nature to culture, then there was a need for historical reconstruction and commentary. It was now all about us. Comparisons were neglected.

Beginning in the 1970s, there has been a remarkable outpouring of publications on family history (Stone 1981:52). Michael Anderson early distinguished two main trends, a 'sentiments approach' and the 'household economics approach' (1980). In broad and crude terms, the sentiments approach is a way of thinking about developments in the eighteenth and nineteenth centuries, when the nuclear family is supposed to have become more emotionally loaded and more isolated. The household economics approach deals with the simultaneous transformation of the household. Once upon a time, every family ran a family business, as farmers or labourers or craftsmen. With the industrial revolution, the household became simply a unit of consumption.

The family business was, of course, the classic vehicle of Victorian entrepreneurship, binding together several generations of cousins in complex, sometimes fraught combinations. The Rothschilds provide a remarkable instance. The five brothers who established the five branches of the great Rothschild Bank were faced with the problem of continuity. Their solution was to institute a system of intermarriage. Between 1824 and 1877, marriages were contracted by 36 patrilineal descendants of the founder of the House of Rothschild. Thirty of these men and women married cousins, of whom 28 were first or second cousins related through the male line only. In other words, 78 per cent of the marriages were with a father's brother's daughter or a father's brother's son's daughter. These marriages were arranged in order to sustain the partnership between the five branches of the family, and they ceased abruptly when the rise of Prussia and the institution of joint stock companies changed the banking environment (Kuper 2001).

But the Rothschilds were a special case. The Wedgwood pottery was a more typical example of the large Victorian family business, and a closer look at Wedgwood marriages suggests that the materialist view of cousin marriage – that it 'keeps the wealth in the family' – is too simple.

---

[9]     Schneider (1968:1984). Cf. Kuper (1999:132–158).

The Wedgwood patriarch, Josiah Wedgwood, had married a cousin in 1764. His wife's father was a particularly successful potter. He did not want his daughter to marry Josiah, who was struggling to establish himself. Josiah was made to wait for years until – as his uncle put it – he could match his cousin's dowry of £4,000 'guinea for guinea' (Wedgwood and Wedgwood 1980:11).

Having started off at the age of fourteen as an apprentice to his brother Thomas, Josiah Wedgwood went on to become the most successful of all the potters in Staffordshire. He innovated, experimented with new processes and materials, organised his production along modern lines, and introduced fresh designs. His factory at Etruria made Wedgwood pottery world-famous. And it was very much a family business. However, Josiah's children did not marry cousins. His eldest sons, John and 'Jos', married two sisters, who were daughters of a wealthy country gentleman named Allen. There was no particular financial advantage to either side in these marriages. While an alliance with the country gentry was a step up socially for the Wedgwoods, Josiah was not greatly interested in conventional social prestige. He was much happier when his favourite daughter, Susannah, married Robert Darwin, the son of his close friend, Erasmus Darwin, a doctor, natural philosopher and poet, but not a particularly wealthy man, and no businessman.

Robert Darwin was a particular friend of his brother-in-law Jos Wedgwood, the coming man among the younger Wedgwoods. They had an understanding that Jos's eldest son, yet another Josiah Wedgwood, known as Joe, should marry Robert Darwin's daughter, Caroline. Joe was in no hurry to get married, but he went along with his father's wishes eventually. His marriage to Caroline Darwin was celebrated in 1837. He was 42 years old, Caroline was 37. Obviously they were not slaves to passion. Nor were they simply being pushed around by their fathers. But their marriage did make excellent financial sense. Dr Robert Darwin was not only a prosperous physician, like his father Erasmus. He also operated as a private banker, and he had lent a lot of money to Jos. The two men were involved in joint speculations in canals and later in railways. And Robert Darwin advised Jos on most of his financial arrangements, including those within the family. Since Joe was in line to take over the Etruria pottery works, his marriage to Caroline Darwin helped to ensure that important debts and obligations would be kept within the family.

Jos was also perfectly happy when, two years later, his daughter Emma reinforced the alliance with the Robert Darwins by marrying Charles Darwin. Charles had always been a favourite with his uncle. When the engagement was announced, Jos wrote delightedly to Robert Darwin: 'I could have parted with Emma to no one for whom I would so soon and so entirely feel as a father, and I am happy in believing that Charles entertains the kindest feelings for his uncle-father' (E. Darwin 1915:3). And now he and his friend would be quits. 'You lately gave up a daughter – it is my turn now' (E. Darwin 1915:2). Nevertheless, the business interests of the two fathers were marginal to this marriage. Charles had no intention

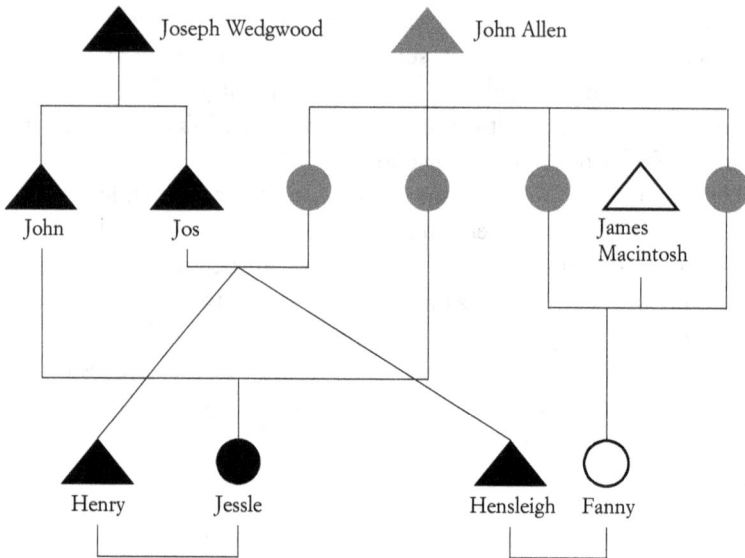

of taking on Robert Darwin's banking activities. Emma was not involved in the pottery business. And the fact that she married her cousin made no difference to her marriage settlement. Jos made similar provision for all his married children, some of whom married cousins while others did not.

Two of Jos's other children, Henry and Hensleigh, also married first cousins. Both these cousin marriages were poor financial risks, and they were resisted by prudent fathers. John Wedgwood had been Jos's partner in the pottery, but he was a hopeless businessman, and Jos had to get rid of him. John then went into banking, failed, and had to be bailed out by Jos. Jos was therefore not best pleased when Henry, the least promising of his own sons, married John's daughter, Jessie Wedgwood. Another of his sons, Hensleigh, fell in love with his mother's sister's daughter, Fanny Mackintosh. Fanny's father thought – as it turned out, rightly – that Hensleigh's prospects were poor, and he opposed the marriage for years before eventually giving in and arranging for him to get a civil service post.

So fathers generally paid close attention to financial considerations when their children married, but this was not a necessary reason for cousin marriage, certainly in the Darwin-Wedgwood clan. Nor was it a sufficient reason. In any case, fathers did not always have the last word on marriages. Mothers and sisters were also closely involved in courtship negotiations, and they were less concerned with the family business. Family sentiment mattered more to them. The relationship between siblings was typically very close in middle-class families, particularly between sisters, and between brothers and sisters. Brothers and sisters often formed joint households and maintained close emotional relationships. Cousins were often raised very much in and out of one another's houses, and as they grew up they quite often formed romantic attachments. Their aunts took a great interest in their marriages.

Sister exchange was also common, and quite often two brothers married two sisters. For example, Jos Wedgwood and his brother John married two Allen sisters. Although the relationship between the brothers cooled because of John's failure in the business, the sisters remained close. When Jos's son Henry wanted to marry John's daughter, Jessie, Jos resisted. However, the two mothers, who were, of course, each other's sisters, were all in favour of the match, and they carried the day. Jos's youngest son, Hensleigh, married the daughter of a third Allen sister. His aunt supported him, against her husband (Kuper 2009:129).

By the late twentieth century kinship theory had become unfashionable in anthropology, and most English people had long forgotten that their grandparents or great-grandparents found cousin marriage perfectly respectable. Yet just at this moment, the debates of the 1870s acquired a fresh relevance. Medical researchers remarked a high incidence of disorders in babies born to recent immigrants to Britain from Pakistan. Was this connected with a preference for cousin marriage?

The general view among geneticists today is that the risk of birth defects or infant mortality is roughly doubled for the children of first cousins. That is not a high level of risk. The geneticists, A.H. Bittles and G. Makoff conclude that 'the risks to the offspring of inbred unions generally are within the limits of acceptability. For first cousin progeny, it also must be admitted that they appear to be in remarkably close agreement with the levels calculated by [George] Darwin in 1875' (Bittles and Makov 1988:164). However, some studies are less reassuring. The authors of a recent prospective survey of Pakistani families in Birmingham suggest that if they 'ceased to marry relations, their childhood mortality and morbidity would decrease by 60%' (Bittles and Makov 1988:216).

George Darwin would have been interested to discover that the medical evidence is still by no means conclusive, but we might well suspect that this debate is not only about health risks. At any rate, it helps to sustain another, broader argument about immigration. Father's brother's daughter marriage is taken to be a defining feature of Islamic culture, and it is blamed not only for overloading the health service but for resistance to integration and cultural stagnation. It is also associated with patriarchy, the suppression of women and forced marriages. An American commentator, Stanley Kurtz – who has a doctorate in social anthropology from Harvard – has even argued that this marriage preference is 'an unexamined key to the war on terror' (2007).

Realistic ethnography is the best antidote to this sort of rhetoric. In Pakistan, and in the Pakistani diaspora, a preference is commonly expressed for marriage within the extended family or *birādarī*. Close relatives do often marry in most regions of Pakistan, although for a variety of rather down-to-earth reasons, and not because the ideology tells them to do so (Hastings 1988). Perhaps unexpectedly, the rate of cousin marriage among Pakistani immigrants to Britain is higher than the rate in rural Pakistan. And the rate of cousin marriage is particularly high among younger British Pakistanis. Around a third of the marriages of the immigrant generation were with first cousins, but well over half the marriages of the British-born generation are with first cousins (Shaw 2001). This is a consequence of British immigration regulations. It is very difficult for people to enter Britain unless they are married to people already here. In most cousin marriages, one partner immigrates to Britain from Pakistan. Alison Shaw found that 90 per cent of the first-cousin marriages in her sample of British Pakistanis in Oxford involved one spouse who came directly from Pakistan (Shaw 2001:327). There are often debts to family members back home who helped to finance the migration, and Roger Ballard points out that if a British-based family refuses a marriage offer from relatives in Pakistan, 'they are likely to be charged with having become so anglicized that they have forgotten their most fundamental duties towards their kin' (1987:27).

I feel a special kinship with these people. My background is Baltic Jewish, and my ancestors emigrated from Lithuania to South Africa at the end of the nineteenth century. My father's parents were first cousins. My great-grandfather had come to South Africa together with five of his brothers and a sister. His son married the daughter of one of those brothers. My mother's parents were also first cousins. I believe that when my grandfather had established himself he went back home to find a wife, and was then, presumably, pointed in the direction of his cousin.

Once upon a time, British emigrants behaved in the same way. Twenty per cent of marriages among protestant Northern Irish immigrants to the Midwest were with first cousins in the first half of the nineteenth century (Reid 1988:iv). Highland Scots migrants to New Zealand were also strikingly endogamous. What Maureen Molloy calls 'kin group endogamy' reached 70 per cent in some areas, and she remarks that 'it is quite common to find three siblings marrying two sibling cousins and a third cousin or cousin's cousin' (1986:232).

Scots abroad, Berber villagers, Pakistani and East European Jewish migrants, Tswana aristocrats and Victorian élites marry cousins for different reasons, but there are clearly common threads in the marriage strategies in all these cases. However, the analysis of marriage choices is not enough. Marriage preferences have structural consequences. It is probably not a good idea to look for these at the level of a total society, since marriages are very often limited by class or minority status, and political boundaries are unlikely to coincide with barriers to intermarriage. The structural implications of cousin marriage become evident on a smaller scale, at the level of a social network. Systematic intermarriage may guarantee the trust on which complex financial relationships depend, or it may foster patronage. No doubt there are other pay-offs. Often a sense of another sort of affinity, an affinity of values, of social situation, underpins intermarriage. In any case, families that can count on sustained alliances of this sort enjoy a powerful competitive advantage.

Cousin marriages in nineteenth-century England did not, of course, bind an entire society. However, they did contribute to the formation of a new social stratum, which Noel Annan called the 'intellectual aristocracy' (1955). This was not so much a class as a set of clans that persisted for several generations, each with a characteristic occupational speciality and specific political and religious tendencies – the Wedgwood-Darwins, for example. Such clans were highly endogamous. I believe that the rise of the new English ruling class, the Victorian intellectual aristocracy, may be ascribed very largely to their remarkable preference for cousin marriage and sister exchange.

Some final reflections may be in order. First of all, we must include ourselves in our comparisons, and on equal terms. Comparisons must not pit us against them: we and they must always both be included, treated within the same framework. Second, we should pay more attention to these banal encounters, to the taken-for-granted habits of everyday existence, to the 'many little traits of character', in which we find ourselves most alike. Malinowski once remarked that when he came into anthropology the emphasis had been on the differences between peoples. 'I recognized their study as important, but underlying sameness I thought of greater importance & rather neglected. I still believe that the fundamental is more important than the freakish' (quoted in Young 2004:76). Comparisons should surely focus on the commonalities, at least in the first place. We should therefore compare practices rather than conceptions.

Social anthropology can still aspire to extend the range of the social sciences by testing their propositions in other conditions. Ethnographers should engage ethnocentric social scientists in discussions about the less familiar social processes and views of the world they have studied. Perhaps as we come to know others better, as people with similar capacities, forming societies of a comparable sort, faced with common dilemmas, we may also understand more about ourselves.

*REFERENCES*

ANDERSON, Michael
1980     *Approaches to the history of the Western family 1500–1914.* Cambridge: Cambridge University Press

ANNAN, Noel
1955     "The intellectual aristocracy", in: J.H. Plumb (ed.), *Studies in Social History*, 241–287. London: Longmans

BALLARD Roger
1987     "The political economy of migration: Pakistan, Britain and the Middle East", in: J. Eades (ed.), *Migrants, workers and the social order*, 17–41. London: Tavistock

BARNES, John
1967    *Inquest on the Murngin*. London: Royal Anthropological Institute

BITTLES, A.H. and E. MAKOV
1988    "Inbreeding in human populations: an assessment of the costs", in: C.G.N. Mascie-Taylor and A.J. Boyce (eds.), *Human mating patterns*, 153–168. Cambridge: Cambridge University Press

BOURDIEU, Pierre
1977    *Outline of a theory of practice*. Cambridge: Cambridge University Press

BROWNE, Janet
1996    *Charles Darwin: voyaging*. London: Jonathan Cape
2002    *Charles Darwin: the power of place*. London: Jonathan Cape

BURKHARDT, Frederick and Sydney SMITH (eds.)
1986    *Correspondence of Charles Darwin*. Volume 2. Cambridge: Cambridge University Press

DARWIN, Charles R.
1833    *Letter to Caroline S. Darwin, 30 March–12 April 1833*. Letter 203; Darwin Correspondence Project; Cambridge University Library
1839    *Journal of researches into the geology and natural history of the various countries visited by H.M.S. 'Beagle'*. London: Colburn
1868    *The variation of animals and plants under domestication*. Volume 2. London: John Murray
1874²   *The descent of man, and selection in relation to sex*. London: John Murray
1875²   *The variation of animals and plants under domestication*. Volume 2. London: John Murray
1876    *The effects of cross and self fertilisation in the vegetable kingdom*. London: John Murray
1877    *The various contrivances by which orchids are fertilised by insects*. London: John Murray

DARWIN, Emma
1915    *A century of family letters*. Edited by Henrietta Litchfield. Volume 2. London: John Murray

DARWIN, Francis (ed.)
1887    *The life and letters of Charles Darwin*. Volume 3. London: John Murray

DARWIN, George H.
1874    *Letter to Charles R. Darwin, 6 February 1874*. Darwin Correspondence Project; Cambridge University Library
1875a   "Marriages between first cousins in England and their effects", *Journal of the Statistical Society* 38:153–184
1875b   "Note on the marriages of first cousins", *Journal of the Statistical Society* 38:344–348

FIRTH, Raymond, Jane HUBERT, and Anthony FORGE
1970    *Families and their relatives: kinship in a middle-class section of London*. London: Routledge and Kegan Paul

FITZROY, Robert
1839    *Narrative of the surveying voyages of His Majesty's ships Adventure and Beagle between the years 1826 and 1836, describing their examination of the southern shores of South America, and the Beagle's circumnavigation of the globe*. Proceedings of the second expedition, 1831–36, under the command of Captain Robert Fitz-Roy, R.N. London: Henry Colburn

FRAZER, James George
1909²   *Psyche's task*. London: Macmillan
1918    *Folklore in the Old Testament*. Volume 2. London: Macmillan

HASTINGS, Donna
1988    *Marriage among Muslims: preference and choice in Northern Pakistan*. Delhi: Hindustand Publishing Corporation

HAZELWOOD, Nick
2000    *Savage: the life and times of Jeremy Button*. London: Hodder and Stoughton

KEYNES, R.D. (ed.)
1988    *Charles Darwin's Beagle diary*. Cambridge: Cambridge University Press

KUPER, Adam
1987    *South Africa and the anthropologist*. London: Routledge
1999    *Culture: the anthropologists' account*. Cambridge, MA: Harvard University Press
2001    "Fraternity and endogamy: the House of Rothschild", *Social Anthropology* 9:273–287
2009    *Incest and influence: the private life of bourgeois England*. Cambridge, MA: Harvard University Press

KURTZ, Stanley
2007    *Marriage and the terror war*. National Review Online, February 15. http://article.nationalreview.com/?q=OWYyMDhkOWYwOWU4YWZlMTkwMWEzMDY0MTA0MGM0YmY

LASLETT, Peter
1989    "Marriage's ups and downs", *Times Literary Supplement* August 4

LÉVI-STRAUSS, Claude
1949    *Les structures élémentaires de la parenté*. Paris: Mouton
1959    "Le problème des relations de parenté", in: *Systèmes de parenté: entretiens interdisciplinarires sur les sociétés musulmanes*, 13–20. Paris: EPHE, Vie section

MAINE, Henry
1883    *Dissertations on early law and custom*. London: John Murray
1861    *Ancient law*. London: John Murray

MALINOWSKI, Bronislaw
1929    *The sexual life of savages*. London: Routledge

MOLLOY, Maureen
1986    "'No inclination to mix with strangers': marriage patterns among highland scots
        migrants to Cape Breton and New Zealand, 1800–1916", *Journal of Family History*
        11(3):221–243

MEDICAL RESEARCH COUNCIL
1935/36 *Report*. London
1936/47 *Report*. London
1938/39 *Report*. London

MORGAN, Lewis Henry
1878    *Ancient society*. New York: Henry Holt


NEEDHAM, Rodney
1971    "Introduction", in: Rodney Needham (ed.), *Rethinking kinship and marriage*, xiii–
        cviii. London: Tavistock

OTTENHEIMER, Martin
1996    *Forbidden relatives*. *Urbana*, IL: University of Illinois Press

RADCLIFFE-BROWN, A.R.
1927    "The regulation of marriage in Ambryn", *Journal of the Royal Anthropological
        Institute* 57:343–348

REID, Russell M.
1988    "Church membership, consanguineous marriage, and migration in a Scotch-Irish
        frontier population", *Journal of Family History* 13:397–414

SAHLINS, Marshall
1976    *Culture and practical reason*. Chicago: University of Chicago Press

SCHEFFLER, Harold W.
1978    *Australian kin classification*. Cambridge: Cambridge University Press

SCHNEIDER, David
1968    *American kinship: a cultural account*. Chicago: Chicago University Press

SHAW, Alison
2001     "Kinship, cultural preference and immigration: consanguineous marriage among British Pakistanis", *Journal of the Royal Anthropological Institute* 7(2):315–334

STONE, Lawrence
1981     "Family history in the 1980s", *Journal of Interdisciplinary History* 12:1–52

TRAUTMANN, Thomas
1987     *Lewis Henry Morgan and the invention of kinship*. Berkeley, CA: University of California Press

TYLOR, Edward
1871     *Primitive culture*. Volume 1. London: John Murray

WEDGWOOD, Barbara and Hensleigh WEDGWOOD
1980     *The Wedgwood circle 1730–1897*. London: Studio Vista

YOUNG, Michael W.
2004     *Malinowski: odyssey of an anthropologist 1884–1920*. New Haven: Yale University Press

# 3

## WHAT ENDS WITH THE END OF ANTHROPOLOGY?[*]

### Patricia Spyer

What ends with the end of anthropology? The spirit in which my own question is posed is as follows: Let us take the provocative challenge that informs the question 'the end of anthropology?' at face-value and answer it affirmatively. Anthropology as a discipline, and even more importantly, I would argue, as a practice, is coming to an end. But does this really matter in the larger scale of things? Is this something we should worry about? And, if so, how or what should we worry about? To say that anthropology ends is really, in other words, to say what? What ends or comes to an end with the end of anthropology?

Would the end of anthropology correspond to the end of otherness as we know it? Or does such otherness rather proliferate today as it spills out of the niches to which it has thus far been more or less comfortably confined? What happens when the major force in peoples' lives is change and not continuity, as so often seems to be the case under contemporary conditions? What continued value can anthropology have vis-à-vis the novel, the unfamiliar, the uncanny? How does one even recognise the sites of such revamped and released otherness? What is the fate in such a world of hard sociological notions such as race, class and gender, or, for that matter, of such anthropologically canonical ones as tradition, religion, culture and kinship? What becomes of these when the others to which we long have grown accustomed themselves make the world, crafting not only their own possibilities but ours as well, as, for instance, in the amazing phenomenon of an African-American president being in the White House? For all of its terrible on-going continuities, race will never be the same – indeed, this important instance suggests that it already is not.

When I asked myself 'What ends with the end of anthropology?' I came up with more than just a few things. I consider several of these here. First, I offer a brief overview of some of the more familiar, often celebrated aspects of the anthropological stock-in-trade; subsequently I single out one salient dimension of our practice that

[*] I would like to thank the members of the Institute of Cultural Anthropology & Development Sociology at Leiden University who participated in an afternoon seminar discussion that I organised on this topic in order to try out some of my ideas for the memorial lecture. I also thank my colleague Franklin Tjon Sie Fat for his suggestions and references on the topic of serendipity. I am most grateful to Webb Keane, Rosalind Morris and Rafael Sánchez for their comments on a previous version of the essay.

nonetheless is considered a bit infrequently. But first, our more familiar stock-in-trade. To begin with, there is the critical transformative power that is often ascribed to the anthropological encounter, or at least to the quest for transformation with all the implications thereof for knowledge production and the mutual understanding of different persons and collectivities.[1] Countless examples of such valued and often explicitly enjoined transformation abound in the anthropological literature. In the recent ethnography "Politics of piety: the Islamic revival and the feminist subject" (2004), for instance, Saba Mahmood describes the intellectual and personal benefits that issue from such transformations as follows:

> Critique, I believe, is most powerful when it leaves open the possibility that we might also be remade in the process of engaging another world-view, that we might come to learn things that we did not already know before we took the engagement. This requires that we occasionally turn the critical gaze upon ourselves, to leave open the possibility that we may be remade through an encounter with the other (Mahmood 2004:36).

Or as James Siegel puts it in his book "Naming the witch", foregrounding the challenge and thrill that such an encounter can bring with it, 'without the frisson that comes to the anthropologist, and that, in my experience, is one of the pleasures of ethnography, when one has to take seriously that which one cannot accept, anthropology, as the study of the other, would change its nature' (Siegel 2006:17). Taking seriously what one cannot accept is one version – albeit a somewhat more radical one – of anthropology's canonically sought-after engagement with otherness. The difference here, as Siegel intimates and as I elaborate below, is that any attempt to domesticate such otherness by either explaining it away or reducing it to something already known and commonsensical is eschewed.

In more general terms, though, this sought-after engagement along with the frisson that comes with an encounter with otherness pertains, of course, to the very oldest of the anthropological stock-in-trade. At the same time, I believe that such an open stance towards engaging with other lifeways and being potentially remade in the process assumes an even more urgent value in our current age of globalised flows and modernity at large, the latter, of course, being Arjun Appadurai's felicitous formulation (1996). Being 'remade' through encounter today and offering generosity and hospitality towards one's others seems, if anything, more pressing than before. To be sure, nowadays, such potentially transformative and literally unsettling encounters are perhaps less explicitly sought after than in previous times. Less and less, at any rate, do they inhabit the realm of choice. Lest I be misunderstood here, what I have in mind are those anthropologists and others of similar persuasion who, for whatever reason, actively sought out encounters with otherness or, conversely,

---

[1]     The concomitant defamiliarization of the familiar is also referred to by Jebens in the present collection.

those inhabiting such privileged places and circumstances that they could or could at least imagine that they might opt out of unwanted confrontations with one or another Other.

Today, by contrast, such encounters – variously violent, devastating, unsettling, transformative, creative, or indifferent – are frequently flung in one's face. They press in upon one's lifeworld, inflect, encroach upon or enhance one's existence, regardless of whether one welcomes and seeks them out or aims to cancel or avoid them. This, to be sure, is a situation that increasingly applies more generally to persons and populations scattered around the globe, including those who, until recently, could by and large shield themselves from unwanted otherness. One consequence, it would seem, of such potentially devastating collisions is either submission or wholesale violence, as so many trouble spots in the world unfortunately remind us. The main difference today is not that such devastating collisions did not transpire before or that situations of submission or wholesale violence were either unknown or uncommon – think only of the many colonial situations, including their often devastating aftermaths – but that now these are more generalised, less restricted in their ramifications or, in short, delocalised and more at large than ever before, neoliberalism's ravaging inroads being a prime example.

Call it, on a more celebratory note, as the conveners of the Jensen Memorial Lecture series do, 'the dazzle of the new heterogeneity' that marks our contemporary world. Or call it, as they also do, 'the crisis of anthropology',[2] a discipline both founded within and constitutive of a Western episteme that turned upon the radical distinction between the West and the Rest, an episteme that in recent years has fallen into crisis and crumbled in correspondence with a world, as Clifford Geertz would have it, 'in pieces', which, more often than not, are antagonistically interlocked and juxtaposed (Geertz 1998). Anthropology's crisis, in short, is not simply the result of internal critique on the part of its own practitioners or of academic turf warfare waged amongst ourselves and our colleagues in cultural studies nor even of the rising competition between anthropologists and journalists or NGO activists, as anthropology's current emphasis on contemporaneity and Internet-driven up-to-dateness replaces the discipline's former predilection for locating its subject matter in 'out-of-the-way' places as well as out of time.[3]

But what else ends with the end of anthropology? Related to the inclination to be remade in the process of ethnographically engaging the lifeworlds of others are at least two additional dimensions that I want to note here as constitutive of the disciplinary stock-in-trade. The first is the very ability or even propensity to engage and think other lifeworlds and lifeways. Bronislaw Malinowski's evocative opening to his "Argonauts of the Western Pacific" 'imagine yourself suddenly set down [...]

---

2       On the 'crisis of anthropology', see also the contribution by Jebens in the present collection.
3       Tsing (1993). See also Fabian (1983).

alone on a tropical island' is a foundational example (Malinowski 1922:4). To be sure, this 'heraldic arrival scene' has all the trappings of the heroic individualism that underwrites anthropological fieldwork (Visweswaran 1994:15). At the same time, the scene from the veranda signals a departure from something known and an opening onto the imagining and partial inhabitation of something radically different. As we all know, this ability not simply to observe or study difference but to participate in the lives of others and thus ideally at least, to come to inhabit this otherness partially over time, constitutes the very core of anthropology. As the linking of the term for the key disciplinary method of anthropology, 'participant observation' intimates, such a subject position is inherently unstable, far from easy, and allows for both provisional engagement and privileged withdrawal. This is a delicate arrangement, as all the cautionary tales about 'going native' warn, since the anthropologist should also not emerge from the encounter untouched or unsettled: at this engagement's core remains the much valued possibility that we might be remade – though crucially not undone – through the serious entertainment of otherness.

Secondly, I would argue that, at its very best, the anthropological encounter entails the ability to listen rather than simply understand, in which understanding, following the French philosopher Jean-Luc Nancy, would aim to reconstruct in the sense of defining and thereby circumscribing and placing the 'object' of study. Listening, by contrast, would engage otherness without trying to subsume or tame it (Nancy 2007). Notwithstanding its deservedly celebrated merits, an example of the former, of the taming of ontological otherness, would be Edward Evans-Pritchard's interpretation of Azande witchcraft (1976), following James Siegel's incisive reading of it. In "Naming the witch", Siegel returns to the famous granary scene in Evans-Pritchard's work and to the latter's argument that witchcraft serves the Azande as a natural philosophy that domesticates what lies beyond reason – namely, the granary's collapse at a certain moment when certain people are sitting under it.[4] This philosophy, Evans-Pritchard argues, provides stereotypical ways of thinking about the relationship between humans and accident or the occurrence of singular events. It offers an answer to the 'why me' question, or to why this singular event happened to m e and not to someone else. Evans-Pritchard, according to Siegel, introduces the witch via the Azande to rob such singularity of its excessive, unfathomable dimensions, as condensed in the figure of the witch. Yet in doing so he turns the

---

[4]     In his book, "Witchcraft, oracles, and magic among the Azande" (1937), Edward Evans-Pritchard refers to the collapse of a granary on raised pillars onto a man sleeping under it. Although the Azande recognise that the pillars had been eaten away by termites, only witchcraft could explain why the granary collapsed at that particular moment with that particular person under it. Witchcraft therefore and not the termites or the weight of the granary was the cause of death.

witch into a purely logical cipher, disregarding the incalculable, disruptive force that he or she is. In Siegel's words,

> this cheerful understanding of the witch follows (or perhaps established) the anthropological tendency to avoid thinking both the violence of witchcraft and the fear it inspires. The anthropological predilection to explain in local terms, which I share, risks losing sight of certain aspects of witchcraft. The contextualising of it risks its denaturing. One glides over the killings that often accompany witch hunts and the extreme fear they can produce as one unravels the logic of the beliefs and the reasons one might have to murder. Furthermore, this logic, unacceptable to the anthropologist him or herself – we do not ordinarily end up practicing witchcraft or protecting ourselves against it – becomes merely the beliefs of others in a place where everyone, it seems, believes in witches (Siegel 2006:17).

Although I will not pursue this line of argument, I offer it here as a new, less colonially inspired, and more nuanced approach to otherness, and therefore as one intimation of how anthropology might productively revamp parts of its classical heritage and methodology to meet the challenges presented by today's 'dazzling heterogeneity'.

Siegel's example suggests a novel opening inspired more by 'listening' than by conventional 'understanding' in Nancy's sense of these terms and, as such, it can be seen as one crucial dimension within a possible refigured future social terrain. In contrast to this example, however, and before moving on to my main topic, I note in passing two additional longstanding aspects of anthropological practice that would end with anthropology's coming to an end. The two final aspects I single out here are the discipline's characteristic privileging of everyday nitty-grittiness – in the sense of finding virtue and instruction in it – and the tendency to make visible what is invisible, in particular with respect to those life forms and lifeways that are marginalised, forgotten, downtrodden or exploited. But, equally importantly, in anthropology's newer terrains such as the "Media worlds" documented in the book of this title edited by Faye Ginsburg, Lila Abu-Lughod, and Brian Larkin (2002), our particular way of doing things often brings to light practices and understandings that remain hidden from the representatives of other disciplines. As the editors observe in the book's introduction,

> the kind of alternative circuits that we routinely encounter in our work – the spread of illegal cable networks or the widespread presence of pirate videos as a means of media exhibition outside the West – are rarely counted in the statistics about the U.S. or global media industries on which many accounts of transnational media are based. Indeed, it is one of our arguments that the construction of media theory in the West, with rare exceptions, has established a cultural grid of media theory with the effect of bringing into visibility only certain types of media technologies and practices.[5]

---

5    Ginsburg, Abu-Lughod, and Larkin (2002:2). See Larkin (2008) for an original analysis of video piracy's complicated infrastructure in contemporary Nigeria.

Anthropology, in short, in no small measure due to the combination of the open, reflective stance that is an explicit part of the discipline's constitution and methods tends to come across and entertain dimensions of distinctive lifeways through which the future unexpectedly arrives.

Rather than focus on any of the topics I have touched upon thus far, however – all of which have been amply discussed by anthropologists in the context of the discipline's internal critiques of itself, as well as by its intellectual interlocutors – I turn now to what will be the focus of the remainder of this essay, namely one aspect of our anthropological methods that I have always found especially illuminating as well as crucial to how we go about our work. It is also something that has received less attention than the other aspects of our practice named here and that, at least in the context of my own work, has been a recurrent source of the frisson invoked above that makes doing anthropology not just an on-going intellectual challenge but also a continual source of pleasure. To put it simply, this is the role of 'accident' in ethnography – yet, importantly, 'accident' of a very particular kind, and as something that, while forming a crucial component of sound ethnographic research, has not exactly been banished from our writing, but nor has it, to my knowledge, explicitly been developed as a constitutive element of a good deal of what we do.[6]

What I have in mind here is a very fortuitous kind of 'accident', enabled and in part prepared by the intimate ethnographic engagement with the everyday nitty-gritty and by the 'deep hanging out' (Clifford 1997:90) and extended fieldwork that, to this day, continues to characterise much of our practice and that allows or, more strongly yet, m a k e s   f o r  the often happenstance and serendipitous nature of our findings. These aspects of our practice, I argue – and I will offer examples from my own fieldwork experience – enable encounters and i n s i g h t s that often remain beyond the purview of other disciplines and knowledge practices. I also propose that, in comparison to other disciplines, and as a result of its particular methodology and open stance towards the objects of its intellectual inquiries – in short, as a discipline in principle surrendered to the Other – anthropology is characterised by a surplus of serendipitous insights. As long as we regularly assess and reinvent what lies at the core of anthropology's 'classical approach' and methodology, I suggest that this kind of serendipity, as a crucial component of the ethnographic imagination, can serve us as well today, within current globalised conditions, as it did during the earlier years of our discipline. And this, I argue, is a good thing.

Coined by Horace Walpole in 1754 in a letter he wrote to a friend living in Florence, the term 'serendipity' refers to instances of what he described as 'accidental

---

6       On the importance of serendipidity, see also the contribution by Crapanzano in the present
        collection.
7       Cited in Merton and Barber (2004:2; emphasis in the original).

sagacity', subsuming 'no discovery of a thing you are [actually] looking for'[7] but only those things that bump up against you inadvertently or that cross your path while you are looking for something else. Besides serendipity (*sérendicipité* or *sérendipité*), the French call such occurrences 'heureux hasard' (happy or fortunate chance). Absolutely crucial, when it comes to such 'happy chance', is that you can spot and recognise its value when you run across it or, as the case may be, it runs across you. Regarding such occurrences, the French scientist Louis Pasteur once famously opined, 'in the fields of observation, chance favours only the prepared mind'. Another, often neglected dimension of serendipitous discovery, following Horace Walpole's original formulation, is the requisite 'sagacity' or wisdom that allows a person 'to link together apparently innocuous facts to come to a valuable conclusion' (Merton and Barber 2004:22). As I hope you will agree, this statement could serve as a description of the best ethnography that our discipline has to offer. For, if anything, what good ethnography does is to lift out and trace the connections among apparently incongruous domains of life from religion and bureaucracy to food and sex or kinship and ecology, and so on, and so on ad infinitum.

To be sure, serendipitous discovery plays a part in the advancement of science generally, where it often establishes the foundation of important leaps of scientific understanding and intellectual insight.[8] Much more could obviously be said about serendipity's felicitous, creative place in intellectual production. This, however, is not my particular take on the topic. I refer you instead to the long-awaited book authored in the 1950s by the sociologist Robert K. Merton and Elinor Barber, "The travels and adventures of serendipity: a study in the sociological semantics and the sociology of science" (2004). What I do want to insist on is that while anthropology has no special claim on serendipity, our methods and approach vis-à-vis our objects of study – in which, at least ideally, we surrender ourselves to others – make us especially prone to serendipitous encounters. As anthropologists, I suggest, we are more likely to run up against and learn from serendipity. I turn now to substantiate this claim through ethnographic examples drawn from my own career as an anthropologist.

I begin at the beginning – my own, at least. In 1984, as a young graduate student, I made my first trip to Indonesia, where I have worked since as an anthropologist, concentrating primarily on the Moluccas or that eastern part of the archipelago featured in Adolf Ellegard Jensen's book "Die drei Ströme" (1984) about the religious life, among other aspects, of Seram Island's Wemale peoples. 1984 was also the year in which I first travelled to the Southeast Moluccas in the context of a preliminary survey trip to the Aru Islands, where, between 1986 and 1988, I

8    For an interesting piece on the workings of insight – scientific and otherwise – from the perspective of a cognitive neuroscientist, see Lehrer (2008).

spent close to two years conducting the fieldwork for my doctoral dissertation. As a student of Valerio Valeri, who, following in Jensen's footsteps, carried out extensive fieldwork in Seram, but also of Marshall Sahlins, Nancy Munn and Barney Cohn, I arrived in Aru attuned to the traffic in material things, to issues of exchange and circulation, but also to history, colonialism, commerce and communication. Armed with this orienting background, I set foot in the first village I visited on Aru's eastern pearl-diving shores to discover, a day or so after my arrival, an elephant tusk and gong carved in the centre of the village space. Although, as I have already suggested, I was certainly disposed by my training to find value in material things, nothing had prepared me for these objects, which jumped out, as it were, from their silhouettes so prominently outlined in the rocky cliff on which the village was built. Exorbitant even with respect to any expectations I already had, this highly serendipitous encounter with the privileged objects of multiple local transactions was not to be repeated again in such an explicitly foregrounded and objectified form. In no other village, among the many I spent time in thereafter in Aru, did I see these socially central things thus amplified and celebrated in communal space. No mere graffiti or casual carving, as I already knew from my study of the colonial sources on Aru, elephant tusks and gongs were not only among the most highly prized of trade goods that had been imported into the islands during the nineteenth century (if not earlier), they were valued precisely because of their productive agency within the marriage transactions that created and consolidated the most privileged of bonds among large groups of kin both within and across Aruese communities. Since such ties, in turn, formed the building blocks of other social exchanges and lifecycle performances, from the launching of new sailboats and the appeasement of the sea spirits to the ceremonies surrounding death, it was indeed a revelation to run across them so explicitly monumentalised in public space.

This early instance of 'happy chance' or serendipity in my career as an anthropologist served subsequently to orient my proposal for doctoral research, which, taking off from the importance of material things, prefigured in many respects – though, to be sure, in a much less sophisticated fashion – some of Arjun Appadurai's insights in "The social life of things" (1988). This was hardly surprising, since Nancy Munn's groundbreaking work on the *kula* exchanges of Papua New Guinea's Massim region (Munn 1986) was a major inspiration for both of us. What this serendipitous encounter did was not simply to highlight the need to take such things seriously, but to underscore their absolute centrality to the very enablement and contouring of social life. Thus, the encounter with tusk and gong pushed me to put into practice what Appadurai, in his seminal work on commodities and circulation, terms a certain 'methodological fetishism' (1988:5). In my subsequent writings on Aru, for instance, I repeatedly situate distinct things in motion – pearl oysters and store-bought white plates, for example – in relation to each other, following comparisons made by Aruese themselves. Also, I systematically track how these objects circulate between the trade stores on land, run by and large by Chinese-Indonesian merchants, and the undersea transactions between male Aruese divers and their sea-spirit wives. In following the Aruese cue to fetishise things, I was able to nuance and complicate the crass distinction that is so frequently asserted between the pragmatic realm of economics and, in Aru too, the debt relations that bind divers to traders on the one hand, and the more elevated domain of ritual and native belief on the other. This was hardly original since, as mentioned earlier, tracing such incongruous connections has long been part of the anthropological stock-in-trade: of relevance here, for instance, would be Malinowski's foundational work on the *kula*. Yet by homing in on the complex entanglements between a gendered undersea of seductive 'sea wives' who provide their diver husbands with pearl oysters and, in turn, demand store-bought goods (especially fake gold jewellery), thereby contributing to the indebting of divers to the traders a n d via their own beautification producing the surplus desire that animates commodities, I also undermined prevailing assumptions about global and local, central and remote, and the like, which, at least at the time, appeared a worthwhile contribution. All of this, however, only followed from both fetishising and pursuing the thing in motion and thus at least can be understood, at least in part, as an outcome of my early encounter with a tusk and gong in an Aruese village centre. Regarding these insights, I write in "The memory of trade":

> Analytically, the sea wife personifies what might be called the paradox of trade in Aru – the fact that in the context of debt relations wealth is inevitably drained in the same move that it is gained. But if the undersea spirit woman subsumes or even collapses what in actuality are often moments in a more drawn-out process, she also embodies the promise of a surplus that transcends the double bind that debt commonly describes. The seductive side of things surfaces prominently in divers' descriptions of their undersea consorts when they linger over their alien richness, getting caught up in the excess that […] constitutes in Aru the origin of trade itself. Nor surprisingly, while Barakai men and women speak in many ways alike in general terms of these figures as 'female', as 'wives', and as coupled with a diver in what more often than not is construed as a monogamous relation analogous to a man's marriage on land, conversations with Barakai men about their sightings and transactions with sea wives summons forth a more diverse gallery of women. Across a variety of settings and situations, men's talk about 'sea wives' ranges from highly eroticized fixations on the oyster itself in which the trade product assumes an active, seductive role – its opening move, as it were, read as an invitation extended by a woman to a man – [or as one diver put it]: 'when pearl oysters open up like that, men go crazy for them, because these oysters are women, women with reddish hair' – to somewhat more fleshed out portraits that tend to focus on the flowing coppery red hair with which these figures cloak themselves as they float about the undersea on their pearl oyster perches, to – less frequently – more sober fishwives who only, and then rarely, appear to their diver husbands in the guise of a fish – usually something a bit out of the ordinary (not to mention potentially dangerous) like a stingray.

But whatever specific form their apparition assumes for individual Barakai divers, sea wives, at least in good times, provision their men with the most prized of trade products destined to pay off debts in island stores [the oysters, in other words]. By the same token, these spirit women are themselves credited with a desire for things of the 'splendid and trifling' kind: in addition to generic white plates, the sea wives covet 'gold' jewelry. If, then, sea wives can be seen as entangled in the networks productive of debt in Aru, they are also (in)vested – at times quite literally – with an aura of alluring wealth. The varying investments of islanders in the figures of the undersea spirit women, the tantalizing, often eroticized influence that sea wives exert sporadically on land as they enter the homes of divers and into the relations between Barakai women and men with a range of repercussions, and the promise of surplus they embody makes these figures much more than a sanction that serves to enforce a certain system of debt or simply a form of false consciousness reproductive of exploitation (Spyer 2000:144–145).

In subsequent passages of the book, I go on to show how much more is both at stake and imagined with regard to these undersea transactions. To be sure, many other experiences in these islands, including those of learning a local language (Barakai) and of interacting intimately and over an extended period of time with Aruese men and women, with traders and a host of others – in short, the myriad, complicated relations, exchanges, conversations, events, insights, doubts, troubles and joys that we subsume under the rubric of fieldwork – all of this, along with a Ph.D., a postdoctoral position, a first job, a return to Aru, and the turning of a way-too-long dissertation into a published book – all of this mediated my first visit to the archipelago and my serendipitous confrontation with the gong and tusk pair that jumped out at me from a pearl-diving village's rocky centre.

You may object, perhaps, that, even without this initial encounter, I would have arrived at many of the same conclusions. Perhaps. At the same time, in my career as an anthropologist, some serendipitous event seems often to mediate, dramatically-à-vis reorient or refine the terms of my ethnographic engagement vis-à-vis a particular problem in a particular place. Such serendipity, crossing my path in this way, may not only provide an initial framing of the problems pursued and the questions asked – more often than not, it offers a sense of that crucial frisson, which, as Siegel puts it, is one of the great pleasures of ethnography, 'when one has to take seriously that which one cannot accept' or that, at any rate, seriously confounds one.

I turn now to a more clear-cut instance of this, of 'taking seriously that which one cannot accept' and of listening that is more along the lines of Jean Luc Nancy's understanding of that term, mentioned earlier. To be sure, in the previous example, for me to discern an elephant tusk and gong in their bare if symbolically potent outlines meant that someone had to show me the way. I only came to recognise these objects – and it was only then that they 'jumped out' at me – when, in answering my questions, some of the village's inhabitants helped me see what they themselves saw.

When I returned to Aru in 1994 for a visit of two months, a great deal had transpired since I last left the islands in 1988 upon concluding the fieldwork for my doctoral dissertation. Of relevance here is especially the combination of overfishing of the oyster beds, the effects of shrimp trawling and shark fishing in these same areas, and the turning of the Chinese-Indonesian traders to the employment of divers from elsewhere, the so-called *deba-deba*, who in contrast to the majority of Aruese would dive with 'bottles' and ventured therefore deeper and further from shore where, notwithstanding the increasingly depleted circumstances, shells could more easily be found. Complicating all of this was a disease that had struck and ravaged the oyster beds, further depleting an already diminishing supply. Many explanations for this combined disaster circulated among the islands' pearl-diving populations. A popular one was the claim that the large-scale 'disappearance' (as it was termed) of shells was a temporary affair, even something that they had experienced before, if less dramatically.

> 'One year', explained an older man recalling his own pleasured encounter with the resurfaced shells, 'there are almost none; but then another year – hey, these things are here again!' Still others, confronted with the massive devastation of their oyster beds in the early 1990s ensuing, as noted above, from a deadly combination of disease, overfishing and the incursions of especially the *deba-deba* teams employed by their own traders into Barakai community diving areas, denied the shells' 'disappearance' altogether. Introducing some local initiative into this dismal process, many of these women and men saw the oyster depletion as disappearing acts or willed protests on the part of undersea spirits against the reckless trespasses into their territory by unauthorised persons who ventured there without heed to the etiquette and claims that regulate its entry and use (Spyer 2000:115).

My return, incidentally, in the context of these dramatic events wreaking havoc in Aru's pearl-diving communities also hints at how the particular moment of field research, the 'ethnographic present', is itself in a sense serendipitous. Unlike historians, who may choose the periods in which they work, anthropologists enjoy no such luxury, constrained as we are not only by the times which we and our coeval others inhabit, but also by the happenstances of our own biographies that put us in particular places at particular times.

Returning now to the attitude of many Aruese regarding the oysters' decline, this suggests how pearl diving's shifting contours are creatively and variously construed by Barakai peoples. At the same time, however, the prevailing attitude at the time also suggests some of the limits that this particular discourse runs up against. These limits were driven home to me – forcefully, poignantly, but also serendipitously – by the adamant objection of a diver, a close friend and ritual specialist, whose daughter was also my research assistant. This arose when I proposed – indeed, even insisted, driven by my own fears about the impending ecological exhaustion and the general Aruese' refusal to entertain it – that the valued shells might not just disappear, but more dramatically and conclusively, die out. Contrary to local expectations, they might, I argued, never return again. I still recall my friend's response, equally vehement, in the face of my assertions, as one of the most moving exchanges of my fieldwork. 'How could these pearl oysters disappear', he reasoned, 'if this is what we live off?'

It took some days for me to realise that what he had articulated was not only an existential investment in a particular order of things – days, incidentally, that were the only time in our long, enjoyable and fruitful collaboration when he avoided and did not address me. What my friend voiced with his protest against my assertions was also the extreme limit of a way of understanding beyond which it becomes impossible to think – a limit, in some respects, like that of the Azande witch, following Siegel's critical reading thereof. In short, the imaginative field in which the sea wife enjoys such prominence has its own limitations. The same reason that allows the figures of divers' undersea consorts to subsume and do so much symbolic work in the lives of Barakai islanders – namely, that they are crucial embodiments of surplus – forecloses for Aruese any idea of ecological exhaustion insofar as the sea wives stand in the way of admitting that even 'surplus' can sometimes end.

My next and last two examples of serendipity are taken from my current book project on the mediations of violence and what I call post-violence in the aftermath of the murderous conflict that racked the provincial Moluccan capital of Ambon from early 1999 until official peace in 2002, with sporadic violence continuing thereafter. When the war broke out in this Indonesian city, less than a year after former President Suharto stepping down and the tumultuous series of crises that precipitated this event, scholars from Indonesia, the Netherlands, Australia and elsewhere quickly weighed in with arguments explaining why the conflict, defined rapidly in religious terms as Muslim versus Christian, had been inevitable. Without the opportunity, given the circumstances, to visit Ambon, I took in these writings and commentaries, but found myself little satisfied with the kinds of explanations the majority of them had to offer. This is not the place to detail my dissatisfactions, which I discuss elsewhere (Spyer 2006). Suffice it to say here that, while many of these writings marshalled a slew of enabling backgrounds that allegedly explained the conflict – things like the former colonial situation, increasing land shortages on the island, population pressure, rising numbers of Muslim migrants in the city, the skewing of the former numerical balance between Muslims and Christians or the recent arrival in Ambon of a hundred or so thugs in the wake of a battle surrounding a Jakarta gambling den – these were all explanations of why the conflict s h o u l d have happened, not necessarily of why or how it in fact did happen. I tried instead to discern the precise conditions that might help clarify why and how the conflict d i d happen at that particular time, in January 1999, and in the particular way it did. In other words, much like Evans-Pritchard's example of the Azande granary, I was interested in contingency and particularity, in the nitty-gritty of a particular place and circumstances at a particular moment in time.

Starting from what I could glean from the perspectives of ordinary Ambonese, I homed in on the creation of and conditions for 'the climate' that helped to produce the violence and, crucially as well, how the sedimentation or consolidation of violence in the city in turn provoked additional violence. In so doing, and for reasons that I can only gloss here, I came to understand the violence, in many respects, as emerging out of what I characterised as a situation of blindness or a mobile, dense and murky terrain in which something that is waiting to happen does, in fact, happen. I described this terrain as built out of spirals of information, misinformation and disinformation, the revamping of criteria of credibility, customs of trust and accountability, and knowledge forms that blur that boundary between what is seen and what is heard, what is known and what is suspected, what is feared and what is fantasised, what is fact and what is fiction. This is what I meant in taking the word 'climate' – often invoked, but not further specified in the literature on violence – as an analytical point of departure. I came to understand this 'climate's' composition as an infrastructure comprising the overt and covert representations and mobilisations of both mass and smaller scale, politically-driven 'tactical' media, the circulation of ideologically potent images and hard-edged reified positions, in addition to rumours, graffiti, some unknowables and even unmentionables. These, I argued, haunted the terrain in which various Big Men, regular folk and the shadowy characters of war moved, and in which these structured – equally but differently – their varied perceptions and actions. I also went on to detail what I call anticipatory practices as part and parcel of a larger 'aesthetics of depth', since these practices home in on the disguises and deceptive identities that are held to be prevalent during the war and the counter-moves such surface disimulations would, in turn, have provoked to penetrate the treacherous appearances of persons and things. What the discourse makes clear is that, while difference may be something you can see – the assumption of many Ambonese, especially since the war, that you can spot not only a fellow Christian or Muslim, as the case may be, but recognise the Other at face-value as well – what you see cannot necessarily be trusted. This is a fine line that can make all the difference – indeed, as some found out brutally during the war, even between life and death. In some respects, then, at this early stage of my research, I was already attuned to seeing Ambon's violence as made up of blindness and uncertainty or as a predicament in which the sense of unseen and faceless danger prevailed, in which the familiar became unfamiliar, and where everyday appearances concealed unknown horrors.

Still, I was in no way prepared for what I encountered in Ambon's streets on my first trip back to the city since the war's conclusion. In this first visit since the mid-nineties, in 2003, I was amazed to see murals of Christ surrounded by Roman soldiers stretching out on public walls, a monumental replica of his face after a

Warner Sallman original in front of the city's Maranatha Church, a Christ mural opposite a motorbike taxi stand with an Israeli flag as backdrop, and a billboard showing a tearful Jesus overlooking over a globe oriented to Ambon Island at a Christian neighbourhood gateway where none of these had ever been before.[9] Later trips revealed more such productions. They range from the billboard of Christ under a crown of thorns, which greets the visitor on the highway running from the island airport into Ambon, to others dispersed across the city, commonly marking entrances to Christian neighbourhoods and flanked by murals with scenes from Jesus' life and Christian symbols (cf. Spyer 2008).

Though especially striking in the city's postwar public space, painted Christs recently began rising up behind Protestant church altars, and not just those of the colonial-derived Protestant Church of the Moluccas or Gereja Protestan Maluku (GPM), but also, for instance, the Salvation Army. Domestic space is also being transformed as painted prayer niches and even small prayer rooms are carved out in some Ambonese Protestant homes. These are modelled on or draw inspiration from print examples taken from Christian calendars and the occasional Last Supper posters that were the main religious embellishments in such homes until the recent war. Remarkably, the pictures and painted spaces fly in the face of the aniconic Dutch reformed Calvinist tradition from which Ambon's mainstream Protestant church, the GPM, historically derives.[10] Equally remarkable is the fact that the paintings in the streets are neither organised, supported or encouraged by any centralised authority, including the Church. And while they differ in certain respects ethnographically from those in churches in the general import of Christ's depiction, the diverse painted sites scattered across the city share a common origin in violence and fear. In an immediate sense, as I have argued elsewhere (Spyer 2006), they register the sense of a community not only under extreme duress but also, generally speaking, seeing itself at risk of annihilation.

In terms of my larger project, this totally unexpected and, in light of Calvinist Protestantism's aniconic tradition, unlikely encounter with the pictures – which only proliferated as I tracked down the painters and their productions in the city and on surrounding islands – was highly serendipitous. The pictures, and the various ways in which I have come to understand them, clinched my earlier argument about blindness and, more generally, made me see how Ambon's postwar situation provides

---

9      Quite a number of Ambon's billboards and murals draw upon calendars and illustrated books
       that feature the world of Warner Sallman, whose paintings of Christ were a crucial component
       of popular religiosity and Christian visual culture from the mid-twentieth century, especially in
       the United States. In Ambon, for instance, I have seen such Sallman classics as "Head of Christ"
       (1940), "Christ at heart's door" (1940), "The Lord is my shepherd" (1943) and "Christ in
       Gethsemane' (1941), reproduced both accurately and more approximately. See Morgan (2005).
10     This is the Calvinist Dutch Reformed Church or Nederlands Hervormde Kerk, not to be confused
       with its later, nineteenth-century orthodox offshoot, the Reformed Church or De Gereformeerde
       Kerken.

an especially pregnant site for thinking the place and diversified manifestations of the 'visual' today. The turn to picturing in the city – or what I analyse more theoretically, beyond the simple emergence of billboards and murals, as a wider process of becoming image – brought home to me, via the 'happy chance' encounter with Ambon's huge multiplying Jesuses, how visibility emerges in sharpest relief within conditions that I have already described as those of a generalised blindness, much as in a situation where seeing is prohibited and invisibility enforced (Mitchell 2005). From this perspective, the city's novel Christian pictures are simply the most literal manifestation of a much wider thematisation of the visual on the part of segments of Ambon's traditional Christian population. Suffice it to say here that the enabling factors of the thematisation of the visual range from those that are more immediately rooted to globally inflected processes that were amplified and aggravated during the recent war. Among such factors are the growing presence in Ambon, as elsewhere, of a highly public Islam, the relative withdrawal of the Indonesian state and the partial revamping of modes of governmentality in post-Suharto Indonesia, which many Christians perceive as their general abandonment during the war not only by their own government, but by other imagined potential sources of support as well, like the United Nations, the Dutch government and European Union and, last but not least, the effects of the mediation of the city's 'crisis' by the wider humanitarian aid industry and national and international mass media. Taken together, along with other influences and ingredients too complex and numerous to go into here, these prepared the wider valorisation and, by extension, thematisation of the visual and the visible in relation to issues of authority, community and futurity among some of Ambon's Christians.

If in this case serendipity was, at least in the first instance, visual – my own startled encounter with the city's new pictures on the ruins of recent war – my final example again follows Jean-Luc Nancy's invitation to l i s t e n in the sense of engaging otherness without aiming to domesticate or tame it. In other words, this example is less circumscribed by prior 'sagacity' than the way in which my qualification of Ambon's violence as a blindness had in a sense already prepared me to see the new Christian pictures in a particular way. This last example of serendipity surfaced in an interview I conducted with a Protestant minister of the GPM, a man who also headed the church's Pastoral Counseling Office. He spoke of Ambon's new street paintings as, among other things, a direct counter to what scholars increasingly describe as a burgeoning 'public Islam'.[11] In Ambon, as across Indonesia generally, Islam's growing public presence registers visibly and audibly in the many new mosques being built, as well as the popularity of Qur'anic reading sessions and typical Muslim fashions. To this can be added the rise in the number of Indonesians performing the *hajj* or pilgrimage to Mecca, the resurgence of Islamic

---

[11]    See, for instance, Hasan (2007).

print media, the development of new forms of *da'wa* or proselytising like cyber-*da'wa* and cellular *da'wa,* and the rise in new Islamic economic institutions. As the minister put it, invoking an oppositional logic that defines the Christian pictures as a kind of counter-public to the dominant one in Indonesia of Islam: 'It's the same. They don't make pictures much, but they wear headscarves as their own kind of special characteristic. To show that "we are Muslims". Yes, that's what stands out'.

Like others I conversed with in Ambon, his comments drew a stark contrast between Muslims and Christians on multiple fronts, including their post-war territories in the city, their general behaviour, their respective misdeeds or martyrdom, but also their alleged appearance, inherent characteristics and even, according to many Christians, the presence of light rays or illumination enhancing their own faces as opposed to what the minister, like others, described as the dark illegibility of the Muslim. To be sure, one way of understanding the new Christian pictures would be to uphold this rigid understanding of the main terms of relations between the two religiously defined populations. Rising up along the highways leading into the city, or monumentally at the entrances to Christian neighbourhoods, the billboards and their companion murals brand particular neighbourhoods as Christian, gate them against outsiders and appear as amulets to ward off the Muslim Other. Yet, when the minister turned to relate the story of a spate of possessions that had afflicted some among the city's Christian population in the very midst of war, I caught a serendipitous glimpse of how things might in fact be much more complicated.

To make a long story short, the possessions began in a Christian prayer group of five persons when the protagonist of the story – a Javanese convert to Christianity and city resident – introduced its members to a small stone that had been given her by a Muslim woman clad solely in black. The convert obtained the stone from the Muslim following a fight between them in the city's Ahuru neighbourhood. When the Javanese prevailed, the Muslim leader surrendered the stone to her opponent. Once it began to circulate within the Christian prayer group – like others of its size formed during the war, along with multiple extra prayer sessions convened in churches, homes and even in Ambon's streets – strange things began to happen. Whoever held the stone fell ill. More unsettling, though, was the fact that whenever the group sat down to pray they found that they could not, or felt themselves lifted out of place, or prayed as Muslims with their hands held out flat and open in front of them as if they were holding the Qur'an. The first to be possessed was the Javanese convert at the refugee camp, where she had fled as the latest in a series of displacements; the other group members quickly followed suit. Exorcism conducted by two ministers at the GPM's head Maranatha church – including the one who disclosed these events to me – and backed by the congregation's alternate singing and praying revealed that the possessed convert was not only possessed by the Muslim woman she had defeated in battle but by the Muslim daughter of the Sultan of the North Moluccan city of Ternate.

Relevant here, briefly, is how Ambon's possession appears to lay bare the fault lines of a highly fraught, religiously mixed urban society under radical revision. It came via a Muslim convert to Christianity, turned a Christian prayer group into a Qur'anic reading session and introduced the formerly powerful, ancient North Moluccan sultanate of Ternate – in 2001 the new capital of an almost wholly Muslim province – into the core of Christian worship.

One part of this story unfolds into a larger account of this societal revision, comprising, among other things, the changing status and location of religion today, not just in Ambon, but more broadly in Indonesia and beyond. The source of this instance of serendipity, however, is foregrounded in the scene of possession itself – its revelation of the permeable, wavering fault line between Ambon's Muslim and Christian communities against the backdrop, as it were, that was so insistently conjured up in post-war conversations of the stark and absolute contrast between them. For me, this serendipitous encounter provoked the following questions: what does it mean when a Muslim spirit – a force that cannot be ignored – seizes upon and usurps the place of a Christian subject? What kinds of concerns might be at stake when such Muslim agency can interrupt the space not only of an individual Christian but of the larger Ambonese Christian community by hollowing out its most intimate sites of worship? How does the status of the event's protagonist – a Muslim convert to Christianity, and thus a split subject from the start – complicate the character of possession? What might these multiple layerings and porous co- and inhabitations tell us about the interfacings and entanglements of the city's Muslim and Christian populations as these have evolved both historically and in recent years, and as they were shaped and aggravated in the context of war? Crucially, what claim of a Muslim Other is being articulated vis-à-vis a Christian Self? And lastly, if most urgently, what might we take from all of this to suggest how the inhabitation of possession might contain or not contain possibilities for the cohabitation or future living together of Christians and Muslims?

Using these four examples from my ethnographic fieldwork, I hope I have not only shown how productive a serendipitous encounter can be and how central to anthropological practice such encounters are, but also offered some sense of anthropology's relevance to the challenges and problems that correspond to the 'dazzling heterogeneity' that marks our contemporary world. I also hope that the serendipitous encounters I describe here may offer insights into how a previously privileged population, in this case Christian Ambonese, confront their fears of marginalisation and even physical obliteration, yet aim to insert themselves via the Christ pictures – let it be said, in many respects, conservatively and dangerously – back on to the Indonesian national stage and into the international spotlight that makes or breaks the media 'hot spots' and fleeting foci of international attention and thus potential opportunity around the globe. Similarly, I hope that the example from Aru may indicate the complexities that can afflict the coming together of different perspectives on ecological disaster, a pressing concern of our time and especially fraught, too, since, as we all know, the environment acknowledges no borders. And finally, my last example – call it if you like the construction of difference in conflict – may suggest how, alongside the hard-edged enmities of war, other constructions of otherness, however strange and oblique, may be at work as well, and, if in a complicated fashion, offering an alternative to figuring what otherwise may appear to be an intractable situation.

In choosing to emphasise what would end with anthropology's ending, I have concentrated on what I consider to be of continued relevance and value in our discipline. Although I have not addressed the discipline's diminishing public role, or even its widespread institutional troubles, I hope I have suggested how there is much that we, as anthropologists, still have to offer. To be sure, there is a great deal in today's world – as, indeed, in previous times – alternately to 'dazzle' or dismay and confound one. Yet anthropology's particular ability, at least in the very best of the tradition, to take 'that which one cannot accept' seriously as a point of principle and *modus operandi* describes an increasingly urgent position that should be assumed – politically as much as, if not more than, academically. Seen in this light, serendipity, so central if not so celebrated within the discipline, can at times provide a point of entry into this position. From 'accident', *heureux hasard* or intimations of the future arising in the most unexpected places, to taking seriously what one cannot accept, anthropology offers strategies, forms of knowledge and methodologies for inhabiting and cohabiting in our fraught, dazzlingly heterogeneous world.

## References

APPADURAI, Arjun
1988    *The social life of things: commodities in cultural perspective.* Cambridge: Cambridge University Press
1996    *Modernity at large: cultural dimensions of globalization.* Minneapolis: University of Minnesota Press

CLIFFORD, James
1997    *Routes: travel and translation in the late twentieth century.* Cambridge, Mass.: Harvard University Press

EVANS-PRITCHARD, Edward E.
1976    *Witchcraft, oracles and magic among the Azande.* New York: Oxford University Press

FABIAN, Johannes
1983     *Time and the other: how anthropology makes its object.* New York: Columbia
         University Press

GEERTZ, Clifford
1998     "The world in pieces", *Focaal* 32:91–117

GINSBURG, Faye D., Lila ABU-LUGHOD, and Brian LARKIN (ed.)
2002     *Media worlds: anthropology on new terrain.* Berkeley: University of California Press

HASAN, Noorhaidi
2007     *The making of public Islam: piety, agency, and commodification of the landscape of the
         Indonesian public sphere.* Unpublished paper presented at the program seminar "In
         search of middle Indonesia", Royal Netherlands Institute for Southeast Asian and
         Caribbean Studies, Leiden, March 2007

JENSEN, Ad.E.
1948     *Die drei Ströme.* Züge aus dem geistigen und religiösen Leben der Wemale, einem
         primitiven Volk in den Molukken. Leipzig: J.W. Goethe-Universität, Frobenius-
         Institut (Ergebnisse der Frobenius-Expedition 1937–38 in die Molukken und nach
         holländisch Neu-Guinea 2.)

LARKIN, Brian
2008     *Signal and noise: media, infrastructure, and urban culture in Nigeria.* Durham: Duke
         University Press

LEHRER, Johan
2008     "The Eureka hunt", *The New Yorker* July 28

MAHMOOD, Saba
2004     *Politics of piety: the Islamic revival and the feminist subject.* Berkeley: University of
         California Press

MALINOWSKI, Bronislaw
1984     *Argonauts of the Western Pacific.* Prospect Heights, IL: Waveland Press ([1]1922)

MERTON, Robert King and Elinor G. BARBER
2004     *The travels and adventures of serendipity: a study in sociological semantics.* Princeton,
         NJ: Princeton University Press

MITCHELL, W.J.T.
2005     *What do pictures want?* The lives and loves of images. Chicago: University of
         Chicago Press

MORGAN, David
2005     *Visual piety: a history and theory of popular religious images.* Berkeley: University of
         California Press

MUNN, Nancy D.
1992    *The fame of Gawa: a symbolic study of value transformation in a Massim (Papua New Guinea) society.* Durham: Duke University Press

NANCY, Jean-Luc
2007    *Listening.* New York: Fordham University Press

SIEGEL, James
2006    *Naming the witch.* Stanford: Stanford University Press

SPYER, Patricia
2000    *The memory of trade: modernity's entanglements on an Eastern Indonesian Island.* Durham: Duke University Press
2006    "Some notes on disorder in the Indonesian postcolony", in: Jean Comaroff and John L. Comaroff (eds.), *Law and disorder in the postcolony*, 188–218. Chicago: University of Chicago Press
2008    "Blind faith: painting Christianity in post-conflict Ambon, Indonesia." *Social Text* 26(396):11–37
2008    "Christ at large: iconography and territoriality in postwar Ambon, Indonesia", in: Hent de Vries (ed.), *Religion: beyond a concept*, 524–549. New York: Fordham University Press

TSING, Anna Lowenhaupt
1993    *In the realm of the diamond queen: marginality in an out-of-the-way place.* Princeton: Princeton University Press

VISWESWARAN, Kamala
1994    *Fictions of feminist ethnography.* Minneapolis: University of Minnesota Press

# 4

# THE END OF ANTHROPOLOGY, AGAIN
## On the future of an in/discipline[*]

John Comaroff

In May of 1971, I underwent an initiation rite, one that stripped me all but naked before the world. This was the day on which I had finally to deal with the trauma of becoming adult. I refer to my very first job interview, at the University of Wales. To be honest, I had some forewarning. It came in the guise of an ethnographic film. Actually, the movie was styled as a farce, but I know high realism when I see it. Entitled "Only two can play", its high point was a job interview for the position of sublibrarian in a Welsh town.[1] Both the committee and its questions were notable for their absurdity: a few involved plumbing; one, how best to treat a woman who asked to borrow "Lady Chatterley's lover". This should have primed me. When my turn came to meet my inquisitors, I faced a dean, a priest, an archaeologist, and an elderly matron, who, I think, represented the local community. Her name was Mrs. Evans. Their queries ranged widely. Had I, as a youth in South Africa, played rugby? This, clearly, was a job requirement. Did I take drugs? Whether that was also a requirement was less clear. What was my political past? In Wales, rugby is politics, so those two questions were really the same. The clincher came from Mrs. Evans. 'I read somewhere', she said, 'that anthropology is becoming extinct'. I waited for the interrogative. There was none. Instead, excruciating silence. I was caught totally unawares. Could this everywoman from the Celtic fringe have read Margaret Mead, Claude Lévi-Strauss, and others who believed that our discipline might die with the demise of the last primitive? Had she come to the same conclusion by a parallel process of induction? Of course, she could simply have been confusing anthropology for something else with the prefix 'anth-'. Like anthropophagy, cannibalism. That,

[*] Many of the ideas in this article have been developed in collaboration with Jean Comaroff. My title – which invokes a well-known essay by Peter Worsley (1970) – also plays, ironically, on her "The end of history, again: pursuing the past in the postcolony" (Comaroff 2005). Thanks, too, to Andre Gingrich, for his insightful reading of an earlier draft article, and to Molly Cunningham, my excellent research assistant. Finally, I acknowledge the anonymous reviewers for the American Anthropologist and, above all, its editor-in-chief, Tom Boellstorff, for their gently critical, highly constructive comments of the draft submitted to the journal. Its talented managing editor, Mayumi Shimose, tolerated my innumerable questions and editorial alterations with grace and good humor. I am immensely appreciative of her efforts.

[1] Directed by Sidney Gilliat (1962), the film was based on Kingsley Amis's novel, "That uncertain feeling" (1955).

however, did not occur to me at the time. My reply was wholly vacuous. As it happens, I got the job, probably because I was the only candidate who actually had played rugby. But I left the room deep in thought: What are the conditions that kill off a discipline? Or ensure its continued life? So, although Mrs. Evans is long dead and I am almost forty years late, here at last is my answer to what I take to have been her question: Is anthropology about to die? Wherein lies the future of its extinction?

Few believe any longer that our continued existence depends on the perpetuity of the primitive or the survival of *le savage*. As long as there are human beings living on the planet, we will, in principle at least, have an object of study. And after that, who cares? More seriously, the real question is not external to anthropology. It is internal. (Well, largely internal. As we all know, some of its 'natives' have long censured the subject for being a brute instrument of Empire; or worse, the regime of knowledge on which colonial capitalism was founded. Which, in turn, has ensured our exile from a good part of the post-colonial world – although now that the politics of identity have made a return, so has anthropology, the human science that dignifies difference.) As Clifford Geertz (1988:71) once suggested, we do seem to suffer from a proclivity for the autopathological; he referred to it as 'epistemological hypochondria'. And yet, while we appear to stagger from one self-inflicted crisis to the next, anthropology lives on to tell the tale: it evinces palpably more rigor than mortis. Indeed, it is almost as though we actually require to look disciplinary death in the face to survive. Perhaps, with apologies to vampires and antifunctionalists everywhere, imminent demise is our necessary lifeblood. After all, as Greg Beckett (2008:50) observes in his analysis of the long history of the concept, recalling Reinhart Koselleck (1988) and Raymond Williams (1983:84–86), crisis and critique are closely connected, both alike a potential source of animation and emancipation. To the degree that ours is a critical practice, then – and it is not always that, by any means – it will always be imbricated in crises. Perhaps intermittent iterations of the end of anthropology do not portend oblivion so much as prevent it.

I shall not dwell on the archaeology of anthropological crisis here; it is the future with which I am primarily concerned. But just a few words. As Matti Bunzl (2008:54–55) reminds us, the 1960s and 1970s brought an end to the hegemony of British structural functionalism and U.S. culture and personality, the two enduring orthodoxies of twentieth-century anthropology. Both decomposed under the cumulative insurgency of colonial and post-colonial literary theory, early feminist anthropology, anthropological hermeneutics, various species of Marxism, Derridean deconstruction, and Foucauldian poststructuralism. For my own generation, though, it was the colonial critique that was most devastating. It held that the entire theoretical scaffolding of anthropological knowledge was rotten to the core: its commitment to closed systems, holism, and homeostatic models; its representation of the social by analogy to the biological; its stress on reproductive processes rather than dialectics; its inherent idealism; and, in the United States, its ahistorical, apolitical concept of culture were all said to be corollaries of the racialisation of difference, not to mention of the radical 'othering' (cf. Fabian 1983), at the dark heart of the discipline.[2] Hence Peter Rigby's (1996) "African images: racism and the end of anthropology", a critique simultaneously political, ethical, epistemic. It called for a new kind of praxis, another metanarrative to replace the liberal idealism that had entrapped anthropology: for less cryptoempiricism, more critical theory; less localism, more contextualisation in both space and time; less hermeneutics, more materiality; less description, more explanation.

By contrast, for the next anthropological generation, especially in the United States, crisis talk gave voice to a very different sensibility – one that, in retrospect, was not unrelated to the rise of neoliberalism. It began, famously, with the publication of "Writing culture",[3] which congealed into a single discourse many of the diverse impulses that had led to the implosion of prevailing paradigms (cf. Bunzl 2008:54–55). Whatever may be said on either side of the debate, it had a palpable impact on the discipline – largely by railing against metanarratives sui generis, against the authority of the authorial, against the finality of any representation, against generalisation and, for the most part, explanation. Against culture, except in the most anticoherent, contingent, contested sense (Abu-Lughod 1991:147). Against exoticism, closure, dialectics, determination. Against theory. For partial truths (Clifford 1986) and provisional readings (Capranzano 1986). For ethnography as textuality. Toward a new empiricism of ever greater descriptive complexity.

There have been counterarguments, of course. They stress the depoliticising, dematerialising, unwittingly conservative tendencies of this kind of anthropology. And its reduction of ethnography to a solipsistic literary practice, one so obsessively reflexive as to be of no interest to anybody outside of itself (cf. Sangren 1988). There has also been a great deal written since 1986 that has looked elsewhere for its theoretical and critical inspiration: notably the important work, in the 1990s, of feminist (e.g., Behar and Gordon 1995) and black scholars (e.g., Harrison 1991). I shall have more to say about anthropology after 1986. My point here, simply, is that much present-day talk of the future of the discipline – and the substantive responses it has elicited – is haunted by some of the issues that surfaced during the writing culture moment (cf. Marcus 2008). To be sure, there is a direct line to be drawn between that moment and the symptoms taken by disciplinary pessimists, of which I am emphatically not one, to be prognostic of the end of anthropology.

---

[2]    See, for example, the essays in Asad (1973), especially Forster's "Empiricism and imperialism".

[3]    Clifford and Marcus (1986). Cf. also Marcus and Fischer (1999), Marcus (2008).

*TRIAGE: THREE SYMPTOMATOLOGIES OF CRISIS*

Let me deal briefly with just the three most commonly cited of those symptoms.

The first is that the discipline has lost its brand – I use the commodity metaphor pointedly – in the form of its signature method, ethnography; its root concepts, especially culture; its research terrain, namely, comparative societies, and in particular, non-Western societies; and its paradigmatic theoretical landscape. In respect of method, goes the angst, many sociologists, political scientists, social psychologists, humanists, even some economists, claim these days to 'do [...] ethnography', the practice constitutive of our discipline (Geertz 1973:5). What is more, ethnographic technique itself – which, like all qualitative methodologies, has long been under siege from the 'hard' social sciences – has become more inchoately imagined than it was in generations past, which may be why so many 'how to' manuals are being produced,[4] why so many anthropology departments have added courses on the topic over the past decade,[5] why anthropologists sometimes lament how 'thin' has become its modal practice,[6] and why so much institutional effort is being given to its defense. In the United States, the National Science Foundation has created what it calls, appositely in our market-driven academy, a "Cultural Anthro Methods Mall": an online facility intended 'to provide skills to current and future colleagues who are conducting scientific research in cultural anthropology'.[7]

As with method, so with concepts. 'While emblematic of [...] the discipline', argues George Marcus (2008:3), echoing many others, culture 'is longer viable analytically'; to wit, its use is typically hedged around with caveats about what it is not being taken to signify.[8] Furthermore, as it has become commonplace to point out, the concept has disseminated itself quite promiscuously. Corporate law firms have courses on it. Sports teams invoke it. Nations brand it. But, most of all, 'natives' insist on claiming it for themselves, often trademarking it, sometimes even charging scholars who study it (Comaroff and Comaroff 2009). Worse yet, other disciplines have muscled in on it. And, if that were not enough, our research terrain, 'society' and its cognates (social order, system, organisation), have been eroded

---

4      E.g., Atkinson *et al.* (2001), Hobbs and Wright (2006).

5      I base this statement in the fact that, when I first designed a graduate course in anthropological methods at the University of Chicago in 1998, I actively sought syllabi both online and from other departments. But few were available. A recent Internet search produced a remarkably large number, most of recent vintage.

6      See, for example, Ortner's (2006:61–62) critique of the anthropological study of resistance on grounds of its ethnographic thinness.

7      See http://www.qualquant.net/training/ (accessed May 30, 2008); a 2009 online version was announced by e-mail circulation from H. Russell Bernard on December 8, 2008.

8      Perhaps because this text is the transcript of an interview, Marcus does not justify his claim. Presumably, it is founded on the critique of the concept in "Writing culture" (Clifford and Marcus 1986) and other contemporary publications; see above.

from a number of sides. Existentially, for one. 'There is no such thing as society', Margaret Thatcher, organic voice of the 1980s, said famously to "Woman's own" magazine (Keay 1987), anticipating Bruno Latour by several years. It was a view that had deep echoes across both the lay and the scholarly world, heralding not merely the age of the market but also an age in which nonsocietal metaphors would come to describe the domain vacated by a Durkheimean sense of the social: terms like 'network', 'community', 'civility', 'citizenship', and 'biosociality'; terms, again, that cannot be claimed as its own by anthropology.[9] But even if we leave the existence of society aside, it is impossible, in this epoch of antisystem, of antitotalisation and indeterminacy, to envisage any anthropologist believing that she would be taken seriously were she to rest an analysis on the concept. As with everything else, we can use it in its adjectival form to describe a contingent practice or a process but not as an abstract noun – we may speak of the social, not of society, of the cultural, not of culture (cf. Appadurai 1996:13) – which, I shall argue, actually does have a positive point to it. And something to say about a distinctive future for anthropology.

The adjectivalisation of our concepts – the suspension of the noun form, and, with it, the flight from abstraction – points toward the idea that anthropology is threatened as well by the erasure of its theoretical landscape. Harri Englund and James Leach (2000) have argued, in effect, that any theory work that does much more than serve as a vehicle for vernacular voice, consciousness, or cognised experience is the illegitimate spawn of '[Euro-metropolitan] modernity', of its 'metanarrative'. As such, it undermines the authority, and the claims to an authentic identity, of our 'native' subjects (Englund and Leach 2000:225) – and, hence, calls into question our raison d'être. As Jean Comaroff and I (2003) have countered, this is a position at once incoherent and self-negating. But it has some real support among those scarred by accusations of 'othering'. And among those unwilling to be tarred as 'modernists', let alone as functionalists, structuralists, or Marxists. Perhaps it is this unwillingness that has made so much of the discipline theory averse and – beyond descriptive analysis of the most limited, self-referential sort – explanation phobic. Perhaps it is this, too, that has led Marcus (2008:2) to declare that anthropology is 'in suspension': that it has 'no new ideas, and none on the horizon, [that there is] no indication that its traditional stock of knowledge shows any signs of revitalization', and that its best work has been energised less from its interiors than from its borders with feminist studies, media studies, post-colonial studies, science studies, and the like. To the extent that this is true – a matter to which I shall return – it is unlikely that our concepts and constructs, our propositions and dispositions, will ever again be subsumed within a specifically disciplinary paradigm. They may be political or philosophical or ethical or social, generically speaking, but not distinctively anthropological.

---

9    The term 'biosociality' was coined by Paul Rabinow (1992). It has since taken on a vigorous life of its own beyond anthropology.

The second symptom said to prognosticate the end of anthropology follows closely. It is that, in contrast to other disciplines that retain well-defined empirical terrains, we have no real subject matter of our own any longer. Why can an account of, say, the Indian advertising industry (Mazzarella 2003) not be as authoritatively done in cultural studies? Or one of fraudulent elections in Nigeria (Apter 1999) by a political scientist? Or one of *fatwa* councils in Egypt (Agrama 2005) by an Islamic law and society specialist? Or one of clothing and adornment in Africa (Hendrickson 1996) by an art historian? Or one of casino capitalism in Native America (Cattelino 2008) by an economist? The answer is that they could be. Some have been, which simply compounds the angst.

Hence the third symptom of crisis: that, having relinquished its object of study – namely, local 'societies' or 'cultures' – the subject matter of anthropology has diffused itself into anything and everything, anywhere and everywhere, and hence is about nobody or nothing or nowhere in particular. Marshall Sahlins commented recently that anthropology appears to have become little more than the production of 'thin' ethnographic accounts of the myriad, dispersed effects of global capitalism.[10] These days, he added, there are forensic journalists who cover the same topics as do we – and often do so more thoroughly, more insightfully. It is true that, in South Africa, the most memorable recent ethnography of prison gangs is the work of one such journalist (Steinberg 2004), who treats their symbolic economy, their iconography, their legal anthropology, and their sociomaterial existence with extraordinary 'thickness'.

The point? That, while Sahlins may have exaggerated somewhat to make a rhetorical point, his remark – which arises out of a genuine fear for the extinction of anthropology – packs a powerful punch. Prima facie, a discipline that takes to doing work that could as well be done, and be done as well, by journalists, technicians of ephemera, is indeed one without a distinctive subject, distinctive theoretical concepts, distinctive methods, or a distinctive place in the disciplinary division of labor. A discipline that hardly exists at all, in fact, other than as an institutional trace waiting to be erased.

How, then, is anthropology responding to the threat of its banalisation, its dissipation, its annihilation, real or imagined? What may we make of those responses? Are they likely to avert the end of anthropology by charting new ends for anthropologists? Or are they merely deferring the inevitable?

Before I answer, two parentheses.

---

[10]   Marshall Sahlins, June 2, 2008. The comment was made in a faculty discussion at the University of Chicago. I cite it with his permission.

One is this. While we attend here to the end of anthropology, other disciplines may equally be said to be in crisis. Take economics. It may have become the most influential knowledge regime on the planet. But, to the degree that its theoretical models seek to account for and predict outcomes in the real world, it remains, well, a pretty dismal science. Hence the growing recognition, exacerbated by the global meltdown of 2008, that most economists get things badly wrong most of the time. This, says James Galbraith, is because they remain wedded to a 'theoretical model that has been shown to be fundamentally useless' (Solomon 2008). Even Richard Posner (2009:231), leading scholar-ideologue of the law and economics movement, speaks of the 'crisis of '08' as a 'wake-up call to the economics profession', a view recently echoed by the Economist (2009). Not that its spectacular capacity for error has had much practical effect: it continues to perpetrate its theories on living societies, whatever the consequences – among them, the political, social, ecological, and moral havoc wrought as a result of rising corporate power and the massive concentration of wealth in relatively few hands in recent decades. Thus, for example, a 2008 survey by the UN Food and Agriculture Organisation reported that a billion people would go seriously hungry in 2009, despite 'bumper harvests', primarily because they cannot afford the cost of food; because currency depreciations in the global south have prevented those who most need it from benefitting from falling basic commodity prices; because, despite soaring agrochemical and biotech profits, fertiliser and seed are priced beyond the means of most non-Western farmers; because, with shrinking labor markets across the global north, migrants are losing their jobs and, with it, their ability to send remittances home. Because, in other words, because the confident axioms of free-market economics have been proven catastrophically untrue.[11] This, in part, is why the so-called post-Autistic movement of French economists seeks to 'liberate' the discipline from its 'obsession with formal models [with] no obvious empirical reference' (Fullbrook 2003:17, 22f.). Post-Autism challenges the 'neoclassical mainstream' to embrace the analysis of nonmarket phenomena, of human intersubjectivity, and of 'cultural and social fields' (Fullbrook 2003:17, 22f), a view, apparently, shared by a growing number of economists elsewhere too. Could it be that the next step for them, their way out of their own crisis, is to sidewind silently onto our terrain?[12]

Or take sociology, a house deeply divided. As Joseph Lopreato and Timothy Crippin (1999:xi–xii) note, it stands accused of having 'produced "no [...] theory" of worth', of importing much of its methodology from other disciplines, of 'failing

---

[11]   See Lean (2009). This account, first printed in the Independent (U.K.), was widely syndicated. For the original report from which Lean drew his information, see FAO (2008).

[12]   Or onto the terrains of bioscience (vide the rise of behavioral economics) and human psychology (especially its nonrational, noneconomic dimensions, a.k.a. its 'animal spirits'; see, e.g., Akerlof and Shiller 2009).

to define [its] concepts' adequately, of producing knowledge that has 'little or nothing in common [...] [with] the real world'; so much so that it faces imminent 'decomposition', even 'deletion from the academy'.[13] As in anthropology, talk of crisis in sociology is neither new nor a matter of consensus: Raymond Boudon (1980) and Alvin Gouldner (1970) famously wrote about it almost forty years ago. In doing so, each in his own way raised important philosophical, political, and theoretical questions. Contemporary crisis talk tends to be more mundane. The discipline is 'tired', says Satish Deshpande (1994), and lacking in distinction: its qualitative end has become a mere shadow of anthropology, relying increasingly on ethnography; the work of its subfields – politics, economics, law, culture – is more substantially done in other disciplines; and its quantitative end typically celebrates method above all else, evolving ever more exquisite techniques for measuring phenomena that are often poorly conceptualised or reduced to their most superficial manifestations. Hence Lopreato and Crippin's anxieties about both the epistemic and the empirical scaffolding of contemporary sociology. This is not to deny that it, or economics, yields much of value. It is to observe that, as regimes of knowledge, other disciplines too have critical challenges to meet.[14]

The second parenthesis. Many prognoses of the end of anthropology have presumed a rather monolithic view of the discipline, one circumscribed by its 'traditional' concepts, objects, and methods. And yet it was never so bounded, so self-limiting. After all, contemporary network theory had one of its sites of origin in the Manchester School in urban Central Africa (see, e.g., Mitchell 1969), whence it found its way into U.S. organisational sociology – and beyond; Godfrey Wilson's (1941–42) economics of detribalisation, also in Africa, was a remarkable harbinger of world-systems theory; Frederik Barth's (1997) deployment in 1959 of 'the theory of games' to Yusufzai Pathan political processes foreshadowed later applications of rational-choice models and transactional analysis; and so on and on. Ours has long been an undisciplined discipline, whose heterodoxy has always made its future hard to predict. And ultimately, to its great advantage, irrepressible.

I shall return to both of these parentheses.

---

13    Observe here the parallel with the critique of economics, especially (but not only) from the post-Autistic movement. Given the convergence between the two disciplines in some areas – not least those that resort to rational choice models and the analyses of very large, highly abstract data sets – this parallel is not altogether surprising.

14    This is itself part of something more general. With the epochal changes in economy and society of the late twentieth century, the social sciences have found their received division of labor, their subject matter, the boundaries between them, and many of their concepts called into question. As a result, they are scrambling to recast their horizons. Hence the explosion of knowledge communities defined either as supradisciplinary 'studies' (gender studies, race studies, queer studies, science and technology studies, area studies) or by means of the conjunctural (law and society, law and economics).

Back to my question, then: How have anthropologists reacted to talk of the imminent demise of their discipline? Most do not bother with it at all. Like the vast majority of sociologists (Lopreato and Crippin 1999), they treat it as so much background noise. Among those who have chosen to react, however, three primary tendencies are discernable.[15]

The first is a retreat back into the local – often still, although we rarely admit it, the exotic local. This is owed to the fact that, for many anthropologists, the uniqueness of the discipline remains its 'ability to get inside and understand small-scale communities, to comprehend [their] systems of knowledge' (Graeber 2002:1222). Herein lies our sense of security, our source of solace in the face of epistemic or ethical uncertainty. This is in spite of the fact that much contemporary anthropological practice deviates far from the foundational fiction of fieldwork: the conceit that, given sufficient time 'on the ground', it is possible to comprehend 'the totality of relations' of a 'society' or the essential workings of 'a culture' (cf. Gupta and Ferguson 1997). The elemental faith in fieldwork nonetheless survives because it rides on the methodological myth that ethnography may 'function well without a theory to guide it' (Marcus 1994:44).[16] It is also buttressed by a long-standing chimera: that anthropological wisdom consists of generalisations about the particular that are also particularisations of the general – in short, empirical aggregates, not propositions or explanations. Hence the oxymoron 'descriptive-analysis' so strongly favored by my teachers' generation.

One corollary of the fetishism of the local has been a denial of the relevance to anthropological concerns of macrocosmic forces and determinations in the world, forces and determinations referred to, dismissively, under the sign of globalisation. This, in turn, is founded on two assertions: one, of the efficacy of indigenous agency against those global forces; the other, of the banal truism that different peoples do things differently.[17] What follows is a species of relativism, and an intractable realism, that repudiates any 'general' theory and method grounded in political economy, history, philosophy, whatever; indeed, any form of knowledge that threatens our distinctiveness. Thus, for example, in the early 1990s, when rural South Africa was awash in mystical violence – in the murder of alleged witches and other technicians of evil – a few social scientists, Jean Comaroff and myself included (1999a, b), argued that these outbreaks were local effects, figurations really, of changes in the production of social, moral, and material life. Those changes had been occasioned

---

[15]   This triangulation, I hasten to add, is not correlated with the triangulation of symptoms discussed earlier.

[16]   The original sentence in Marcus's text (1994:44) has been truncated for purposes of quotation.

[17]   This paragraph borrows heavily from Comaroff and Comaroff (2003).

in part by the impact on the countryside of so-called structural adjustment. They manifested themselves in growing joblessness, in a crisis of social reproduction, and in the emergence of a virulent occult economy, all of which bespoke the modernity of witchcraft.[18] The details are not important here. What is, though, was the skepticism of anthropologists both within the country and outside.[19] They countered that the phenomenon had a profoundly parochial character, which is self-evidently true – and that, therefore, to pursue explanations beyond the local is to court the dual dangers of abstraction and theoreticism. Which does not follow logically at all. In point of fact, our argument was that contemporary African witchcraft is reducible neither to 'the local' nor 'the global' – that it has to be understood with reference to the complex, multilayered mediations in between.

For Arjun Appadurai (1997:115), the refusal of explanation beyond the compass of the immediate is owed to anthropological angst over the loss of the 'space of intimacy in social life', classically the stock-in-trade of the ethnographer. Whether or not this is so, it certainly is true that the ethnography of the local is being depicted as an endangered art. Englund and Leach (2000:238; see above), for instance, argue that 'it' is engaged in mortal struggle with 'generalising perspectives'. In other words, with Theory, upper case: Theory represented by an ensemble of 'familiar sociological' – note, sociological – 'abstractions', among them, commodification, modernity, disenchantment, neoliberalism; theory that seeks not merely to describe the world but to account for what goes on within it; theory that opens our scholarly patrimony to the encroachment of an ever-more-generic social science. This sort of self-ghettoisation, it seems to me, is less likely to stave off the end of anthropology than to assure its death by descent into an exquisite form of irrelevance.

The second reaction to perceptions of disciplinary crisis complements the first. It is a retreat into fractal empiricism: the description of acts, events, experiences, images, narratives, and objects in the phenomenal world – in all their concrete, fragmentary, unruly manifestations – without reducing them to any more coherence than is required to render them into words, without imposing any authorial order on them, without seeking meaning 'beneath' their surfaces, thus to allow them to speak for themselves. Matti Bunzl (2008:56) offers as the prime exemplar of this species of anthropological practice Anna Tsing's "In the realm of the diamond queen" (1993). In it, Tsing, a prose poet of rare gift, lays before us a wealth of descriptive detail, enunciated from a variety of vantages and voices. On principle, however, no gesture is made toward integration or explanation. Which raises a problem: Wherein lies the anthropological value-added? Why call this anthropology at all? Why not literary nonfiction? Literary nonfiction of the highest quality, no question. But unless we

---

18    Comaroff and Comaroff (1993); cf. Geschiere (1997).
19    E.g., Moore (1999); Niehaus with Mohlala and Shokane (2001).

ask what it is that gives shape to a social world – how it is imaginatively made social in the first instance; how its internal incoherencies and fractiousness are to be understood; who in it can speak or cannot; what is or is not thinkable and actionable within it; how its realities are constructed, negotiated, empowered, embodied; how its materialities materialise – what makes this particular text, any text, specifically anthropological? And how might it serve to sustain the singularity, or the raison d'être, of the discipline?[20]

The same might be asked of contemporary anthropological writing that shares a commitment to the empiricist but eschews the fractal by resorting to ordering metaphors. Metaphors, I stress, not explanations. Network analysis is a case in point. Here the use of the fecund imagery of reticulation, of the assemblage or the ensemble, stands in for theory, the descriptive tool being an alibi for the presentation of the particular as if it might portray something beyond itself. From this vantage, the concrete itself is the highest permissible form of abstraction. But, again, there is nothing anthropological about this. Network analysis might have had one of its points of origin in the Manchester School (see above) – where, incidentally, it was never mistaken for theory – but it has dispersed itself widely across the social sciences.[21] For all the fact of it being a response to epistemic crisis, in other words, a resort to empiricism does not, even when coupled with a focus on the intimacy of the local, add up to disciplinary distinction.

This brings me to the third response, especially manifest in the United States. It is to return to basics, so to speak: to the concept of culture – albeit hedged about by caveats, albeit transposed into a lexicon of more contemporary vintage, most usually that of semiotics, of image, representation, voice. Or of phenomenology, of experience, belief, being-in-the-world. A vivid instance has been the recent effort to essay something called the 'anthropology of Christianity'.[22] This endeavor, Chris Hann (2007) has argued, is reductionist, incoherent in defining its subject matter, contradictory in the claims it makes about that subject matter, and unreflective in its idealism. What is more, he adds, it yields little we do not already know from the comparative anthropology of religion. So be it. My own concerns lie elsewhere. Joel Robbins (2007:5f), in making the case for this 'new' field of study, asserts that anthropologists, Jean Comaroff and I being the worst offenders, have taken pains to make Christianity 'disappear' from anthropological discourse, to 'airbrush [it] out' of historical ethnographies, largely by writing it into a narrative that embraces such

---

20   I stress that this is not intended at all to devalue the importance of Anna Tsing's remarkable corpus of work in anthropology. Quite the opposite. Like many others, I hold it in the highest esteem. My point is to pose a generic question about the specifically anthropological value of a particular form of fractal empiricism.

21   Clyde Mitchell, perhaps the leading figure in the development of network analysis at the time, repeatedly emphasised this to us when we were colleagues in Manchester between 1972 and 1978.

22   See, e.g., Cannell (2005, 2006), Robbins (2003, 2007).

things as its connections to capitalism and, in Africa, its imbrication in colonialism; largely, also, by giving too much weight to the ways in which its message has been indigenised by 'native' populations – and too little to its own intrinsic substance and determinations. Robbins concedes implicitly that Protestantism may indeed have been interpellated in these broader historical forces, that its southerly march may have been integral to the rise of colonial capitalism, that some African peoples may have vernacularised its content.[23] But 'empirical adequacy', he asserts, is insufficient (Robbins 2007:8).

Why? Because anthropologists persist in 'assum[ing] that Christianity [is not] culturally important' in its own right (Robbins 2007:7–8). Here is the crux of the matter: what is particular about the anthropology of Christianity is that it treats the faith primarily as culture. Robbins himself appears to 'airbrush out' of it anything other than its putative cultural content, which, at a glance, would seem greatly to diminish its complexity as a world religion. He also presumes that it actually has a cultural content, as opposed to a theology, independent of the social worlds in which, historically, it has sown itself. This is ironic, because the Protestants who exported it in the nineteenth century bore with them a faith heavily inflected by the secular cultural contexts (plural) from whence they came. It was a faith that contained, within its own Euro-ontology, a credo actually called 'Christian political economy' (Waterman 1991), one explicitly embedded in the capitalism of its time. This is why the likes of John Wesley wrote at such length about money and other materialities. And why evangelists thought that teaching Africans to shop and to cultivate cash crops opened a pathway to their souls, whatever their would-be converts made of their theological message. They understood clearly that the political economy, theology, and semiosis of Protestantism were one – and that all alike were embedded deeply in the 'civilisation' of a rising Euromodernity. Neither did it take them long to conclude, in southern Africa at least, that even the most enthusiastic of African Christians, deeply separated from them by culture, seldom shared their ideas of time, personhood, and divinity. Or of conversion.

My object is not to squabble over Christianity or its anthropology.[24] It is to argue that a return to cultural accountancy as the signature of a quintessentially anthropological contribution to the understanding of this or any other phenomenon

---

[23]   McDougall (2009:483) reiterates Robbins's point by arguing that anthropologists 'must engage [the Christian] ideology' of conversion 'because it is shared by the subjects they are studying'. This is an extraordinary piece of Oceanacentrism. Our whole point is that many black South Africans in the nineteenth century did not share that ideology – which would seem to render the critique of our work somewhat beside the point.

[24]   Were I to do so, I would dispute Robbins's assertions about the inattention of anthropologists to Christianity and to its cultural dimensions. I would also debate his understanding of the nature of Christianity itself, which seems to me to be rather narrow. And I would contest his readings of the work of others – including our own, which, as he concedes, was never intended as a contribution to the anthropology of religion.

– and hence as a justification for the continued existence of the discipline – is deeply problematic. Not that culture is unimportant. In dialectical engagement with the sociomaterial, and framed in appropriate theoretical terms (Comaroff and Comaroff 1991:19–31, 1992:27–31), it is indeed critical in making sense of the world. But the reduction of a global religion to it, conceived immaterially and ahistorically, is precisely what gives anthropology a bad name. After all, evangelical Christianity has changed the political and economic face of the planet. All manner of conflict is being conducted under its sign. Christian political economy has returned to haunt us. To distill it to culture is to ensure for the discipline not prolonged life but death by trivialisation.

If, then, the three major panaceas for disciplinary perpetuity – retreat into the local, resort to the empirical, and return to the cultural – are part of the problem not the solution, is there a way to speak of the future of anthropology in different terms?

## ANTHROPOLOGICAL FUTURES: FIRST THOUGHTS, SECOND GUESSES

There is no easy answer to this question, of course. But let me offer a few thoughts. They lead away from received ideas of the discipline toward a sense of indiscipline, a knowledge regime that seeks to rethink the conceptual foundations, the empirical horizons, and the methodological coordinates of anthropology.

To begin with, the claim that we have lost our distinctive subject matter, methods, concepts, theoretical scaffolding – and, with it, our unique place in the disciplinary division of labor – rests on a fallacy of misplaced typification. This has it that anthropology is a species of knowledge defined by its topical reach and received techniques. In sum, we are what we study and how we study it. It goes without saying that many social scientists subscribe to this view; so do lay people, like the late Mrs. Evans of South Wales. For them, our work lies in the ethnographic documentation of small-scale, non-Western cultures. Historically speaking, we have also tended to typify ourselves largely in these terms. To continue to do so, however, is at once anachronistic and counterproductive; worse yet, it leads to silly wrangles over what is or is not properly anthropology. In this day and age, it seems to me – if not to those who seek panaceas in neoempiricism, cryptoculturalism, or brute localism – the discipline ought to be understood as a praxis: a mode of producing knowledge based on a few closely interrelated epistemic operations that lay the foundation for its diverse forms of theory work, mandate its research techniques, and chart its empirical coordinates. They belong, I stress, to the domain of Methodology, upper case: the principled practice by which theory and the concrete world are both constituted and brought into discursive relationship with one another. And they are epistemic in that they entail an orientation to the nature of knowledge itself, its philosophical underpinnings and its notions of truth, fact, value. None of them is new, none of them absent from anthropologies past. Together, they underscore the point that our topical horizons ought to be configured by our praxis, not the other way around.

Let me clear. I am not suggesting that the discipline shares a single episteme. That is patently not so. The contrasts in this respect between, say, anthropological phenomenology and Marxist anthropology, or structuralism and actor-network theory, are all too plain. However, as we shall see, these epistemic operations, because they belong to the domain of Methodology, transect substantive paradigmatic divides: they may as well chart the anthropology of a practice theorist as a structuralist or a Foucauldian. What is more, they permit anthropologists to converse critically across lines of theoretical difference, topical interest, even ethical cleavage. Note, too, that my argument is at once an account and an aspiration, at once description and prescription: it describes what many anthropologists do and makes a case for the kind of anthropology I believe should survive into the future.

First among these operations is the critical estrangement of the lived world, itself founded on a double gesture – on the deconstruction of its surfaces and the relativising of its horizons – thus to pose the perennial question: What is it that actually gives substance to the dominant discourses and conventional practices of that world, to its subject positions and its semiosis, its received categories and their unruly undersides, to the manner in which it is perceived and experienced, fabricated, and contested? This goes way back. Recall Bronislaw Malinowski's (1927) effort to rewrite Sigmund Freud on the Oepidus complex by demonstrating its very different manifestation among the matrilineal Trobriand Islanders. Here boys were said to evince their first love for their sisters (not their mothers) and hostility toward their maternal uncles (not their fathers), a dramatic transposition of affective patterns found in Europe. The corollary? That the phenomenon has less to do with innate human sex drives than with culturally specific relations of authority and their concomitant ambivalences. Whether or not he was right (cf. Spiro 1983), Malinowski's general point was that Western perceptions of family, kinship, sexuality, and desire required critical decentering if they were to be analytically useful, something that only a comparative anthropology might accomplish.

Ever since, anthropologists have insisted, with great profit, on making sense of the phenomenal world by estranging its observable forms. Vide, for instance, Monica Wilson's (1951) extraordinary insight into the McCarthy-era hearings in the United States through the defamiliarising optic of the African occult as ethical etiology. The red agent of 'the Senator's fevered dreams' and the accused witch, she observed, were linked not only metaphorically by the trope of the witch hunt but also by a positional equivalence (1951:313): both were 'standardised nightmares' of a moral order fraught with contradictions that defied ordinary discourse, contradictions sharpened by transformations of scale in the social universe. Her genius, in short, was to discern, and to historicise, the connection between the visible and the invisible, the audible and inaudible, beneath the contours of everyday existence. This is the generic genius of anthropology as a critical practice, one that continues to infuse its most creative work. It is what, for example, led Andrew Apter (1999; discussed earlier) to see behind the elaborately ritualised exteriors of a Nigerian election the same kind of counterfeit – the same play on the disconnect between signifier and signified, the same effort to render imaginative fictions into material facts – on which are based the 419 scams that bombard the Internet daily. These scams are themselves an artifact of the speculative culture of deception pervading the 'casino capitalism' that has come to infuse the global economy (Strange 1986). Here, in short, is a political anthropology that estranges normative discourses of failed states, corrupt regimes, and procedural democracy so as to give account of a politics in which the essential political act, the very essence of power, is to determine what is or is not politics in the first place. A far cry, this, from the usual horizons of a conventional social science.

The second operation involves being-and-becoming: it is the mapping of those processes by which social realities are realised, objects are objectified, materialities materialised, essences essentialised, by which abstractions – biography, community, culture, economy, ethnicity, gender, generation, identity, nationality, race, society – congeal synoptically from the innumerable acts, events, and significations that constitute them.[25] This operation, in other words, is concerned with establishing how it is that verbs of doing become nouns of being – common nouns, collective nouns, abstract nouns, proper nouns – thus to illuminate the pathways by which lived worlds are pragmatically produced, socially construed, and naturalised. Take, for example, Appadurai (1995) on the 'production of locality': it is not the received nature of the local, goes his thesis, but its fabrication that is critical in comprehending the salience of place in social life. Appadurai's (1986) 'social life of things' evokes the same sensibility: namely, an impulse to situate the 'thingness' of objects, their simultaneous materiality and meaning, in the diachrony of their becoming.

There is, again, an archaeology to this: the classic work of E.E. Evans-Pritchard (1940) on the Nuer, one of the most nuanced pieces of conceptual anthropology ever written, albeit one that has not a word of theory in it. Evans-Pritchard's achievement, famously, was to show how, in a stateless polity, an immanent grammar of social formation – inscribed, in the Anthropologese of the time, in patriliny – hardened into actually existing lineages under conditions of conflict. His ethnography pointed to the fact that African descent groups, far from being observable aggregations *ab initio*, existed as a potentiality, contained in

---

[25]    The term 'being-and-becoming' evokes more than one genealogy in classical and modern philosophical thought – perhaps most obviously, although not only, Heideggerian phenomenology. I intend it in a specifically anthropological sense here, however, where it refers to the domain of Methodology.

the semiotics of blood; that they took on their manifest character through material practices occasioned by ruptures in everyday life. Contemporary anthropologists did not all understand "The Nuer" in these terms, seeing in it an empiricist account of African life, but this reading is powerfully present in the text. Similarly, if in counterpoint, alliance theory, developed in Lévi-Strauss's (1969) masterwork on kinship, arrives at an ontology of human society by treating its elementary forms as the sedimented effect of exchanges of conjugal partners and prestations according to a range of grammatical rules. Social order, the noun form, is a predicate here of modes of becoming realised through marriage practices. Each, therefore, has to be theorised as the condition of the other's possibility.[26] Or take, in a different theoretical vein but similar revisionist spirit, Frederick Barth (1969) on ethnicity.[27] Reversing received truths, Barth argued that there is no one-to-one relationship between ethnicity-as-experienced and the sociology of difference (1969:14). It is the act of drawing boundaries among populations, not their inherent 'cultural stuff', that constructs ethnoidentities. The implication? That ethnicity is less a thing than a virtual relationship whose objectification is rooted in a dialectic of identification and contrast (Barth 1969:15); that the cultural content of ethnic consciousness may be a product, rather than the constitutive basis, of 'ethnic group organization' (Barth 1969:11); that, by extension, the concept of identity itself is a historically sedimented abstraction with no ontological substance of its own. And the general point? That mapping process of being-and-becoming is a vital element not merely in our theory work but also in the antiessentialising sensibility of a critical anthropology.

The third operation is the deployment of the contradiction, the counterintuitive, the paradox, the rupture as a source of methodological revelation.[28] Again, this has a long genealogy. It begins with the use of the social drama by the Manchester School; in particular, with Victor Turner's (1957) account of Sandombu, *Homo politicus* incarnate in rural Africa, whose rise and fall was deconstructed through its drawn-out dramaturgy to lay bare foundational contradictions between structure and process in Ndembu society, to disinter the paradoxes and impossibilities inherent in political ambition in that context, and to reveal the aporias in domestic life intrinsic to matriliny; in sum, to make sense of the interiors of the Ndembu world. The story

---

[26]    Back in the 1970s, I made an analogous argument about African marriage payments in an effort to forge a synthesis among structuralist, functionalist, and Marxist perspectives. I suggested that the collection and distribution of bridewealth – critical to processes of social reproduction – sedimented a kinship ideology, to be understood again as a virtual grammar of relations, into concrete property-holding associations (Comaroff 1980).

[27]    Barth's (1969) analytical lexicon is now dated. As a result, I have translated some of his terms into more contemporary anthrospeak.

[28]    In Marxist theory of various stripes, of course, contradiction has a very specific theoretical status, being fundamental to the analysis of class, the commodity, and the dialectic. But that is beyond my present scope.

may have been underhistoricised, the depiction of 'the Ndembu' too mechanistic for present-day sensibilities. But the methodological gesture itself underscored the capacity of the unexpected and the counterintuitive to disclose deep truths about everyday existence. Echoes here of Edgar Allan Poe, who spoke long ago of the forensic value of that which falls 'out of the range of ordinary expectation' (1975:191).

This is why anthropologists have continued to return to them – to the unexpected, the counterintuitive, the rupture – to lay bare worlds both familiar and strange. Noteworthy in this respect is Michael Taussig's (1983) celebrated analysis of a Faustian devil compact to elucidate the contradictions of capitalism, and its misperceived magic, for Colombian cane-field workers. So too, a generation later, is Mateo Taussig-Rubbo's (2007) astonishing image of a one-way mirror in a Californian immigration camp, inverted so that the inmates can see the guards but the guards cannot see the inmates; Taussig-Rubbo commissions this image to interrogate the sorts of sovereignty exercised over 'illegal' entrants to the United States in recent times – and, thereby, to illuminate the increasingly contrarian nature of its borders, which are at once ever more both open and closed. Similarly, Fernando Coronil's (1997) account of two deaths, the demise of a factory and the murder of a lawyer, alike theatrical moments of rupture, are used to great effect in dissecting the 'system of circulation' at the core of the Venezuelan petroeconomy in the 1970s. Patently, recourse to contradiction, rupture, and the counterintuitive as a methodological stratagem is closely related both to critical estrangement and to mapping processes of being-and-becoming. It is often by such means that the other two operations are enabled, that the interiors of the phenomenal world, in space and time, begin to reveal themselves.

Space and time. The phrase itself points to the fourth epistemic operation: the embedding of ethnography in the counterpoint of the here-and-there and the then-and-now – in a word, its spatiotemporalisation.[29] In recent times, the notion of situating almost anything in its broader context has, as often as not, been banalised by reduction to the language of the local-and-the-global; just as the historicisation of almost everything tends to be translated into the argot of the epochal, into framing terms like colonialism, empire, modernity, post-coloniality, and neoliberalism. Blunt instruments, all of them. It goes without saying, or should, that neither spatial nor temporal contextualisation is given empirically, nor is it an a priori. Context is always a profoundly theoretical matter.

---

[29] Although this epistemic operation seems similar to the second, the one involving being-and-becoming, they are not identical. One refers to the mapping of the processes whereby social and cultural phenomena come to be realised; the other, to the contextualization of those phenomena and their production in space and time.

Spatiotemporalisation, as I said earlier, is eschewed by many anthropologists, especially those who repudiate explanation with reference to anything much beyond the enclosed edges of the ethnographic gaze. By contrast, I would argue that anthropology at its most productive is anthropology most comprehensively positioned in the here-and-there and the then-and-now – in proportion, of course, to its analytic object. Thus it is that Jessica Cattelino (2008; see above) embeds her ethnography of the Florida Seminoles, a study of the impact of casino capitalism on their world, in several pasts (U.S. colonialism, local Indian history, recent turns in U.S. political economy) and in several spatial frames (contemporary pop culture, the entertainment industry, rez [reservation] imaginaries, the politics and economics of identity, the realm of the law). As a result, she is able to show how this people have succeeded in deploying their new wealth, despite all the contradictions it has brought in its wake, to reconstruct their indigeneity and sovereignty – in such a way as to belie the notion, characteristic of much on-reservation anthropology, that they are sacrificing their culture to the solvent of capital. Thus it is, too, that Harry West (2005), in explaining why sorcery is so important on the Mueda Plateau in Mozambique, situates the occult in multiple dimensions: in the here-and-there of the regional, national, and global economies and in the then-and-now of a past that begins with Portuguese overrule, moves through the Frelimo socialist period, and ends with the neoliberal reforms imposed by the IMF and the World Bank. For those who live on the plateau, it is these intersecting dimensions out of which arises the mystical, life-threatening evil that they must control to make a habitable future for themselves. Thus it is, as well, that Kaushik Sunder Rajan (2006) accounts for the character of contemporary genomics by contextualising it along two axes: vertically, in the rise of biocapital and bioscience, a corollary of which has been the rendering of 'life [as] a business plan' (2006:138f.); and horizontally, in the market logic and the political sociology of research in the United States and India, respectively, which affect directly what goes on in laboratories. In the absence of this spatiotemporalisation, Sunder Rajan's narrative would be just another addition to science and technology studies.

All of the anthropology I have cited in exemplification of the various epistemic operations underscores the final one: the founding of the discipline on grounded theory, on an imaginative counterpoint between the inductive and the deductive, the concrete and the concept, ethnographic observation and critical ideation; also, in a different register, between the epic and the everyday, the meaningful and the material.[30] This, self-evidently, implies a respect for the real that does not conflate the empirical with empiricism. And a respect for the abstract that does not mistake

---

[30]    I intend 'grounded theory' here quite differently from the manner in which it has been deployed in sociology – and famously criticised by Michael Burawoy (1991a, b) – in the wake of Glaser and Strauss's "The discovery of grounded theory" (1967), which treats it as a purely inductive practice.

theory work for theoreticism. In the absence of one half of this counterpoint (the ethnographic, the inductive, the concrete), we risk becoming second-rate philosophers, or worse, ideologues who deploy 'facts' purely in defense of a priori positions. Without the other (the deductive, the concept, critical ideation), we limit our horizons to forensic journalism, to bearing witness, to literary nonfiction or the poetics of pure description. Elsewhere, Jean Comaroff and I (2003) have made the case in extenso for grounded theory. I shall not rehearse the argument, because it has saturated everything I have said so far, save to suggest that the counterpoint between the empirical and the conceptual offers the most productive pathway for the discipline, maybe the only one, between the Scylla of brute descriptivism and the Charybdis of bloodless abstraction.

Also between triviality and obscurity. Hence the anthropological value added of, say, Andrea Muehlebach's (2007) ethnography of ethical citizenship and the 'new' voluntarism in Italy, which informs, and is informed by, a theoretically provocative analysis of the changing nature of labor and nationhood in neoliberal Europe. Or of Rocio Magaña's (2008) thick description of death in the Arizona desert, which, in telling of the dramaturgy of immiserated Mexican migrants, theorises anew the relationship between the violence of the law, sovereignty, the politics of the body, and the paradox of national borders at once porous and policed. Or of William Mazzarella's (2003; discussed above) account of advertising in India, a narrative of condoms and commodity aesthetics that rewrites key elements of European critical theory by grounding them in the exigencies of situated cultural practices. Or any number of other recent works written with a similar eye to the fecund counterpoint of the concept and the concrete.

I reiterate that the epistemic operations of which I have been speaking lie at the core of much contemporary anthropological praxis. Self-evidently, moreover, the various ways in which those operations have been and are given analytic life have begotten different theoretical orientations and species of explanation – and, with them, the kinds of argumentation that animate disciplinary discourses, which, inflected by world-historical conditions, have, in turn, shaped the content of anthropology, its intellectual trajectories, its inner turbulence, its intermittent transitions, its futures-in-the-making. This is why I have illustrated them with instances drawn from both the past and present, from diverse ethnographic domains, and from a variety of paradigmatic approaches. Together they underscore the fact that our praxis is capable of yielding a wide spectrum of theory and method; hence, my parenthetic point earlier about its long-standing heterodoxy, about anthropology as an immanently undisciplined discipline. Ours really is an indiscipline whose conceptual foundations and techniques of knowledge production have almost infinite potential to open up new horizons.

*INDISCIPLINARITY: TOWARD INCONCLUSIVE CONCLUSIONS*

Without a principled praxis, I submit, what pretends to be anthropology is not. Without it, the discipline would indeed be nothing in particular. And difficult to distinguish from others. This is true, too, when it conceives of itself in purely topical terms. That way lies anachronism or indistinction at best, extinction at worst. Conversely, if it remains epistemically grounded in the manner I have described, there is little by way of subject matter that anthropologists cannot take on and address in a distinctive manner, whether it be the Indian advertising industry, Nigerian electoral politics, Egyptian *fatwa* councils, African adornment, or casino capitalism – or, for that matter, Islamic banking (Maurer 2005), vigilantism and death squads (Abrahams 1998), the U.S. nuclear uncanny (Masco 2006), the changing nature of money (e.g., Guyer 2004, Hart 1999), and many things besides. This is why we are not forensic journalists, even when journalism and anthropology cover similar things; why we are not simply creative writers and poets, even though we may aspire to write creatively. And why we are not dissolving into the other social sciences.

In point of fact, from the perspective advanced here, the difference between us and them could not be more marked. Normatively speaking, those disciplines continue to be topically driven – which abets their crises (see above).[31] For the most part, they are not given to critical estrangement or the deconstruction of their ur-concepts. Political scientists, by and large, study political institutions and processes, conventionally understood, just as economists study economic institutions and processes. They rarely ask what politics or economics actually are.[32] Anthropologists do, repeatedly. Unlike political scientists, we also spend a great deal of time trying to discern what taken-for-granted terms like democracy or the rule of law might mean for 'natives', both as signifiers and as species of practice, which often turns out to be anything but obvious. Likewise, most sociologists presume the concrete existence of such 'social facts' as, for instance, ethnicity. While they may differ over definitional details, they see no epistemic problem in taking the measure of its manifest significance or its material impact on human lives, usually by means of survey instruments. We, however, are more likely to begin by calling into question the very notion of 'identity' and then proceed to interrogate the production of ethnic consciousness, the objectification of ethnic populations, the phenomenology of 'being ethnic', and the like – which, parenthetically, is why we are such a pain to the policy industry.

---

[31]     This is by partial contrast to 'the studies' – gender studies, cultural studies, critical race studies, and the like (see fn. 14) – which, although topically named, have been sites of deep epistemic self-reflection and autocritique.

[32]     Of course, political theorists do address such things. As my colleague Lisa Wedeen has reminded me, so do some political scientists who work on comparative politics from an interpretive vantage. Institutionally, these scholars tend to find homes in political science departments. But, for the most part, critically important although their work may be, they inhabit the margins of their discipline, not its normative core.

The contrast is stark. And this is not even to mention the vexed matter of quantification, which many social scientists take as the evidentiary basis of all truth, paying no heed whatever to foundational critiques of statistical knowledge or the means of its production. Anthropologists don't count. But we like to think we know what does – and it is rarely measured numerically. For many of us, numbers are a fetish. Although they may reveal important things, they are just one mode of construing the world, one that often reduces complexity beyond recognition, one based on the occulting of probability. Even history, which, in its mainstream is predominantly qualitative, has a very different relationship to topicality, epistemology, and facticity from that of anthropology. For its orthodox practitioners, who are empirically driven to a fault, the divine is in the detail, in fealty to the fact; the devil lurks in interpretation. This is why analysis-heavy historical anthropology is such a scandal to them, why it has provoked such bitter attacks in defense of their discipline against ours.[33] Those historians who are theory prone, who indulge in the imagination beyond the narrowest confines of the datum, risk being accused of 'committing' ... anthropology. So do political scientists and sociologists who concern themselves with 'soft' political and social phenomena: the cultural, the meaningful, the phenomenological.

Of course, there are others who engage in critical estrangement, in mapping processes of being-and-becoming, in the methodological deployment of rupture, contradiction, and the counterintuitive, in spatiotemporalisation and grounded theory. The more they do, however, the more they become like us. There are increasing, if unacknowledged, signs of this in diverse places; recall the rise of post-Autism in economics and the ethnographic turn in sociology. But that – the anthropologisation of other social sciences – is a topic for another time. Here we are concerned with our futures, not theirs – except to say one thing. To the extent that anthropology is a critical in/discipline, this ought to chart its scholarly practice in university and other institutional settings, vexing the social sciences at large about the production of knowledge, about pedagogy, about the human predicament – and how best to make sense of it in the perplexing history of the present. To be sure, it is only by essaying our praxis in positive, even provocative, terms that anthropology, the generic study of the human, may claim a unique place for itself in the world. How, precisely, are we to configure our indiscipline as a scholarly practice in educational and other contexts? That, it seems to me, is what we ought to be arguing about among ourselves right now.

There is much more to say, patently. I have merely scratched at surfaces. And, no doubt, will elicit some angry reactions. This is all to the good. What is most likely to assure the Future of Anthropology is that those who inhabit its Very Small Planet continue to argue with one another. As long as we do, we will remain a

---

[33]    See, for example, Vansina's (1993) attack on historical anthropology at the University of Chicago.

scholarly community. For my own part – and here I return to my prescriptive voice – I should like to see the discipline perpetuate itself by recourse to the praxis that I have sketched above. While we ground our work in its various epistemic operations, there is every reason to believe that we shall not kill ourselves off by trivialisation, irrelevance, or indistinction, which is more or less assured by a retreat into neoempiricism, cryptoculturalism, or brute localism. Or by repudiating ethnography altogether, which has manifested itself in a few powerful places of late. For me, there is no such thing as a postethnographic anthropology just as there is no such thing as a posttheoretical one.

But there is a more positive basis on which to prognose the future of the discipline. It lies in a younger generation whose work distinguishes itself by its sheer energy, by the imagination that drives it, by its critical edge. I have offered many examples of their work along the way. Others that come immediately to mind – an invidiously small, random selection from a substantial body of work – include Cori Hayden (2003) on bioprospecting and the uneasy tapestry of relations to which it has given rise among local communities, scientists, and drug companies in Mexico; Janet Roitman (2004) on the economics and ethics of (il)legality, militarised commercial networks and organised crime, and sedimentations of the state in the Chad Basin; Caitlin Zaloom (2006) on the operations of global finance, from the trading pits of Chicago to the digital dealing rooms of London; Daniella Gandolfo (2009) on urban renewal in Lima, Peru, read through the dramaturgy of struggles between female streetsweepers and a corrupt state over the privatisation of public services; Kim Fortun (2001) on the Bhopal disaster and the litigation that followed it, a process in which the hidden workings of power interpellated themselves awkwardly into advocacy, the rights of victims, and environmental politics; Tom Boellstorff (2008) on the cyberworld of Second Life and its virtual culture, interrogated from the vantage of an avatar. All of them evince a capacity to estrange, to ground their theory in an ethnographic optic at once wide angled and close up, to demystify received orthodoxies. By these means does our own verb-to-be become a proper noun. By these means does the critical practice of ethnography become Anthropology, upper case.

So, in a word, Mrs. Evans: no. Anthropology, into which I was initiated on that grim day in South Wales in 1971, is not about to die. Nor is it 'in suspension'. It is very much alive, producing new kinds of knowledge, new theory work, new empirical horizons, new arguments. The future of the discipline, in short, lies, as it always will, in its indiscipline.

*REFERENCES*


ABRAHAMS, Ray G.
1998    *Vigilant citizens: vigilantism and the state.* Cambridge: Polity

ABU-LUGHOD, Lila
1991    "Writing against culture", in: Richard G. Fox (ed.), *Recapturing anthropology:
        working in the present*, 137–162. Santa Fe: School of American Research Press

AGRAMA, Hussein
2005    *Law courts and fatwa councils in modern Egypt: an ethnography of Islamic legal practice*
        (Ph.D. dissertation, Department of Anthropology, Johns Hopkins University)

AKERLOF, George A. and Robert J. SHILLER
2009    *Animal spirits: how human psychology drives the economy, and why it matters for
        global capitalism.* Princeton: Princeton University Press

AMIS, Kingsley
1955    *That uncertain feeling.* London: Gollancz

APPADURAI, Arjun
1995    "The production of locality", in: Richard Fardon (ed.), *Counterworks: managing the
        diversity of knowledge*, 208–229. London: Routledge
1996    *Modernity at large: cultural dimensions of globalization.* Minneapolis: University of
        Minnesota Press
1997    "Discussion: fieldwork in the era of globalization", in: Sandra Bamford and Joel
        Robbins (eds.), Fieldwork in the era of globalization, 115–118. *Anthropology and
        Humanism* 22(1):115–118

APPADURAI, Arjun (ed.)
1986    *The social life of things: commodities in cultural perspective.* New York: Cambridge
        University Press

APTER, Andrew
1999    "IRB=419: Nigerian democracy and the politics of illusion", in: John L. Comaroff
        and Jean Comaroff (eds.), *Civil society and the political imagination in Africa: critical
        perspectives*, 267–308. Chicago: University of Chicago Press

ASAD, Talal (ed.)
1973    *Anthropology and the colonial encounter.* London: Ithaca

ATKINSON, Paul, Amanda COFFEY, Sara DELAMONT, John LOFLAND, and Lyn H.
        LOFLAND
2001    *Handbook of ethnography.* London: Sage

BARTH, Frederick
1969    "Introduction", in: Frederick Barth (ed.), *Ethnic groups and boundaries: the social organization of cultural difference*, 9–38. Boston: Little, Brown
1997    "Segmentary opposition and the theory of games: a study of Pathan organization", *Journal of the Royal Anthropological Institute of Great Britain and Ireland* 89(1):5–21 ([1]1959)

BECKETT, Greg
2008    *The end of Haiti: history under conditions of impossibility.* Chicago (Ph.D. dissertation, Department of Anthropology, University of Chicago)

BEHAR, Ruth and Deborah A. GORDON (eds.)
1995    *Women writing culture.* Berkeley: University of California Press

BOELLSTORFF, Tom
2008    *Coming of age in Second Life: an anthropologist explores the virtually human.* Princeton: Princeton University Press

BOUDON, Raymond
1980    *The crisis in sociology: problems of sociological epistemology.* Translated by Howard H. Davis. New York: Columbia University Press ([1]1971)

BUNZL, Matti
2008    "The quest for anthropological relevance: Borgesian maps and epistemological pitfalls", *American Anthropologist* 110(1):53–60

BURAWOY, Michael
1991a   "Reconstructing social theories", in: Ann Burton, Ann Arnett Ferguson, Kathryn J. Fox, Joshua Gamson, Nadine Gartrell, Leslie Hurst *et al.* (eds.), *Ethnography unbound: power and resistance in the modern metropolis*, 8–28. Berkeley: University of California Press
1991b   "The extended case method", in: Ann Burton, Ann Arnett Ferguson, Kathryn J. Fox, Joshua Gamson, Nadine Gartrell, Leslie Hurst *et al.* (eds.), *Ethnography unbound: power and resistance in the modern metropolis*, 8–28. Berkeley: University of California Press

CANNELL, Fenella
2005    "The Christianity of anthropology", *Journal of the Royal Anthropological Institute* 11(2):335–356
2006    "Introduction", in: Fenella Cannell (ed.), *The Anthropology of Christianity*, 1–50. Durham, NC: Duke University Press

CATTELINO, Jessica R.
2008    *High stakes: Florida Seminole gaming and sovereignty.* Durham, NC: Duke University Press

CLIFFORD, James
1986    "Introduction: partial truths", in: James Clifford and George E. Marcus (eds.), *Writing culture: the poetics and politics of ethnography*, 1–26. Berkeley: University of Chicago Press

CLIFFORD, James and George E. MARCUS (eds.)
1986    *Writing culture: the poetics and politics of ethnography*. Berkeley: University of Chicago Press

COMAROFF, Jean
2005    "The end of history, again: pursuing the past in the postcolony", in: Ania Loomba, Suvir Kaul, Matti Bunzl, Antoinette Burton, and Jed Esty (eds.), *Postcolonial studies and beyond*, 125–144. Durham, NC: Duke University Press

COMAROFF, Jean and John L. COMAROFF
1991    *Of revelation and revolution*. Volume 1: Christianity, colonialism, and consciousness in South Africa. Chicago: University of Chicago Press
1993    "Introduction", in: Jean Comaroff and John L. Comaroff (eds.), *Modernity and its malcontents: ritual and power in postcolonial Africa*, xi–xxxvii. Chicago: University of Chicago Press
1999a   "Occult economies and the violence of abstraction: notes from the South African postcolony", *American Ethnologist* 26(3):279–301
1999b   "Alien-nation: zombies, immigrants, and millennial capitalism", *Codesria Bulletin* 3–4:17–28
2003    "Ethnography on an awkward scale: postcolonial anthropology and the violence of abstraction", *Ethnography* 4(2):147–179

COMAROFF, John L.
1980    "Introduction", in: John Comaroff (ed.), *The meaning of marriage payments*, 1–47. London: Academic

COMAROFF, John L. and Jean COMAROFF
1992    *Ethnography and the historical imagination*. Boulder, CO: Westview Press
2009    *Ethnicity, Inc.* Chicago: University of Chicago Press

CORONIL, Fernando
1997    *The magical state: nature, money, and modernity in Venezuela*. Chicago: University of Chicago Press

CRAPANZANO, Vincent
1986    "Hermes' dilemma: the masking of subversion in ethnographic description", in: James Clifford and George E. Marcus (eds.), *Writing culture: the poetics and politics of ethnography*, 51–76. Berkeley: University of Chicago Press

DESHPANDE, Satish
1994    "Crisis in sociology: a tired discipline?", *Economic and Political Weekly* 29(10):575–576

ECONOMIST
2009    "What went wrong with economics?", *Economist* July 28:11–12

ENGLUND, Harri and James LEACH
2000    "Ethnography and the meta-narratives of modernity", *Current Anthropology* 41(2):225–248

EVANS-PRITCHARD, Sir Edward E.
1940    *The Nuer: a description of the modes of livelihood and political institutions of a Nilotic people*. Oxford: Clarendon

FABIAN, Johannes
1983    *Time and the other: how anthropology makes its object*. New York: Columbia University Press

FOOD AND AGRICULTURE ORGANIZATION (United Nations)
2008    *Food outlook: global market analysis, November*. http://www.fao.org/docrep/011/ai474e/ai474e00.htm (accessed January 15, 2009)

FORSTER, Peter
1973    "Empiricism and imperialism: a review of the new left critique of social anthropology", in: Talal Asad (ed.), *Anthropology and the colonial encounter*, 23–38. London: Ithaca

FORTUN, Kim
2001    *Advocacy after Bhopal: environmentalism, disaster, new global orders*. Chicago: University of Chicago Press

FULLBROOK, Edward (ed.)
2003    *The crisis in economics: the post-autistic economics movement: the first 600 days*. New York: Routledge

GANDOLFO, Daniella
2009    *The city at its limits: taboo, transgression, and urban renewal in Lima*. Chicago: University of Chicago Press

GEERTZ, Clifford J.
1973    *The interpretation of cultures*. New York: Basic Books
1988    *Works and lives: the anthropologist as author*. Stanford: Stanford University Press

GESCHIERE, Peter
1997    *The modernity of witchcraft: politics and the occult in postcolonial Africa*. Charlottesville: University of Virginia Press

GILLIAT, Sidney (dir.)
1962    *Only two can play*. 106 min. U.K.: British Lion Films, Columbia Pictures

GLASER, Barney G. and Anselm L. STRAUSS
1967    *The discovery of grounded theory: strategies for qualitative research*. Chicago: Aldine

GOULDNER, Alvin
1970    *The coming crisis in Western sociology*. New York: Basic Books

GRAEBER, David
2002    "The anthropology of globalization (with notes on neomedievalism, and the end of the Chinese model of the nation-state)", *American Anthropologist* 104(4):1222–1227

GUPTA, Akhil and James FERGUSON
1997    "Discipline and practice: 'the field' as site, method, and location in anthropology", in: Akhil Gupta and James Ferguson (eds.), *Anthropological locations: boundaries and grounds of a field science*, 1–46. Berkeley: University of California Press

GUYER, Jane I.
2004    *Marginal gains: monetary transactions in Atlantic Africa*. Chicago: University of Chicago Press

HANN, Chris
2007    "The anthropology of Christianity per se", *European Journal of Sociology* 48(3):383–410

HARRISON, Faye Venetia (ed.)
1991    *Decolonizing anthropology: moving forward toward an anthropology of liberation*. Washington, DC: Association of Black Anthropologists, American Anthropological Association

HART, Keith
1999    *The memory bank: money in an unequal world*. London: Profile Books

HAYDEN, Cori
2003    *When nature goes public: the making and unmaking of bioprospecting in Mexico*. Princeton: Princeton University Press

HENDRICKSON, Hildi (ed.)
1996    *Clothing and difference: embodied identities in colonial and post-colonial Africa*. Durham, NC: Duke University Press

HOBBS, Dick and Richard WRIGHT
2006    *The Sage handbook of fieldwork*. London: Sage

KEAY, Douglas
1987    "Aids, education, and the year 2000! [Interview with Margaret Thatcher]", *Woman's Own* October 31:8–10

KOSELLECK, Reinhart
1988    *Critique and crisis: enlightenment and the pathogenesis of modern society.* Cambridge, MA: MIT Press ([1]1959)

LEAN, Geoffrey
2009    "1,000,000,000 People: that is how many will go hungry in 2009", *The Sunday Independent* (South Africa) January 4:15

LÉVI-STRAUSS, Claude
1969    *The elementary structures of kinship.* Translated by James Harle Bell, John Richard von Sturmer, and Rodney Needham. Boston: Beacon ([1]1949)

LOPREATO, Joseph and Timothy CRIPPIN
1999    *Crisis in sociology: the need for Darwin.* New Brunswick, NJ: Transaction

MAGAÑA, Rocio
2008    *Bodies on the line: life, death, and authority on the Arizona-Mexico border.* Chicago (Ph.D. dissertation, Department of Anthropology, University of Chicago)

MALINOWSKI, Bronislaw
1927    *Sex and repression in savage society.* London: K. Paul, Trench, Trubner

MARCUS, George E.
1994    "After the critique of anthropology: faith, hope, and charity, but the greatest of these is charity", in: Rob Borofsky (ed.), *Assessing cultural anthropology*, 40–54. New York: McGraw-Hill
2008    "The end(s) of ethnography: social/cultural anthropology's signature form of producing knowledge in transition", *Cultural Anthropology* 23(1):1–14

MARCUS, George E. and Michael M. J. FISCHER
1999    *Anthropology as cultural critique: an experimental moment in the human sciences.* Chicago: University of Chicago Press

MASCO, Joseph
2006    *The nuclear borderlands: the Manhattan Project in post-cold war New Mexico.* Princeton: Princeton University Press

MAURER, Bill
2005    *Mutual life, limited: Islamic banking, alternative currencies, lateral reason.* Princeton: Princeton University Press

MAZZARELLA, William
2003    *Shovelling smoke: advertising and globalization in contemporary India.* Durham, NC: Duke University Press

MCDOUGALL, Debra
2009    "Becoming sinless: converting to Islam in the Christian Solomon Islands", *American Anthropologist* 111(4):480–491

MITCHELL, J. Clyde (ed.)
1969    *Social networks in urban situations: analyses of personal relationships in Central African towns*. Manchester: Manchester University Press for the Institute of Social Research, University of Zambia

MOORE, Sally Falk
1999    "Reflections on the Comaroff lecture", *American Ethnologist* 26(3):304–306

MUEHLEBACH, Andrea
2007    *Farewell welfare?* State, labor, and life cycle in contemporary Italy. Chicago (Ph.D. dissertation, Department of Anthropology, University of Chicago)

NIEHAUS, Iszak A., with Eliazaar MOHLALA and Kally SHOKANE
2001    *Witchcraft, power, and politics: exploring the occult in the South African Lowveld*. Cape Town: David Philip

ORTNER, Sherry B.
2006    *Anthropology and social theory: culture, power, and the acting subject*. Durham, NC: Duke University Press

POE, Edgar Alan
1975    *The complete tales and poems of Edgar Allan Poe*. New York: Vintage Books

POSNER, Richard A.
2009    *A failure of capitalism: the crisis of '08 and the descent into depression*. Cambridge, MA: Harvard University Press

RABINOW, Paul
1992    "Artificiality and enlightenment: from sociobiology to biosociality", in: Jonathan Crary and Sanford Kwinter (eds.), *Incorporations*, 234–252. New York: Zone Books

RIGBY, Peter
1996    *African images: racism and the end of anthropology*. Oxford: Berg

ROBBINS, Joel
2003    "What is a Christian? Notes toward an anthropology of Christianity", *Religion* 33(3):191–199
2007    "Continuity thinking and the problem of Christian culture: belief, time, and the anthropology of Christianity", *Current Anthropology* 48(1):5–38

ROITMAN, Janet
2004    *Fiscal disobedience: an anthropology of economic regulation in Central Africa*. Princeton: Princeton University Press

SANGREN, P. Steven
1988    "Rhetoric and the authority of ethnography: 'Postmodernism' and the social reproduction of texts", *Current Anthropology* 29(3):405–435

SOLOMON, Deborah
2008    "The populist: questions for James K. Galbraith", New York Times, October 31. http://www.nytimes.com/2008/11/02/magazine/02wwln-Q4-t.html?_r=1&ref=patrick.net&oref=slogin (accessed November 21, 2008)

SPIRO, Melford E.
1983    *Oedipus in the Trobriands*. Chicago: University of Chicago Press

STEINBERG, Jonny
2004    *The number*. Cape Town: Jonathan Ball

STRANGE, Susan
1986    *Casino capitalism*. New York: Basil Blackwell

SUNDER RAJAN, Kaushik
2006    *Biocapital: the constitution of postgenomic life*. Durham, NC: Duke University Press

TAUSSIG, Michael
1983    *The devil and commodity fetishism in South America*. Chapel Hill, NC: University of North Carolina Press.

TAUSSIG-RUBBO, Mateo
2007    *The sovereign's gift: reciprocity and invisibility in U.S. immigration detention camps*. Chicago (Ph.D. dissertation, Department of Anthropology, University of Chicago)

TSING, Anna Lowenhaupt
1993    *In the realm of the diamond queen: marginality in an out-of-the-way place*. Princeton: Princeton University Press

TURNER, Victor W.
1957    *Schism and continuity in an African society: a study of Ndembu village life*. Manchester: Manchester University Press for the Rhodes-Livingsone Institute

VANSINA, Jan
1993    "Review of ethnography and the historical imagination", *International Journal of African Historical Studies* 26(2):417–420

WATERMAN, Anthony Michael C.
1991    *Revolution, economics and religion: Christian political economy, 1798–1833*. Cambridge: Cambridge University Press

WEST, Harry G.
2005    *Kupilikula: governance and the invisible realm in Mozambique*. Chicago: University of Chicago Press

WILLIAMS, Raymond
1983    *Keywords: a vocabulary of culture and society*. London: Fontana (¹1976)

WILSON, Godfrey
1941/42 *An essay on the economics of detribalization in Northern Rhodesia*. Livingstone: Rhodes-Livingstone Institute (Rhodes-Livingstone Papers 5/6)

WILSON, Monica
1951    "Witch beliefs and social structure", *American Journal of Sociology* 56:307–313

WORSLEY, Peter
1970    "The end of anthropology", in: *Transactions of the sixth world congress of sociology*. Volume 3, 121–129. Geneva: International Sociology Association

ZALOOM, Caitlin
2006    *Out of the pits: traders and technology from Chicago to London*. Chicago: University of Chicago Press

# 5

# THE END – THE ENDS – OF ANTHROPOLOGY

## Vincent Crapanzano

There is a significant ambiguity in the title of this collection and in the title of my own contribution: the end of anthropology. Quite obviously 'end' may mean demise – the demise of anthropology – or it may mean goal: the goal of anthropology. It may also mean a boundary or extreme edge, as in the 'the end of town', intention, result, outcome, completion, conclusion and, suggestively, responsibility, as in 'your end of the bargain'. 'End' is derived by way of the Sanskrit *ántas* from the Indo-European *\*ant-* whose basic meaning is 'front' or 'forehead'. In the locative form, *\*ant-* means 'against' with derivative meanings 'in front of', 'before', and 'end'. It is related etymologically to 'ante', 'anterior', and 'advance'. Its Indo-European etymon draws attention to both the spatial and temporal perspective from which an end is envisaged. We are always located before the end: the goal, the outcome, the completion, the demise, the death, for which – I am stretching my point here – we are not without responsibility. Anticipated, the consequences of the end have to be expressed in the future, at times in the future anterior, in whatever mood: as such, they refer back to the position of whoever announces an end and evaluates its effects – its end, the end, so-to-speak, of the end. The future, however predictable its appraisal of what will have occurred, always requires an imaginative leap, which is constrained by the conventions of the present.[1] We have in any event, therefore, to recognise the significance of the position not only from which we appraise the end of anthropology but also from which we pose its very question.[2]

I question the end of anthropology from a radically disquieting position: one that aims at breaking the complacency that comes with the institutionalisation of a discipline which by its very structure – the straddling it demands – ought to resist the deadening effects of that institutionalisation. In so doing I will no doubt tread, if only by indirection, on the work many anthropologists have produced, as I tread

---

[1] My friend Stephen Foster observed on reading a draft of this essay that it is also possible to view the end – the end of anthropology – from after its demise, as 'ruins', he added pessimistically. Or after the fulfillment of its goal, we might add, were its goal not simply an unreachable telos that structures anthropology as a discipline – a telos that, though in practice continually redefined, resists final definition.

[2] My discussion of the etymology of 'end' is based on the entry and appendix (Indo-European Roots) in the "American heritage dictionary of the English language" (Boston: Houghton-Mifflin 1979). I should note that Partridge (1958:182) finds *\*antas* akin to the Indo-European *\*anti* (opposite).

on my own work. I do this out of a deep concern for anthropology's future. I do not want to deny the progress that ethnography has made over the last century. We have gathered an enormous amount of data. Today, there is probably no society in the world that has not been the subject of anthropological investigation. My concern is with the way anthropology conceives of itself and how this self-conception has affected its theorising, the development of which is incommensurate with the data it has collected. We have tended to borrow theoretical paradigms from other disciplines to illuminate our data, often without critical regard for how they influence our research, our conception of anthropological research, and our take on anthropology as a disciplinary practice. I believe we have not recognised how radical a critique of social and cultural understanding we can make, had we the will. We have not given sufficient attention, I will argue, to the effect of our straddling positions (Crapanzano 2004:39–65). We need to develop theories and interpretative strategies that arise from the betwixt and between from which our research proceeds – a position (if 'position' it can be called) that precludes sure footing and, as such, lays bare – or ought to lay bare – the paradoxical temporalities of social and cultural existence and the plays of power and desire that promote the punctuation of those temporalities, that punctuation's artifice. My essay will oscillate between a critique of contemporary anthropology and intimations of other possible anthropological approaches. I will focus on those anthropologies that are primarily concerned with complex societies, especially the anthropologists', and their institutions and socio-cultural arrangements. That I stress these new foci of anthropological research does not mean that I believe we should abandon our traditional research domains and many of our research practices associated with those domains – quite to the contrary. But consideration of the future of anthropologies that preserve this interest merits a paper in its own right. Here I want simply to note that the changes in research domains and the new methods it requires will inevitably affect the research we do in more traditional domains.

As Karl-Heinz Kohl and other contributors to this collection have noted, anthropology has always worried about its end. This sense of an imminent end has been related to the fact that anthropologists have, until fairly recently, studied moribund cultures – those on the verge of total disappearance or subject to such radical change that they lose their identity and even their memory of their past. At least since Franz Boas, but, in fact, long before him, whether through the collection of artifacts, the recording of disappearing languages, the transcription of myths and folklore, or social and cultural description, anthropologists found themselves salvaging the last remnants of dying cultures. Their emphasis was on the timelessness of the traditions they studied, which were often presented in the ahistorical present tense. It seems odd that these societies and cultures should be figured timelessly, as they were subject to changes so radical that their end was imminent. One might say that the ahistorical tense – the ethnographic present – served magically to preserve what was, in fact, dying or dead. Whether the ethnographers' task was, at least in anthropology's early years, one of salvaging or preserving cultures – despite what humility they may have had – they were placed or placed themselves in a heroic position. We must remember that 'salvage' is related to 'salvation', and 'preserve' is derived through the Latin *servare* (to keep, to preserve) from the Indo-European *\*ser*, which may be related to *\*ser-ôs* or hero. Those anthropologists had an impossible task: to save what 'their people' – the Euro-Americans – had destroyed or were destroying.

I should note, parenthetically, that there were anthropologists, like M.J. McGee, the first president of the American Anthropological Association, who wanted to preserve at least some primitive cultures as living museums and research centres. More than sixty years later, I had a brittle argument with Margaret Mead over her desire to isolate some of the Pacific Island cultures so that they would become 'reserves' for future anthropological research! We are, of course, wont to stress the grieving that accompanies the death of cultures, but we have to remember that their preservation at the end of the nineteenth and early twentieth centuries also served the prevailing belief in indomitable progress. As these primitive societies represented stages in the unilinear evolution then in fashion, they attested to America's – the white man's – extraordinary progress (Parezo and Fowler 2007, Crapanzano 2008).

More than any other human science, anthropology's self-understanding, its identity and definition, are embedded in its subject matter in an intensely personal manner. In part this is the result of fieldwork. With the exception of psychoanalysis, the practitioners of none of these sciences have as long and intimate contact with their subjects. Anthropologists see changes that are rarely happy in the societies they study; they witness the death of those they befriended, who were often custodians of their society's past; they empathise with their informants' nostalgias and regrets, their idealisations or rejections of their past, their fears of and (often unrealistic) hopes for the future, and their (nativistic) turns to the past. They feel the pain of departure – the end of what is often the most significant experience in their lives – the loss of immediate contact with friends, the fear of the future for those friends, the question of whether or not those friends will feel their loss as they feel theirs, and the translation of lived experience into memory – memories that will be so worked on that they will lose the force of immediacy and spontaneity. Death and loss have accompanied anthropology in an insistent and uncanny fashion, often resurrecting feelings that the anthropologists would prefer to ignore.

All of these factors intensify the anthropologists' relationship to their defining subject matter. There is, despite the anthropologists' commitment to change, an inherent traditionalism in their understanding of their discipline. Though death and loss may be less salient in the new domains anthropologists are beginning to study, they nevertheless tone that research, especially in its critical reflexivity – the critique – that is attached to it. Though many younger anthropologists are excited by the changes in anthropology's purview, they are not immune to the sense of loss of the traditional objects of research, the actual loss of the subjects of that research, and the loss thereby of the traditional, defining scope of their discipline. To all of these factors that promote a focus on the end of anthropology, we have to acknowledge the fantasies and probabilities of world-ending that are current today. The anthropologist is no more immune to these than any other inhabitant of the contemporary world.

We live in a violent, competitive, war-besotted age that is edged by thoughts of apocalypse, at least of change so radical that it resists confident predictive articulation, and as such promotes less enthusiasm for the future than worry and despair about it. We search for security – freedom from risk – in a world that we find ever more dangerous. Georgio Agamben has argued in "Homo Sacer" that the 'camp' (death camps, refugee camps) has become our social paradigm – 'the *nomos* of the political space in which we are still living' (1995:185). He may be right, but we must not direct our attention only to those inhuman camps our biopolitics justify but also to the fact that that same biopolitics have encamped us. We wall ourselves in when we talk about globalisation, the demographic disruptions it produces, and the threat it poses to our individual and national pre-possessive identities, indeed to our survival. We tolerate crippling defense budgets (54% of the U.S. budget, that is 47% of the world's entire military spending). We find ourselves at the edge of ecological collapse. We are powerless before markets running wild – markets to whose hand-of-God dynamics we have surrendered as we might surrender to destiny, had destiny not been reduced to chance, luck and risk. We are immobilised by political systems that seem unable to grasp the seriousness of the situation in which we find ourselves or which offer us false hopes as, conned by those same hopes, they act in accordance with them. We are helpless before cosmic forces whose mythic formulations can hardly conceal the reality behind them. We focus on the immediate, we miniaturise our horizons, we reduce our goals, we materialise our aspirations, we measure our worth in greedy numbers, we take solace in the habitual and pleasure in the instant, we seem lost in a labyrinth of deflections and evasions of the consequential and, as Jane Guyer recently observed, ignoring the near future, we skip from the immediate future to a future so distant, so dreamlike, so fragile, so lonely that many people are led to an insistently literal or a selfishly allegorical reading of sacred texts they take to be prophetic (Guyer 2007:409–419).

As for the past, we seem, at least in the United States, to have lost a conception of history that lends support to our understanding of the present and future. The historian Tony Judt writes that 'we wear the last century rather lightly' (2008:16). We may memorialise it with heritage sites and historical theme parks, but we no longer give 'the present a meaning by reference to the past': now the past 'requires meaning only by reference to our many and often contrasting concerns'. Though I am not convinced that historical understanding was ever free of 'present and contrasting concerns', I have little doubt that today, fragmented as our historical understanding is, it is incapable of providing a firm and confident vantage point for appraising ends: the end of anthropology. Does the concern for the end of a discipline not resonate with our fragmented and contradictory picture of the past? Is it not conducive to an uncanny coalescence of the two primary meaning of 'end': demise and goal, death and intention? As we look back, are we destined, like Walter Benjamin's (1977:255) famous Angelus Novus, to see only piles of debris growing toward the sky which, however, we, unlike the Angel of History, invest narcissistically with significance?

My depiction of the position from which we ask after the end of anthropology is rhetorical. In fact, I am not concerned with the end of anthropology, however 'end' is understood, but with the ends of anthropology. Indeed, with the ends of anthropologies. For years I have insisted that we pluralise anthropology.[3] By pluralisation I am referring less to anthropology's four fields, sacrosanct in the United States and largely ignored in the rest of the world, or to its ever proliferating subfields than to its diverse theoretical orientations, critical perspective, methods of research, styles of presentation and argumentation, pedagogical techniques, modes of engagement and commitment to one or other differently evaluated audiences. I am referring – more significantly – to the many ways in which anthropologies have developed in different countries and how, in their evolution, they have responded not only to local traditions and conditions, but also to the hegemony of the self-stipulated 'centres' of anthropological thought and practice in Europe and America.

Though the response of many of these 'new anthropologies', as I have heard them called, to these hegemonic centres has ranged from the apologetic to the foolishly defiant, it seems to me that we have moved beyond the era in which anthropologists of the periphery (read, in most instances, the colonies and post-colonies) are simply clones of Oxbridge, Paris, Columbia, Berkeley, Chicago and Harvard. Many of these anthropologists have gained a voice of their own and a perspective that we cannot ignore. Still there are sensitivities. I remember giving a lecture in 1988 at the International Congress for Anthropological and Ethnological Sciences in Zagreb in which my mention of the loss of influence of the hegemonic centres of anthropology on world anthropologies elicited an immediate negative response from a group of Pacific Island anthropologists who thought I was questioning their ability to participate in mainstream anthropology. That very few American anthropologists attended this meeting, I should add, was taken as a sign of American anthropology's indifference to other anthropologies.

I have to take this observation seriously. One of anthropology's virtues is the hearkening to the voice of the Other. We do not – we are not supposed to – impose our ways of seeing things on those we study. Rather, we are meant to listen to and

---

[3]     A 'pluralisation' of anthropology is also referred to by Jebens in the present collection.

observe them with minimal interference. And I believe most of us try, as best we can, to carry out this impossible task, even in our new settings. I will have more to say about this below. Here I want to stress that it is one thing to hearken to the voice of the Other in the field, that is, in a circumscribed situation that, despite the effect of the participation of our subjects, is largely our construction, and quite another to listen to representatives of other societies in other situations, say, among colleagues with different ways of seeing the world and different empowerments. Frequently, despite ourselves, we treat them with a certain condescension, or perhaps more disturbingly simultaneously as colleagues with whom we can freely converse and as representatives of the societies from which they come, that is, as informants. This crude symptomatising stance is offensive and can lead, as I have sometimes observed at international meetings, to their near-breakdown, certainly a loss of colleagueship, which is difficult to repair. One of the most egregious examples of condescending dismissal occurred at the Zagreb meetings in which one of my well-reputed colleagues, now dead, turned to me after listening to a Japanese physical anthropologist discuss the power of *chi* (*ki*) in his discussion of Japanese martial arts, and loud enough to be overheard, called his approach hogwash or something to that effect. He never bothered to ask what the Japanese anthropologist was trying to say, what he was struggling with conceptually, and how he might be calling attention to a dimension of understanding that fell outside his own paradigm.

My worry is addressed to the insistent parochialism of the anthropologies of the centre. Here I will speak of American anthropology from – inevitably – an American critical perspective tempered by my often prolonged encounters with 'other' anthropologies primarily from Europe, Canada, Brazil, and South Africa. Despite its national and international meetings, American anthropology tends to be turned inward, principally addressing American colleagues and those few 'foreign' anthropologists who have done research in their area of specialisation; that is, if they write in English. Looking at the bibliographies in most books and articles published by American anthropologists, one is immediately struck by how few references are in languages other than English. Looking at the syllabuses of graduate (let alone undergraduate) courses and seminars, one rarely sees a reference to any but works in English. I have read ethnographic studies of Italy, Brazil, and Mexico in which there is not a single reference to a work by an Italian, Brazilian or Mexican ethnographer. This is, no doubt, a product of the United State's stubborn monolingualism, but it is also the result, I suspect, of a sense of academic superiority. It certainly reflects the prevailing attitude of superiority held by most Americans and their displays, however bankrupt, of diplomatic, military and economic power. We are, after all, at anthropology's 'cutting edge'.

I must confess that, whenever I hear the phrase 'cutting edge', I think less of a frontier of knowledge than of the aggression that lies behind a singular approach to knowledge, research and innovation. When applied to a discipline like anthropology that relies on intimate relations with informants, it is especially disquieting. What is so extraordinary about this stance is that it is never quite clear what that edge is. Does it edge on what lay before it or on what lies ahead? Is it simply dismissive of the past, the fact of its pastness meaning it is no longer of interest? It reflects not only a particular historical stance – a stance that is not necessarily shared by colleagues elsewhere, say, in Germany, where far greater attention is paid to anthropology's past. But it also reflects an idea of progress, thought dead by many but still operative, which seems at once specific in its immediacy and so open-ended that it is impossible to define its horizon. I speak here not only of anthropology's disciplinary goals, but also of those of the individuals who engage in it.

We cannot escape parochialism, but we ought to acknowledge it and reflect critically on its implication. We have to ask, for example, to what extent our particular parochialism is a defense against the challenges posed by both our informants and other anthropologists.[4] We have to consider the blinkers – the closure – that parochialism promotes, the isolation it can produce, the epistemological terror that may result from that isolation. In her book on the religiously conservative Women's Mosque Movement in Cairo, Saba Mahmood describes the effect that working with women, whose views she found repugnant when she began her research, had on her own outlook (2005:38). She declares that one of the aims of her book is 'to parochialise those assumptions – about the constitutive relationship between action and embodiment, resistance and agency, Self and authority – that inform our judgments about nonliberal movements such as the mosque movement' (Mahmood 2005:38). Though Mahmood does not take critical account of the 'parochialism' of her categories – action, embodiment, resistance, agency, self and authority – her aim is well taken. Expressed in a different language, it has been one of the principal goals of anthropology.

By personalising her reaction, however telling that personalisation may be, Mahmood side-steps what I believe is a singularly important dimension of anthropology: namely, the critical perspective, the self-reflexivity we are in a position to offer (and inevitably do offer) for better or worse the people with whom we work. We may have been over-protective of, indeed have infantilised, our informants in the past when we were dealing with simple, isolated peoples who did not share, so we supposed, our worldliness: but however justified that stance was – personally I find it demeaning – it can no longer be adopted, as we work in complex societies and in marginal ones which are informed and influenced by them. We have, as I have said, to reckon with the voices of those we study and the critique of us presented by those voices, whether at a mundane political level or at a deeply philosophical one.

---

4      I should note that ethnocentrism is not the same as parochialism, for it may be a component of concern for parochialism: an ethnocentrism, for example, that is unaware of its ethnocentricity. Of course, we might well argue the same for parochialism.

Yes, there has been much talk about dialogical anthropology – I have done it myself (Crapanzano 1992: Part Two, especially Chapter Eight) – but the sense of dialogue that is promoted seems to be o u r construct and rather saccharine. Dialogue always has a critical edge, however masked by *politesse*, which has to be acknowledged and even cultivated if it is to be – I hesitate to use the words – sincere, authentic and creative. I think the failure of the 'writing culture movement' to consider the critical dimension of dialogue was and still is symptomatic of an implicitly hierarchical stance in anthropological engagement – in our parochialism.[5]

Anthropology is caught between the openness to the world of those we study and the closure promoted by parochialism. How can we be at once open- and closed-minded? No doubt there are many ways. There is no end to the ingenuity with which human beings accommodate themselves to contradictions in their outlook. One way, which seems particularly relevant to anthropology and to which I have already made reference, is the framing of an endeavour. What we do in the field, what we tolerate, what we listen to and observe, how, in short, we respond to the field situation is determined by the way we frame it, how we bracket it off from our everyday experiences 'back home' or in off-moments in the field, and how responsive our informants are to the terms of engagement we bring to them. We are rarely invited to the field by the people we study. We are rather more like uninvited guests who hopefully, once welcomed, behave with consideration and perhaps even offer our hosts something of value: friendship, perhaps; money; insight; contact with an outsider and the outside, and the advantages this may bring; entertainment; a comic interlude; an escape from boredom; a critical perspective; an opportunity to be irritated and the mastery of that irritation; and – a gift that needs elaboration – counter-ethnography.

It is not only anthropologists who learn from the encounter but also the people with whom they work. It has often been noted that the best of our informants learn to adopt an ethnographic perspective on their own society. It differs from the ethnographer's if only because they do not have his or her anthropological background or distance. They may, however, suffer a painful alienation – a *Verfremdungseffekt* –

---

[5]     It is also symptomatic of the stress we give to the referential rather than the indexical function of language. In a most insightful article, which has been largely ignored, Jane Bachnick (1987) demonstrates how by considering the indexical play in dialogue, we are able not only to capture its progress – a case in point, the movements of deference and distance – but can come to appreciate the way in which interlocutors are included in each others' views. Monitoring indexical switchings (of honorifics in Japanese, in Bachnick's example) allows the ethnographers to appraise their position within the cultural universe of their interlocutors and, presumably, those interlocutors' appraisal of their position in the ethnographer's world. Focusing on the indexically constituted intersubjective dimension of dialogue, Bachnick argues, enables us to avoid problems stemming from the textualisation of dialogue understood in referential terms. Bachnick does not, however, recognise the role that a meta-indexical language, inevitably formulated referentially, plays in the understanding of dialogue by even its participants. See Crapanzano (1992:115–135).

that has been the source of anthropological anguish. The alienation mirrors, in many respects, the alienation that fieldwork produces in the ethnographer when he or she returns home. But what has received far less attention is what I am calling an informants' counter-ethnography: the eye they have on the anthropologist as a representative – a source of knowledge – of the anthropologist's society and culture.[6] However defensive this counter-ethnographic stance may be – after all, informants have to protect themselves from the challenge of their insistent, at times intrusive Other – it is not without its effect on the anthropologist, the progress of his or her research, and on the interpretations he or she makes both in the field and back home, even years after the research was completed (Crapanzano 1973).

The field situation, especially in foreign cultures or unfamiliar settings, lays bare dimensions of ordinary social encounters that, in their ordinariness, are usually ignored. The ethnographic encounter – at least in its initial stages, before it has become routinised – has for all parties an effect that is not dissimilar to the transformation that Heidegger attributes to conspicuousness (*Auffälligkeit*), obtrusiveness (*Aufdringlichkeit*) and obstinacy (*Aufsässigkeit*), to a break from the way the world usually presents itself (Heidegger 1993:72–76). The world, or more accurately objects in the world, can no longer be taken after such a break instrumentally, as tools (*Werkzeuge*) ready-to hand (*zu-handen*) but in a mode of disclosure, as presence-at hand (*vor-handen*).[7] Among other dimensions of interpersonal engagement, what is revealed in the ethnographic and other exceptional encounters is the terror we experience when we are forced to acknowledge the impenetrability of the mind – the thoughts – of the Other. We are no longer protected by habitual social and communicative conventions from the recognition of this impenetrability and its emotional consequences: we are not only confronted with the opacity of the Other, with that Other's penetrating gaze, but also with our own opacity, its vulnerability, and the impotence of our own gaze.

This is perhaps one of the reasons we have ignored the counter-ethnographic stance of our informants. I remember the sensation that Kevin Dwyer's "Moroccan dialogues" (1982:217–223) produced because he asked one of his informants, a *faqir*, what he thought Dwyer was doing, what he thought Dwyer thought of him, and what he thought of Dwyer. It was clear that the *faqir* was embarrassed by the questions and did his best to avoid answering them. They certainly ran counter to Moroccan etiquette, at least as I know it. When Dwyer asked him whether he

---

6    Kevin Dwyer notes that the *faqir* with whom he worked had a 'certain "anthropological" perspective' (1982:230, fn 23). Stoller (1987) and Bachnick (1987) in their different ways have considered the way they were conceived of by the people they worked with, but did not appraise those informants' views of their own culture. – Cf., in this collection, Jebens's reference to indigenous ideas or constructions of 'being white' or of 'whiteness'.

7    To be sure, their instrumentality is not lost but understood from a different perspective.

had ever suspected Dwyer and his project, the *faqir* answered, 'If I reach the point of getting together with someone many times, it means that I no longer have any doubts'. Dwyer (1982:230) pushed him by quoting a Moroccan proverb (one that resonates with my focus on the impenetrability of the Other): 'One third of what is unknowable is inside men's heads'. The *faqir* answers, 'I don't have any doubts about you. My mind tells me, and my heart tells me, that between you and me there is no longer any suspicion'. He adds that he behaves in good faith but can't rely on Dwyer's (or anyone else's good faith). 'Because your good faith isn't going to benefit me, what benefits me is mine. So I have to struggle with myself to make mine good, and I don't struggle to make yours good'. It is God who will judge Dwyer's. Though one might consider the *faqir*'s indifference to Dwyer's good or bad faith an expression of hostility (as at some level it probably was), it is also an affirmation of the *faqir*'s moral stance, his discipline. He answers Dwyer's questions, which, as he said earlier in the interview, are of no concern to him, because they serve Dwyer's purposes. They may test the *faqir*'s good faith.

What is striking about Dwyer's questions and the impression they made on many of his readers is their naiveté. They assumed (at least I assume they assumed) that the *faqir* or anyone else would answer the questions in a straightforward manner. But, as the *faqir* surely knew, if one is forced to characterise oneself to someone else, that characterisation has to be judged as an expression of how one wants to be characterised (Crapanzano 1992:91–112). When Dwyer asked him what he thought Dwyer thought of him, the *faqir* answered, 'You're the one who understands that. Why am I going to enter into your head?' (1982:219) To me, at least, Dwyer's interview breaches not only the conventions of each participant's communicative etiquette, but also, no doubt, the idiosyncratic conventions the two men had worked out over their many encounters before this last interview. Dwyer calls attention to precisely what has to be ignored if an exchange is to be successful – namely the opacity of each of its parties. Of course, my stress on the terror of impenetrability reflects an epistemological tradition that is haunted by solipsism. By stressing both mind and heart in telling himself that he can trust Dwyer, the *faqir* may well be calling attention to a possibly more confident mode of knowledge of the Other – through the heart – that is less susceptible to the threat of opacity. Whatever cognitive function the heart (*qalb*) may have, if it has any, it is perhaps not so very different from the way in which the body and embodiment have come to function rhetorically in the human sciences in recent years.

Dwyer's observations, his *méconnaissance*, the simplicity of his question, and the startle it produced among anthropologists when his work was first published in 1982 reflects the 'Malinowskian' moment in anthropological research.[8] It never occurred to me (nor, I imagine, to most anthropologists) not to try to find out what my informants thought of me and my research, but I – we – did it through indirection, just as I am sure our informants do in trying to discover what we think of them. I should add that, in my research with white South Africans during apartheid, with American Christian Fundamentalists and original-intention lawyers, and even in my most recent research with the Harkis, my informants often made it quite clear what they thought of me and my research. Sometimes they were friendly, sometimes dismissive, fortunately rarely hostile. I make it a practice to discuss with the people I work with, whenever possible, how they would go about doing my research. Some of these discussions have been among the most insightful from an ethnographic point of view.

At this point, I want to address the ends – the future – of anthropology. I do not want to idealise the discipline nor give it a significance it has never had and probably never will have. It is a field of study that has prided itself on its unique methodological stance – a stance that incorporates a wide range of research strategies that are often at odds with one another or, better, whose advocates are often at odds with one another. I do not want to enter into the specifics of these conflicts: they require critical historical reflection that centres on their arenas of contestation, most notably the university, its affiliated institutions, and funding organisations. I should, in fact, pluralise 'university' since there are dramatic differences in the structures, evaluations, styles, support and roles of universities around the world which are among the most significant determinants of the field. Though there have been a few anthropological studies of anthropology, like Mariza Peirano's (1995) of Brazilian and Indian anthropologies or those collected by Thomas Hauschild (1995) on German anthropology during the Nazi era, it is striking that a field that claims to be as critically self-reflective as anthropology and as sensitive to the formative power of institutions has not, to my knowledge, explored in any rigorous and historically sensitive way the relationship between the structure of the university and other relevant institutions and the manner in which anthropology frames, theorises, and conveys its subject matter. Let me be clear – I am not referring to those simplistic postulations such as 'anthropology is the handmaiden of imperialism', without demonstrating in detail

---

8    I am using 'Malinowskian moment' here to call attention to the absurdity of reifying and detemporalising a practice, as George Marcus has done in his discussion of the reflexivity required by anthropology's new research domains (2006, 2008, among his other recent works). Anthropologists may have idealised Malinowski's fieldwork and modeled their own research on it, but that model has a history that anyone attuned to (self-)reflexivity has surely to recognise. Not only has fieldwork, as responsive as it is to the field situation, 'deviated' over the years, but so has the reading of Malinowski's work. Such a history has yet to be written.

what that relationship is and how it has affected anthropological practice, including, importantly, its pedagogy and its consequent theorisations (Hymes 1971). Nor am I referring to the writing culture movement, which, for the most part, was concerned with textual analysis.

Of course blinkers blind the anthropologist to the effect on his or her discipline of the university, the political and, yes, politics. The latter was, in my experience, true of hiring practices in France at least during Mitterrand's presidency. It is my impression that, after a conservative government has been in power for several years, American anthropology takes a positivist – a scientistic – turn. My observation is casual and requires proof. Whether right or wrong, it does call attention to the need to investigate the relationship among anthropological practices, prevailing political currents and mediating institutions like funding agencies. Our discipline is probably not unique in its failure to subject itself to the same scrutiny as it does to its ostensible subjects of investigation.

Like many other academic disciplines, anthropologists are rather more concerned with the responses of their colleagues to their research than to the way that research circulates and is made use of outside the discipline, the university and the scholarly community at large.[9] We have paid scant attention to how anthropology's findings are used in marketing, advertising, journalism, travel guides, tourism, religious services, law, diplomacy, the arts and their promotion, theater, propaganda, policing, and government policy, though we have expressed concern about their use by the military, the CIA, the FBI and other intelligence gathering agencies and anti-terrorist (and perhaps even terrorist) organisations. I remember an agent of the CIA who tried unsuccessfully to hire me complain that of all academics anthropologists were the most difficult to recruit for 'government service'. Whatever we think of the CIA, his observation merits consideration. Why are we so inwardly turned, so indifferent to the use made of our work, except when it proves detrimental to the people we study or is made by organisations like the CIA whose activities we disapprove of and which run counter to our moral responsibility to our informants?

Critical reflexivity seems particularly important, since anthropologists have begun studying not only marginalised groups in complex societies, but also institutions and networks in globalised and globalising societies which had never been – indeed had never even been imagined as being – in anthropology's purview. The subject of these studies ranges from derivatives and other 'new' financial instruments to human rights and the legal institutions that support them; from insurance companies to hospitals; from gated communities to refugee camps; from traffic in human bodies and body parts to NGOs in war zones; from theatre groups

---

9      I am indebted to David Harvey for calling my attention to this lack of concern and what it says about anthropology.

to missile defense systems. In other words, anthropology can no longer be limited to the tribe or village, economic anthropology to the 'stone age', or legal anthropology to tribal councils. Perhaps it ought never to have been. Today it is near-impossible to find societies in which such 'traditional' approaches can be applied with any legitimacy. I am certainly not the first to observe this. Nor am I the only one who suffers a certain nostalgia for their possibility, but such nostalgia should not be exempt from critical regard, for it may well hinder the development of new research strategies demanded by our new domains of research. (I will return to this below.)

George Marcus (1995, 2006, 2008), ever ready to hail a new wave of anthropology – 'second-wave reflexivity' he calls this one – argues that anthropology's new field sites require new methodologies founded on a reflexivity that becomes 'the key means or operation of determining new forms and norms in the evolution of the multi-sited ethnography'.[10] Marcus's description of the new sites, however generalised, is well taken, though he gives, in my view, too much weight to experts and science studies. He suggests that there are three operations of reflexivity that define his new kind of ethnography: (1) in the materialisation of the object and space of study; (2) in defining and managing collaborative relationships within fieldwork; and (3) in the politics of reception of the study. The first of these demands monitoring (a) the role of (initial) personal contacts in constituting the field, and (b) the evolution of the sites of field research in which informants play a more active role in that evolution. The second focuses on the need to keep track of the researcher's relationship with experts who are now taken as collaborators. Finally the third appraises the role of a new readership that extends beyond the anthropologist to the research subjects themselves.

There is no doubt that the new field sites require reflexivity, but, I must confess, the reflexivities that Marcus describes have played an important role in more traditional research. Anthropologists have always had to consider the role of those who introduced them to the field site in the constitution of that site. Psychoanalytic anthropologists, working in 'traditional' settings, have, for example, insisted on the importance of monitoring one's entry point in the field (Hunt 1989:29, Kracke 1987). Anthropologists have always had to monitor the progression of their research and the determinants of that progression. They have always collaborated with their informants, some of whom take on the position of the expert. I am certainly not unique in having discussed my work with my informants and asked them for procedural advice. The writings of anthropologists, like those of all writers, have always been influenced by images of their readership, including, however fantasmatic, even their illiterate informants. Clearly, however, the anthropologist's

---

10      On 'multi-sited ethnography', see also the contributions by Godelier, Jebens and Kohl in the present collection.

writings will be read in a different way by his or her collaborators: namely as a contribution to their purportedly joint endeavour.

The relations between anthropologists and their 'collaborators' present problems that traditional fieldworkers did not usually have to face, but these relate not only to the complexity, fluidity, and multiplicity of research sites, but also to the authority, confidence, class, and privilege of those collaborators. More important, as Marcus (2008) recognises, is the co-planning of research projects and jointly seeking funding. What has to be considered, however, is the function of the anthropologist in such collaborations. Are they actively contributing to the stated goals of the research? Or are they proffering a reflexivity (or the illusion of a reflexivity) that may or may not contribute directly or indirectly to those goals? Serendipity, rather more than systemic programming, is at play here.[11] Or, most cynically, do they serve simply as decoration for funding? What is required here are rigorous studies, rather than off-the-cuff pronouncements of the interaction of the anthropologist and his or her collaborators. To me, the most significant contribution Marcus makes is his stress on the 'within' (or between) from which the field is constituted. His greatest weakness is his failure to consider the defensive role that disciplines and institutions play in the 'evolution' of research. That anthropologists have not always proclaimed their reflexivity does not mean that they have ignored it. It is rather their mode of critique that demands scrutiny.

Critical reflexivity is of singular importance – perhaps not so singular – in a discipline like anthropology which straddles different cultural and social traditions, producing thereby an instability and fragility that seem to demand correction. It is not altogether clear to me why instability and fragility should demand correction. They have their virtues, just as straddling does, despite the groundlessness or, perhaps more accurately, the illusion of groundlessness it produces. It is, in fact, this straddling that lies at the heart of anthropology, and it merits far greater epistemological reflection than it has received. We have been rather too content to decry the pain, the confusions, at least, that the conceptual gymnastics of such a position requires than accept the challenge it poses.

Remember, for example, the hue and cry – the mud-slinging – that surrounded the now-fading declarations of postmodernity, and especially postmodernist approaches to social and cultural reality (if indeed 'reality' were to have a referent). There is no doubt that postmodernism was a conceptual fad just as globalisation has become one. The fact that it has had its foolhardy enthusiasts, who delighted in Nietzsche's play without ever recognising his seriousness and his deep moral concern, or in declarations that all the world's a text or a mess of simulacra does not mean that 'postmodernism' does not challenge some of anthropology's time-worn conceptual apparatuses.

---

[11]     On the importance of serendipity, see also the contribution by Spyer in the present collection.

Despite initial resistance, deconstruction (which, strictly speaking, should not be confused with postmodernism) has not been without its effect on contemporary anthropology, if only by passing through the 'defiles' of post-colonial studies. It is no longer possible to assume without question the totalizations that lay behind the great master narratives that concerned themselves with psyche, history and society, or to ignore the fact that all power is institutionally lodged. Aside from its incorporation of notions like hybridity, the subaltern, heteronomy, and the simulacrum, contemporary anthropological theory and ethnographic description are far more sensitive to the fissures, fragments, disjunctures, transgressions, paradoxes, aporiae, the in-between, the liminality and the multi-perspectivalism of socio-cultural life.

However tempered by disciplinary conservativism and the allure of simpler conceptions of society, these changes have ethical as well as epistemological and observational import. Think, for example, of Homi Bhabha's reconfiguration of 'cultural difference' (1990:312–315). He notes that, although the conceptualisation and consequent policy of multiculturalism serves the interests of the dominant, insofar as it acknowledges socio-cultural difference it opens up a space of resistance for the marginalised. He refuses to understand cultural differences in terms of their eventual assimilation into the dominant culture. 'The question of cultural difference', he writes, 'faces us with a disposition of knowledge or a distribution of practices that exist beside each other'. It does not surmount 'the space of incommensurable meanings and judgments that are produced within the process of transcultural negotiation'. Put rather more simply than Bhabha, if I understand him correctly, the marginalised hold their position – their cultural assumptions – as do the dominant in negotiations and accommodations not in the 'space' of the simple contestation that arises with essentialist stereotypes of each other, but in an 'in-between' of identificatory interdependence that operates in both conscious and unconscious ways.

Bhabha's language is obscure. His argument, moving indiscriminately from one conceptual level to another, is inconsistent if not contradictory. He often fails to distinguish the descriptive from the prescriptive. But his critique of assimilationalist goals and essentialist characterisations of the Other, as well as his acknowledgement of the interdependence of each party's identity in contestatory situations, does demand a rethinking of the binary thought – the coloniser versus the colonised, the host versus the guest, the owner versus the worker, the powerful versus the powerless – that has characterised so much of our social thought. We have, of course, to ask why the ever-shifting interstitial has become so attractive, especially to the formerly colonised; why they are so attracted to the 'perpetual critique' of Derridian thought; and why they move so promiscuously from one mode of conceptualisation to another. In part this is a result of the paradoxical situation in which the post-colonial intellectuals find themselves. They are caught between often dramatically different audiences and audience phantasms, each of which makes different and often conflicting demands on them. They are also weighed down by theoretical paradigms that, in speaking in different ways to different people, put their own identity in question and thereby the possibility of a stable vantage point. Gayatri Spivak (1985) writes of the silence, the voicelessness, of the subaltern and in so doing speaks for them. But how can she? With what right? In what language? She has to deconstruct – 'destabilise' is perhaps a better word – as she writes. She is caught in the midst, as are Bhabha and countless other intellectuals who attempt to speak, to represent, those whose language they themselves do not know in a language that is not even their own but that of the former coloniser – one that is philologically weighted by domination.[12] They, too, have lost their voice as they voice and ventriloquise vociferously. This is more than an epistemological conundrum: it is a seemingly irresolvable moral dilemma – certainly less acute than that of those of whom they speak, but who cannot, so they say, speak for themselves.

Bhabha may write of the negotiations that occur in the space of the juxtaposed, but he offers no concrete picture of how such negotiations would proceed. He fails to give full recognition to the possible, indeed the likely role of power – brute power – in overriding 'incommensurable meanings and judgments' in 'the process of transcultural negotiation'. He has, of course, been criticised, for his failure to produce hard evidence for his argument. Who is to say that the marginalised don't want to assimilate? That is an empirical question, one that anthropologists could and have, in fact, answered. But, as I have already noted, Bhabha, like other postmodernist and post-colonial intellectuals, conflates the descriptive and prescriptive, a conflation that offers them an illusory but rhetorically potent means of escape (see Crapanzano 1991). To condemn them on these grounds is far less interesting than to ask why they conflate the two. Are they offering a new mode of articulating the social? Though I am sceptical, I do believe that this conflation arises out of the interstitial situation in which they find themselves – one in which it is impossible to separate objective description from moral and political engagement.

There is an obvious parallel between the post-colonial intellectual's situation and that of the anthropologist. Both operate in the in-between. In the case of anthropologists, their interstitial position is voluntary – an artifice of their research – from which, despite all the alienation they feel upon their return home, they are able to depart, thus returning to the epistemological if not the ethical comfort of home. Though still concerned with the problem of how to mediate their culture of

---

[12]    By 'language' I am not referring simply to different languages as 'language' is popularly understood, but also to languages which share the same features but are connotatively weighted in different ways: by class, gender, age, wealth, poverty, hegemonic position, authority, lack of authority, power, powerlessness, experience, and history.

orientation with that of their research subjects, they are now able to bracket it off in a way in which, I suspect, the post-colonial intellectual, despite his or her privilege, cannot. They are, I believe, far less comfortable with the authorised positions the anthropologist is afforded: the theoretical, analytical and hermeneutical frames that his or her discipline validates in one manner or another, like science, for example. Still the parallel between the two highlights the difficulties associated with straddling.

It is important to note that straddling does not require equilibrium: the cultures the anthropologist and the postmodern intellectuals straddle never have the same significance. The culture of orientation, however contorted, hybrid and ill-defined it may be, always has greater weight than the culture under study, though the latter, in so far as it challenges the presuppositions of the former, may be more forceful in effect at the time of engagement. We come to the encounter with what Hans-Georg Gadamer (1985:235ff.) calls prejudice and fore-understanding (*Vorverständnis*), which we have to bracket off or open to question as best we can so that they do not predetermine our take on what transpires during the encounter. Engagement and interpretation are temporal processes that are arrested from time to time through reflection, summation, evaluation, judgment, and decisive action. At such times straddling gives way to taking a position, ephemeral though it may be. The culture under study, as well as one's own, is objectified, detemporalized and exoticized. The in-between gives way to polarisation.

Is it possible to found a body of knowledge of theoretical or practical import from within the interstitial? Is it possible to develop a meaningful ethics from within the in-between? Or are we forced to disengage ourselves from that position and accept the reductions and distortions that come with that move? I cannot answer these questions, which are, in any event, rhetorical. But I would like to suggest that one way in which an anthropology of the future can respond to some of them is by stressing the temporal dimensions – note the plural – of social life, including anthropological fieldwork. I am certainly not the first to note the extent to which space and its metaphorisations ground (!) social and cultural description. It has constituted the way ethnographers construct the field! It delimits context, even historical context through placement, which may serve to arrest time. As we begin to study complex societies, institutions whose particular locus is of little impress, given their spread around the world, and networks whose positionality is precipitated by intervention – usage, interpretation, static or break-down – which may itself be spatially without location, how are we to carry out our fieldwork? Multi-sited ethnographies may be an answer to a few of these new research domains (!), but they are still sited.

In a recent paper, the Argentinean-Brazilian anthropologist Rita Segato has argued for a new conceptualisation of territoriality, one which is defined by networks (rather than specific locations), biopolitics and specularisation

(2008:204). She is writing of new patterns in contemporary religions that escape our attention because of the focus on secularisation and religious mobility. She suggests that it is the body that bears participating identity in a network, and that 'competing networks suffocate and stress their unity vis-à-vis other networks by the management of bodies as emblems of belonging' (Segato 2008:210). This new territoriality treats space the way it treats bodies. It is possible to speak here of bodies in their behavioural space, since the territory becomes the outcome of the presence of the plastic human web, imprinting its traces as it expands or consolidates its existence under a new territorial paradigm. Segato's argument is complex, and I am not doing justice to it here, especially with respect to her take on the new ways governments are forced to adjust to these transnational networks. I simply want to illustrate one attempt to offer a new paradigm that breaks with traditional notions of space and territory.

My own approach is rather different. I would suggest an anthropology of the occasion. By 'occasion', I mean a constellation of occurrences that are not yet articulated as an event, which occurs somewhere, in virtual reality even, but whose effect as it spreads may render its site of origin insignificant or simply an icon of its effective spread. By insisting on its location, we may well blind ourselves to that spread – to its radiant effect.[13] The icon – which paradoxically serves, in a counter-movement, to re-affirm the original event – has its own history distinct from the spread, but not without effect on that spread. The (inevitable) translation of an occasion into an event produces its conformity to prevailing takes on the world or, usually within conventional limits, transgressions of that take. In either case the translation is subject to political manipulation. So powerful, so habitual, so culturally and linguistically determined is 'eventing' that my separating the event from the occasion has to be considered an artifice for drawing attention to its socio-political implication and manipulation.

I cannot develop the notion of an anthropology of occasion here. But I do want to discuss in a far too general, too idealised fashion the temporal movement internal to one such occasion, in fact, a coalescence of occasions, namely, fieldwork. It seems to me that that the pictorial quality of most ethnographic description leads us to ignore or dismiss the effect of the complex temporalities of straddling – of living in, or living as though one were in, the in-between – of anthropological research and the conclusions we draw from it. Fieldwork cannot be reduced to a single practice or held to a single perspective. There is dramatic development in its pursuit, and this development is primarily a result of the exchanges that occur in an arena that is spatially demarcated as the 'field'.

---

[13]     Compare Derrida (1967). He is, of course, writing about structures and not networks, but the centring effect on the structure, its re-articulation, is pertinent.

I use 'arena' here, not to stress the contestatory nature of fieldwork – though, as we shall see, it can be of singular importance – but to focus on the changes that occur both within its formal features and to the modes of engagement of all parties to it. These developments affect the mindset of the participants, but, given the opacity of the mind of the Other, we have no unmediated access to their effect, and, given our own immersion in the exchanges, only limited and presumably distorted access to our own. This is not to say that these presumed changes in mindset do not have an effect on the progress of our encounters in the field: on the contrary, they provide a somewhat anxious horizon to our understanding. We presume that what our informants do and say is always accompanied by what I have called shadow dialogues (Crapanzano 1992:213–215) – silent, internal, usually quasi-articulate evaluative conversations they have with themselves and with us. There is then at least a double movement in the encounters: one which is perceptible to the participants and one which is not, though any of the participants may 'intuit' it by reading the perceptible movement as symptoms of the silent thought of the Other.

Since it cannot be fully identified with the shadow dialogues because it is focused on and in the manifest dialogues, reflection requires a move – if I might use Kantian aesthetic vocabulary – from interest to disinterest. The anthropologist's engagement in the field demands interest, for otherwise he or she would not be able to engage. It is purposeful (*zweckmäßig*), in fact multi-purposeful, for the anthropologist has to take an active interest in whatever is being pursued and its research import. Reflection, like aesthetic contemplation, requires a disinterested stance at least toward the immediate transactions but, unlike aesthetic contemplation, governance by the research purpose. Disinterest does not mean indifference or distancing, nor does it imply that that its object is uninteresting, as Kant (1990:41, fn) noted in a footnote in his discussion of the beautiful. Obviously what is interesting is determined by both the quality of the object, its allure and the purposeful orientation of (secondary) reflection. Theodor Adorno argues that disinterest, if it is not to become indifference, 'must be shadowed by the wildest interest'.[14]

It seems quite obvious that interest and disinterest are not simply isolated attitudes, as Kant assumed, but are embedded in the complex social and cultural surround and subject to the constitutive plays of power and desire in that surround

---

[14]    Adorno (1997:11). Unlike Kant, Adorno stresses the fact that works of art necessarily evolve in a dialectic of interests and disinterests. He argues that for Kant the aesthetic becomes 'a castrated hedonism, desire without desire' (1997:11). This is not the place to pursue the role of desire in the formulation of the 'ethnographic', but it certainly merits a critical investigation that was entirely missing from Geertz's and Clifford's pathetically facile notions of ethnography as fiction, as fiction-making. We might well consider ethnography by analogy with Adorno's observation that '[t]here is no art that does not contain in itself as an element, negated, what it repulses': there is no ethnography that does not contain in itself as an element, negated, what it repulses. And we might relate this to anthropology's moralistic stance towards its subject matter. Think of my discussion of Mahmood in this respect.

– plays of power and desire whose import can only be grasped through consideration of their extension over time and how they punctuate that temporal stretch. The temporal flow of field research and its aftermath (not to mention its preparation) is punctuated by the oscillation of interest and disinterest, purpose and purposeless purposefulness, unreflective engagement and reflective disengagement, and, most importantly, the witting and unwitting accommodations to the empowered and empowering demands of each of the symbolically vested interlocutors. Disinterest, purposeful purposelessness, reflection and accommodation serve to arrest time and in so doing enable the static pictures we draw, interpret and explain. There is no way to avoid these arrests, but when, why, and how they are carried out and how they are ideologically supported merits continual monitoring. This attention has to take account of the ethical, political and epistemological consequences of the arrests, and indeed the letting-flow.

Any anthropology of the future will have to engage with ethical questions that extend far beyond the ethics of fieldwork. I do not wish to deny the importance of the ethical dimension of field research, but I think we have to ask why we have so often been content with delimiting our ethical concerns to so tiny a domain.[15] Is it an evasion? Discussions of moral relativism in cultural relativistic terms are also evasive insofar as, in their generality, they avoid concrete situations. Today these evasions are no longer possible, if only because our informants will no longer let us make them. Yes, we have to hearken to their voice, but – and this is important – we have to probe our own moral values before we either accept or reject their position. By position I mean manifest ones, like wearing the veil, stoning homosexuals, ignoring the lives of thousands devastated by natural disaster because the lives of the masses are thought less significant than the maintenance of power or perhaps even a game of golf, respecting national boundaries and sovereignty despite what one believes to be heinous practices, or invading countries to foster one's own values, like those of democracy American-style or of one religious fundamentalism or another. I am also referring to the underlying epistemological assumptions of moral outlooks, like the separation or non-separation of description from prescription. We cannot simply look to an ethics of practice, essentially a descriptive one, which does not take account of serious cross-cultural differences in practice.

There are no easy answers to these problems. I certainly don't have any. I do want to note that some of them arise from – or are at least foregrounded by – the way we frame our research. We have been wedded to a field methodology that has given preference to supposedly objective observation, that is, to an observational mode that demands minimal interference from the observers. There are virtues in this approach, but it should not be fetishised. While there is a time for this observational

---

15      I am not considering here the ethico-political position our professional societies take in their pronouncements and lobbying, if only because they require far more attention than I can give them here. Central to them is human dignity and the rights that follow from it.

perspective (provided that it is treated with a certain scepticism), there is also a time for a more critical, more argumentative approach. Agonising over the moral dilemmas posed by one's reaction, say, to the Woman's Mosque Movement when that movement is described in a way in which critical engagement – in conversation and debate – is either avoided or eliminated in its presentation is, in my view, a morally dubious reaction to the objectification of the movement. I am not denying the ethical problems, but rather the way in which the anthropologist, in adhering to the objectivistic methods condoned by the discipline, has failed to provide a sound basis for such agonising. It seems to me that we owe the mosque women and ourselves the opportunity to engage in a respectful debate with us about our respective beliefs and practices. (As researchers, we have of course the luxury of not coming to a decisive conclusion.) Apologetics are always addressed to an opponent. Moralising agony aside, apologetics itself, as it is displayed in such engagements, is certainly a social fact. It can best be elicited through critical encounters.

I certainly do not want to deny the delicacy of carrying out ethnographic debate. Timing is of the essence. It took me months of research with American Christian Fundamentalists before I felt comfortable enough to engage in a critical conversation. I was interviewing an elderly professor of New Testament theology who had just completed an enormous commentary on Revelations. He was a gentle, understanding man, warm but not particularly charismatic, who had to cancel our first appointment nearly a year earlier because of an emergency heart operation. I could not help thinking that his confrontation with death had given him a wider perspective than most of his colleagues. I told him that one thing that troubled me about evangelical Christianity was its focus on Christ's Second Coming: it seemed to ignore His First Coming and His message of love. The professor was startled by my observation. He remained silent for what seemed to me ages. The room darkened for me; he suddenly seemed frail and very old – vulnerable. I regretted my question and was sure that I had hurt him deeply. Finally he spoke. 'I've never thought of that. You may be right. I'll have to think about it'. The room brightened; the professor lost his frailty, his vulnerability, and became a man of wisdom, spiritual wisdom. Not only was I relieved by his answer, but I felt open to him, as I believe he felt open to me. From that point on I was able to engage in critical discussions with some of my informants. They were willing enough and, in fact, seemed relieved by my (our) change in style. These discussions were perhaps the most insightful I had.

I believe an anthropology of the future, particularly one that focuses on the anthropologist's own culture, risks losing this edge, which is fundamental, in my view, to the anthropological endeavour. It might be asked how essential this straddling will be to an anthropology of the future as the world homogenises, as anthropologists devote more and more attention to their own cultures. I believe it is essential. The anthropological stance rests on real or artifactual alterity and distance. It gives anthropology its particular angle on both the society under study and the anthropologist's. It serves as a corrective to unquestioned cultural assumptions and provides a 'basis' for social and cultural critique. It impedes the replication of a society's self-understanding, as is the case with so much sociology, by distressing that understanding, often, though not uniquely, by revealing its negative undersong. Anthropology has an important iconoclastic dimension. [16]

In the past it has been the exoticism – the often profound differences between the anthropologists' own culture and that of the people they were studying – that gave them an edge, or at least the illusion of an edge, on those people, their culture and by extension the anthropologists' own culture, their people. For those anthropologists who are not completely charmed by their own interpretive strategies and socially condoned explanations, that edge produces, ideally, a conceptual anguish that demands a critical rethinking of the categories and values prevailing in their society of orientation. It calls attention to the way in which the metalanguage of social and cultural description and critique refract and are refracted in their social and cultural understanding.

If Wittgenstein and the deconstructionists have taught us anything, it is that a metalanguage wholly independent of its target language is impossible. But – and to me this is perhaps anthropologists' most important role – we can t r o u b l e that language and its metalinguistic presumption. In so doing we not only call attention to the limits of our social and cultural assumptions, but may even open up other possibilities (though I must admit a certain scepticism in this regard).

Now, before I am called to account, I should note that I am not claiming that the edge produced by our engagement with an exotic culture – I use this inflammable word here and above purposely, to inflame – is not itself subject to the force of our hegemonic understanding and to our complex and often contradictory projective capacities. But it is safe to say that those exotic cultures resist (in the phenomenological sense) that understanding and those projections in a way in which our own culture and society cannot. Herein lies a serious danger: how do we evaluate the edge we have on our own society, the distance, the difference, the alterity we assume? Are they simply refractions of our own culture that give us the illusion of a critically independent edge?

From my first field research, I have been impressed by the social role of the trickster, as well as the metaphorical role that the trickster may have for suppressed dimensions of ethnographic research and interpretation. Over the years I have met many tricksters and have come to admire their savvy. They know, at least the best of them, that they themselves can be conned by their own tricks. They recognise, in effect, their artifice and the power of that artifice to deny its own artifice. They

---

[16]     On cultural difference, critique and the 'in-betweenness' of the anthropologist, see also the contributions by Godelier, Jebens, and Kohl in the present collection.

are caught not between artifice and reality, but between artifice and artifice's denial of itself. They are in a position that is not unlike that of the anthropologist, who is caught, so it can be argued, between two artifices, that of her or his own culture and that of the culture under study. They have no firm footing. But unlike the trickster who is liberated by his or her savvy and takes delight, at times painful delight, in the plays it afford, anthropologists are often tortured by the complex straddling in which they find themselves. They straddle not just two or more cultures but two or more artifactual realities – call them social constructions if you prefer – that proclaim their reality as their contingent juxtaposition (brought about by the anthropologists' presence) disclaims that reality. (Their situation may even be more complex if the people they are studying, like certain Sufi mystics, or my hypostasised trickster, delight in artifice.) We may seek firm footing in what we assume to be reality – that is, in naive empiricism or positivism or a realism that we assume gives direct access to reality without our acknowledging that realism is only a style. But if the anthropology of the future is not to end in a deadening academicism that, however quickened by nostalgia, sentimentality and an elegiac sense of belatedness, is destined to repeat again and again its 'tried and true wisdom' – the uncritical litany of class, gender, race and ethnicity, for example – it must, I believe, reckon with its artifice and the ethical, as well as the political and epistemological consequences of that reckoning.

## REFERENCES

ADORNO, Theodor
1997     *Aesthetic theory.* Minneapolis: University of Minnesota Press

AGAMBEN, Georgio
1995     *Homo Sacer.* Il potere savrano e la nuda vita. Torino: Einaudi

BACHNICK, Jane M.
1987     "Native perspectives of distance and anthropological perspectives of culture", *Anthropological Quarterly* 60:25–34

BENJAMIN, Walter
1977     "Über den Begriff der Geschichte", in: Walter Benjamin, *Illuminationen*, 251–261. Frankfurt am Main: Suhrkamp

BHABHA, Homi
1990     "DissemiNation: time, narrative, and the margins of the modern nation", in: Homi Bhaba, *Nation and narration*, 291–322. London: Routledge

CRAPANZANO, Vincent
1973    "The writing of ethnography", *Dialectical Anthropology* 2:69–73
1991    "The postmodern crisis: egalitarianism, parody, dialogue", *Cultural Anthropology* 6:431–446
1992    *Hermes' dilemma and Hamlet's desire: on the epistemology of interpretation*. Cambridge: Harvard University Press
2004    *Imaginative horizons: an essay in literary-philosophical anthropology*. Chicago: University of Chicago Press
2008    "Geronimo's buttons", *Times Literary Supplement* August 8:9

DERRIDA, Jacques
1967    "La Structure, Le Signe, et Le Jeu", in: Jacques Derrida, *L' Ecriture et la Différence*, 409–428. Paris: Editions du Seuil

DWYER, Kevin
1982    *Moroccan dialogues: anthropology in question*. Prospect Heights, Illinois: Waveland Press

GADAMER, Hans-Georg
1985    *Truth and method*. New York: Crossroad

GUYER, Jane I.
2007    "Prophecy and the near future: thoughts on macroeconomic, evangelical, and punctuated time", *American Ethnologist* 34:409–419

HAUSCHILD, Thomas
1995    *Lebenslust und Fremdenfurcht*. Ethnologie im Dritten Reich. Frankfurt am Main: Suhrkamp

HEIDEGGER, Martin
1993    *Sein und Zeit*. Tübingen: Max Niemeyer Verlag

HUNT, Janet C.
1989    *Psychoanalytic aspects of fieldwork*. Newbury Park, CA: Sage Publications

HYMES, Dell (ed.)
1974    *Reinventing anthropology*. New York: Random House

JUDT, Tony
2008    "What have we learned, if anything?", *The New York Review of Books* 55(7)

KANT, Immanuel
1990    *Kritik der Urteilskraft*. Hamburg: Felix Meiner

KRACKE, Waud
1987    "Encounters with other cultures: psychological and epistemological aspects", *Ethos* 15:58–82

MAHMOOD, Saba
2005    *Politics of piety: the Islamic revival and the feminist subject.* Princeton: Princeton University Press

MARCUS, George
1995    "Ethnography in/of the world system: the emergence of multi-sited ethnography", *Annual Review of Anthropology* 24:95–110
2006    "Reflexivity unbound: shifting styles of critical self-awareness from the Malinowskian scene to the emergence of multi-sited ethnography", in: Ursula Rao, and John Hutnyk (eds.), *Celebrating transgression: methods and politics in anthropological studies of culture*, 13–22. New York: Berghahn Books
2008    "The end of ethnography: social/cultural anthropology's signature form of producing knowledge in transition", *Cultural Anthropology* 23(1):1–14

PAREZO. Nancy J. and Don D. FOWLER
2007    *Anthropology goes to the fair: the 1904 Louisiana exposition.* Lincoln: University of Nebraska Press

PARTRIDGE, Eric
1958    *Origins: a short etymological dictionary of modern English.* New York: Macmillan

PEIRANO, Mariza
1995    *A Favor da Etnografia.* Rio de Janeiro: Relume-Dumará

SEGATO, Rita
2008    "Closing ranks: religion, society, and politics today", *Social Compass* 55(2):203–215

SPIVAK, Gayatri Chakravorty
1985    "Can the subaltern speak? Speculations on widow sacrifice", *Wedge* (7/8):120–130

STOLLER, Paul
1987    "Son of Rouch: portrait of a young ethnographer by the Songhay", *Anthropological Quarterly* 60:114–123

# 6

## WHATEVER HAPPENED TO THE SPIRIT OF ADVENTURE?

### Signe Howell

Are we witnessing the end of anthropology? To judge by the ever increasing membership of the European Association of Social Anthropologists – especially from universities in countries where there previously was little academic interest in the discipline, such as Germany and Eastern Europe – the answer would be a resounding 'no'. But, to judge from the kind of research projects engaged in by Ph.D. students and academic staff in countries where the discipline has been established for many years, such as the United Kingdom, France and the Scandinavian countries and where the basic disciplinary issues and principles were developed, I feel more uncertain about my answer. Certainly, the practice of social anthropology as we have known it since the time of Malinowski – and which set it apart from the other social sciences, characterised as it was by long-term fieldwork and participant observation in remote and unknown parts of the world and informed by the inductive approach – is changing. This may, indeed, be contributing to the end of anthropology as the discipline used to be understood. What we are witnessing today is a trend marked by an increase in research projects that deal with clearly defined topics for investigation, that increasingly are located in the anthropologist's own country of residence, and that are multidisciplinary.

Does this matter? I think it does, not least because there are clear signs that the trademarks of anthropology that underscored all ethnographic fieldwork are by many no longer perceived as essential. Our particular method – open-ended participant observation – the sole purpose of which was (and is) to achieve understanding of local knowledge 'from the native's point of view' in unknown parts of the world and to contextualise it in wider local significations, is losing its theoretical centrality. The alien gaze, once held to be highly important, is no longer emphasised. This quest, which was (and is) epistemologically linked to the comparative study of human social and cultural life, is undergoing serious redefinitions. While the old methodological terminology is still in use, the actual practice of many ethnographers is giving it new meanings. Among the more striking changes I have observed are the following: actual time spent in the field is shorter than it was a few decades ago, often no more than twelve months; the local language is used less; interviews and questionnaires are used more; topics for investigations are more sharply delineated; more projects are undertaken in the anthropologist's own country and are multidisciplinary; and the holistic ambition seems to be on the wane.

I wish to argue that this demise may be attributed to both internal and external factors – factors that reinforce each other. These I wish to characterise as a loss of the spirit of adventure among graduate students combined with new demands from universities and the institutions that fund research. In what follows, I will deal with each of these. My presentation will be rather personal and guided by my worries about the changes that I perceive to be taking place. I must emphasise that I do not paint a nuanced picture of the current situation. I ignore the many exceptions to my critical statements. I disregard examples of exciting and thriving research projects carried out according to all the cherished ethnographic criteria, whether 'at home' or elsewhere. I am looking for patterns of what I regard as decline.

When I was a post-graduate student at the University of Oxford in the mid- and late 1970s, the common understanding among the students – and our teaching staff – was that we would undertake sustained fieldwork in some distant and unknown part of the world. Here we would seek to acquire an understanding of local ideas, values and practices, primarily through the use of the local language (however imperfectly mastered) and by hanging around twenty-four hours a day. Our projects were open-ended, holistic in their ambition, and, whatever 'social facts' we uncovered, our unquestioned ambition was to interpret them contextually. It was not a question of s h o u l d we do this, but w h e r e we would most like to settle for eighteen months of participant observation. The choice of where was often dictated by two considerations: a place that we felt would be congenial to our taste, perhaps a place we had heard or read about and which appealed to our imagination and sense of adventure and discovery, and a place that we thought might help us answer some theoretical quandaries that, through our readings and the lectures of our teachers, had aroused our intellectual curiosity. Together these two concerns added up to a general desire to explore the unknown: geographical, social, cultural or intellectual. Through rigorous and persistent study of the various social values and practices that we encountered, we would seek to provide a study of the community that was both informed and anthropologically relevant, as well as contribute to fundamental intellectual questions inherent in the discipline of anthropology about the nature of social institutions and social life. Perhaps I have an unrealistic and rather romantic notion of the anthropological ambition, but it was one that I – and most of my contemporaries – believed in and that we tried to live up to.

It is a notion that I still cherish today, but one that I observe is in the process of being undermined for a number of different reasons. In what follows, I want to examine what I mean by 'undermine' and explore some of the reasons for this. They range from external factors attributable to current political thinking about what constitutes 'useful' knowledge, linked to recent trends in the understating of the nature of universities and how this effects research funding, as well as to internal factors within the discipline of social anthropology itself. Certainly in the UK and Scandinavia, where I know the situation best, all these factors threaten to undermine the practice of social anthropology as it used to be practiced. I believe the time has come for senior anthropologists everywhere to examine the current situation and ask some tough questions. Are we allowing our unique contribution to the understanding of human social life to be undermined? If we do not like what we see, what can we do to prevent the discipline from slowly losing its identity and being merged with a number of related disciplines, such as sociology, cultural geography, media studies, ethnology, social psychology, cultural studies and education – several of whose members increasingly proclaim to be 'sort of anthropologists' and to 'really be doing ethnography because we do qualitative studies'. The question is, do we agree that they are 'really doing ethnography'? If not, why not? The topic of this collection is, therefore, an important first step in helping to clarify what some senior anthropologists from different countries actually think about the situation.

## INTERNAL FACTORS OF CHANGE

### Small places, large issues

In order to rescue what many of us agree is the heart of the anthropological enterprise, namely to immerse oneself in unknown 'small places' and thereby address the 'large issues', as my colleague Thomas Hylland Eriksen has aptly called his introductory book, we anthropologists must become more proactive in the defense of our methods and the insights and results we claim they give rise to. On the home front we can best do this in the syllabuses we offer our students – what we teach and how we label and organise our courses; in how we work in grant-giving and selection committees at different levels; and what kind of projects we demand from our graduate students. At the same time, we have to confront the aftermath of the work by the fifth column within our own ranks, the so-called postmodernists who, through their 'critique of anthropology' – more precisely, of ethnographic practice – knocked away the foundations from beneath the discipline. Their criticism had the effect in some influential circles of rendering fieldwork in the world outside Euro-America politically incorrect, indeed illegitimate. The spirit of adventure itself was made suspicious. Although their influence is abating, it had an effect from which many anthropology departments are struggling to recover, namely the loss of prospective Ph.D. students' desire to explore the unknown in distant and unknown places.

   In order to highlight some of the changes that seem to me to be the most serious to have occurred during the past twenty years or so, I will run quickly through those I have observed first hand in British and Scandinavian universities. I will probably emerge as old-fashioned and conservative, refusing to face the 'realities of contemporary life'. But I am willing not only to face such accusations but also to argue against them because I feel that, if we do not fight these current trends, it could easily mean the end of anthropology as I and my generation learnt and loved it – anthropology as it developed from Malinowski and Boas to Firth, Evans-Pritchard, Mead, Leach, Douglas, Needham, Lévi-Strauss, Dumont, Geertz, Sahlins, Strathern and many, many others, who, despite important theoretical differences, had one thing in common: a commitment to exploring social, cultural, mental and moral forms of life in places far from home and to use that knowledge to address overarching theoretical questions concerning the meaning and role of human life as this is manifested through kinship, religion, classification, economic and political life. Where are their future successors? Where are the daring grand theories that we once could engage with? Nowhere. Rather, anthropologists, including those who engage in the old-style fieldwork, have become timid, fearful of grand theories of all descriptions, tending to stick to their ethnographic or topical expertise and avoiding the big questions.

It is true that the important journals such as the "Journal of the Royal Anthropological Institute" (JRAI), "Ethnos", "Social Anthropology", "American Ethnology" and "American Anthropologist" continue to publish articles of high quality, articles in which authors use their carefully amassed ethnographic knowledge to consider and critique the 'eternal perplexities' of theoretical issues. Indeed, for example, the 2008 special issue of the JRAI was devoted to a consideration of what constitutes 'evidence' in our research and how anthropologists construct the objects of their knowledge. These notable efforts notwithstanding, the broader picture suggests that it is precisely the survival of the anthropological approach to knowledge that is at stake. And it is this approach that, ultimately, is most 'useful' in a broad sense of *Bildung* – not researching narrowly defined topics of more or less policy relevance, however well this may be done. In fact, I want to suggest that the latter will not be well done if we abandon our understanding of the former.

We cannot afford to relax. In his epilogue, "Notes on the future of anthropology", to the volume of the same title edited by Akbar Ahmed and Cris Shore (1995), Anthony Giddens argues that anthropology has nothing unique to offer, that with the 'disappearance of the exotic' and the fall of colonialism the distinctiveness of anthropology is under threat. He goes on to state that

> [a] discipline which deals with an evaporating subject matter, staking claim to a method which it shares with the rest of the social sciences anyway, and deficient in theoretical traditions [...] does not exactly add up to defensible identity of anthropology today (Giddens 1995:274).

I disagree with Giddens in most respects and feel enraged by his lack of understanding of the anthropological aims and methods, but I also read the warning signs in his statement. His critique gives legitimacy to all those others who claim to 'be really doing ethnographic fieldwork'. It is only by adhering to the unique features of our methods that we may be able to contribute 'relevant' and 'useful' knowledge that is different from that of other social sciences. Moreover – contra Ahmed and Shore – I maintain that it is after the experience of long-term fieldwork outside our own country that we can best engage with the study of current issues at home (I return to this at the end). If we continue on the path that is discernible today – of avoiding geographically distant and unknown social settings for our research in favour of demarcated research projects at home, of dropping participant observation in favour of 'qualitative research' – then Giddens may be proved right in his assertion that we are indistinguishable from the other social sciences. In this regard, let me remind you of what participant observation entails beyond the purely academic and intellectual. I will quote Jonathan Spencer from an article criticising some of the arguments emanating from the writing culture critique:

> Anthropologists wade into paddy fields, get sick and read bad novels rather than confront another day of mounting misapprehensions; they also take photographs, make films and tape recordings […] the fact that they mainly do it by themselves in strange places is another oddity that passes unremarked upon in Writing Culture (Spencer 1989:160).

However much sociologists, ethnologists, cultural studies students and others insist that they 'do ethnography', I will bet my bottom dollar that this is not what they mean by it, expect or experience. What about the new generations of aspiring anthropologists?

*The spirit of adventure*

The teaching and degree structure at British and Norwegian universities used to be organised in a manner that supported the classical aims. Having passed various tests that satisfied a department that a Ph.D. student would be able to complete eighteen to twenty-four months of fieldwork in a disciplinarily responsible manner, students set off for all parts of the globe. Not everybody went to the jungles of South America or Southeast Asia, the villages of sub-Saharan Africa, India or the Middle East, the islands of the Pacific or the far-flung Arctic settlements. Some went to urban areas on the same continents, or in their own country or another European country. But unlike much research undertaken there today, earlier anthropologists usually undertook a local micro study of some kind. However, I want to argue that from the time of Malinowski and his students until the late 1980s and early 1990s, regardless of the chosen field sites, the majority of British anthropologists (and my Norwegian colleagues) were driven by a sense of personal and intellectual adventure along the lines I have outlined. Although most had some kind of formulated research aims, these were often vague, like a desire to investigate religious practices, or the kinship system, or to learn about the dynamics of political institutions, shamanistic practices, etc. What they (we) all had in common was that the fieldwork task was open-ended and inductive: the anthropologist allowed him- or herself to be guided by the preoccupations of the people he or she studied. They (we) wanted to be amazed, to be stretched to our physical and intellectual limits, to experience the unexpected and to make anthropological sense of it. Is the situation like this today? I think not.

Two major changes amongst graduate students can, broadly speaking, be observed to have taken place. Firstly, students' motivations seem to be more pragmatic and goal-oriented. They want a Ph.D.; they want a job. Many seem to think that this is best achieved by exploring some relatively narrowly defined topic arising out of contemporary life in their own country. They are less interested in going to uncomfortable places to see what presents itself; they prefer urban areas if they go outside their own national boundaries; and their projects are not open-ended, but have clearly enunciated research aims. If this trend continues, what will easily be lost is the experience of total immersion, the realisation that 'the field' can never be just a physical site, but is a social and a moral one too. The experience of the field as a total social fact where, to paraphrase Mauss, all kinds of events and factors promote simultaneous impressions in the head, the heart, the body, and linking the religious, the moral, the economic, the political and the aesthetic will be lost by a narrowly defined and narrowly pursued 'research proposal'. Having read and evaluated a number of research proposals over the past years, I am struck by precisely the absence of a desire for this kind of experience. Rather, I often ask myself why this particular person wants to investigate his or her particular stated problem, since they already seem to know most of the answers they expect to find. This is not entirely their fault, as the format for submitting research applications streamlines the proposals in such a direction, but this does not excuse, to my mind, the lack of genuine curiosity about the venture – the sense of excitement and of a spirit of adventure that I think all anthropological research proposals ought to demonstrate.

## EXTERNAL FACTORS OF CHANGE

### The Economic and Social Research Council benchmarking exercise

This brings me to some external constraints upon the anthropology of the future. They are not insignificant. Two years ago, I was invited by the UK Economic and Social Research Council to be part of an international panel of anthropologists to consider the state of social anthropology in Britain. It was not an evaluation – something British academic departments have been regularly subjected to for the past couple of decades – but a 'benchmarking exercise'. It involved travelling to twelve major departments throughout the country in order to ascertain the state of affairs there. We were not interested in numbers (numbers of publications, research grants, etc., which increasingly have become the markers of quality in the eyes of the authorities), but in how the academics in those departments perceived their current situations and the prospects for the future. Was social anthropology in a good state of health? And if not, why not? These were the main questions to which we sought answers. The result was mixed. In our report we stressed the consistently high quality of disciplinary engagement by British academic anthropologists, as well as their expressed desire to continue the traditions of holistic fieldwork and inductive research. So far so good.

However, it emerged that the British anthropologists were also experiencing a profound disquiet with regard to the future, largely due to the changes in funding. Increasingly, grant-giving bodies discourage self-initiated, long-term individual research in favour of team-work, preferably inter-disciplinary, the research aims of which are largely dictated by the grant-givers. Frequently the overarching need for 'useful' research is stressed. More often than not useful research is thought of as useful to the grant-giving country itself, and there is a tendency to identify policy areas within fields that are currently perceived as 'problematic' in some way or other, such as health, education, urban development or the multicultural population. Although such topics may, of course, be studied anthropologically with benefit, it is unfortunate that these have become the main topics of anthropological research. Furthermore, grant-givers in several countries fail to appreciate that a comparative dimension will enhance the understanding of the local situation and are reluctant to fund research abroad, even if it is on the same topic.

European Union research-funding policy is similarly focused upon 'relevant and useful' projects undertaken within the EU. This kind of research policy has several serious consequences. It limits the geographical region to the home domain, defines the research focus, presupposes a multidisciplinary approach, limits the time available for fieldwork and demands much reporting along the way. British anthropologists were fully aware of these constraints, but they chose not to elaborate upon them in our meetings. In the words of our report, 'the colleagues seemed at times focused on presenting a brave and unified face rather than addressing broader issues about the future of the discipline rather than the department' (Economic and Social Research Council 2006:7). That in itself I regard as disturbing. Is the 'audit culture' (Strathern 2000) rendering academics fearful of criticising its effects? If so, they are contributing to the strangulation of anthropology.

Furthermore, in the UK today, most Ph.D. grants for British students (and there are very few) come from these sources, making self-initiated, inductive ethnographic doctoral research that is carried out beyond the home country and deals with central disciplinary issues almost a thing of the past. An added fact is that, with today's high university fees, British students without a grant are unable to embark upon a Ph.D. project. In so far as more traditional doctoral research is undertaken, this is done almost exclusively by non-British students with grants from their home countries. Due to the constant pressure to generate income, departments do not exercise the earlier stringent demands on qualifications for acceptance to post-graduate studies. Those from outside the EU, many of whom do fieldwork in their own country, are particularly sought after, as they have to pay even higher fees. Moreover, in order to make money, most British anthropology departments have abandoned a previous disinclination against so-called hyphenated anthropology. Master's courses – mainly directed at foreign students – in such fields as medical anthropology, or the anthropology of migration, childhood, obesity, development, refugees, gender, etc. are offered. Many students who take these twelve months courses have little or no previous training in anthropology. Those who continue to the Ph.D. level tend to continue with the hyphened specialisation. Pressure to complete a Ph.D. in a maximum of four years further discourages classical fieldwork. In response to the direct question whether their current students undertook fieldwork of the same duration and quality as those which the staff themselves had done ten or thirty years previously, the answer, with a couple of exceptions, was 'no'. This is disturbing. Perhaps more disturbing is that teaching staff tend to identify themselves more and more with hyphenated anthropology and, just like their Ph.D. students, tend to take an interest only in research and writing which corresponds with their own. One effect is that the weekly departmental seminar – previously the high point of the week in all British anthropology departments – is no longer attended by all staff and research students. This, I argue, will have a debilitating effect on an anthropology which used to pride itself – in distinction to the other social sciences – on being one inclusive discipline, in which all research questions were, in principle, of equal interest and relevance to all active researchers.

Our report further stressed the 'British tradition of a strong commitment to grounded, analytical, investigation in interaction with an eclectic range of interpretative resources', and went on to say that this notwithstanding, 'British social anthropologists are amongst those theorists within the discipline most frequently cited worldwide' (Economic and Social Research Council 2006:15). The report (whose authors were mostly from American universities) stressed that this particular tradition differed somewhat from the American one, where 'theory' is more in evidence. The point about the intertwined nature of theory and fieldwork in the British tradition is one that Giddens failed to appreciate.

The situation in the Scandinavian departments, and also I think in Germany, is not quite as dismal as in the UK. First, there are minimal tuition fees, so that the cost of embarking upon a MA and Ph.D. degree is limited to living and fieldwork expenses. Secondly, the grant situation is not quite as bleak. Although in Norway too there is an increasing tendency to prioritise large interdisciplinary research teams whose focus is on some topic of direct interest to the Norwegian state, with one or more Ph.D. studentships included, it is still possible to obtain individual Ph.D. grants to undertake the kind of research that I outlined at the beginning, in which the classical concerns and methods can prove their worth. However, two other factors have emerged that threaten the continuation of the old ambitions, namely students' reluctance to do that kind of research, and the fact that the same requirements for stringent fieldwork are not applied in many cases when the students engage in research at home. A prime example of this is that none of the anthropologists who have studied immigration and ethnicity in Norway have troubled themselves to learn a relevant immigrant language. In contrast, an anthropologist who failed to study the language of a people researched in a distant place would have little or no credibility. Yet, different criteria appear to be applied to anthropological research at home. What is going on?

*MORE INTERNAL FACTORS: THE HERITAGE OF POSTMODERNISM*

Anthropologists have always engaged in soul-searching regarding their disciplinary practices. In this regard they differ from their colleagues in the other social sciences. Debates about methods, the status of findings, the profoundly personal and idiosyncratic nature of fieldwork have all been hotly discussed – in and out of print – since the famous LSE seminars under Malinowski (Firth, personal communication). In light of this, I find it surprising that the critique launched by postmodernism of the social sciences and some of the humanities in the late 1980s and early 1990s for their lack of reflexivity regarding the research process hit anthropology very hard. The two volumes that appeared in America in 1986 – "Writing culture", edited by James Clifford and George Marcus, and "Anthropology as a cultural critique", edited by George Marcus and Michael M.J. Fischer – marked the start of raging debates about the practice of anthropology (participant observation in distant and exotic places, usually places that were or had been subject to colonial rule) and the way the research findings were presented – mainly in ethnographic monographs. The debate went in two directions, both of which hit the identity of the discipline hard. Firstly, the critique concerned the validity of our findings, criticising much ethnographic writing as being positivistic, expressed in what was called ethnographic realism. John Borneman and Abedellah Hammoudi (2009) have characterised this apects of the postmodernist critique as an accusation of three denials: that ethnography is a literary genre which denies itself as such; that reliance on observation leads to a denial of the role of the ethnographer in shaping the object or subject studied; that ethnographers tend to deny the constructed character of their objects and of the knowledge they produce.

While no doubt this was a valid criticism of some publications from the pre- and postwar periods, it was far from relevant – or fair – as regards many of our most influential predecessors. Let us not condemn a whole profession because of Radcliffe-Brown! Evans-Pritchard, for example, inspired to a large extent by

Collingwood and Marcel Mauss – no propagators of empiricism – argued that we should not apply scientific criteria to our investigations, that anthropology had more in common with history and the moral sciences. His own ethnographic writings bear this out. I have observed how many advanced students (and colleagues) who read "The Nuer" (1940) for the first time are amazed at Evans-Pritchard's relentless questioning of his methods, findings and interpretations. In his "Witchcraft, oracles and magic among the Azande" (1937), one of the most influential studies on indigenous epistemology inside and outside the discipline, he openly acknowledges his confusion regarding Azande explanations of causality and places himself in the middle of his text. The same can be said of numerous so-called 'realistic ethnographies' (Marcus and Fischer 1986). Nevertheless, the discussion in the wake of the writing culture debates did alert anthropologists to the demand that they be open in their texts about the actual nature of their fieldwork, their analysis and interpretations. It was helpful to take a critical look at the use of the notion of culture (or society or community), at a-historical presentations, at a tendency (perhaps) to exoticise, etc. However, this does not mean that ethnographic fieldwork is an impossible task and had better be avoided – only that we take care to more deliberately integrate reflexivity in our interpretations.

The other thrust of the postmodernist critique concerned anthropology as a colonial practice: it became politically incorrect and morally unacceptable to study supposedly powerless small communities in former colonial domains, to make them, the argument went, into the reified 'Other'. As a result of these two aspects of the po–mo critique, many went in for historical archival studies or studies at home (Borneman and Hammoudi 2009). Borneman and Hammoudi are also critical of the solution offered by Marcus, called 'putting things together' – an approach that relied heavily on vignettes, travelogues, media images, texts and literature of the most diverse origins (2009). In addition, a rather obscure notion of dialogue was promoted, giving fieldwork a veneer of morally acceptable interaction, especially when carried out in one's own country. However, similar criticism might be levied against both scenarios; as methods they can lead to superficial insights, quick analyses informed by the latest trendy concepts. More recently, discourse analyses performed on the media, such as interaction on the Internet and television, have in many cases become a popular substitute for engaging with immediate face-to-face social life.

Policy-oriented research may seem more ideologically correct today, more 'useful' and relevant in a rapidly changing world than setting off for the Highlands of New Guinea. However, it is worth bearing in mind that much innovative theoretical insight has been gained in recent years that emanates precisely from high-quality ethnographic fieldwork carried out in New Guinea and the Pacific, not least inspired by the work of Marilyn Strathern. Gender studies have been revitalised, a new-found interest in indigenous ontologies and concepts of personhood has inspired much exciting theorising generally, and novel interpretations of exchange and classification owe their sources to ethnographic fieldwork from these parts. Let me make two more points in connection with the postmodern critique of ethnographic practice. Most of us who have carried out fieldwork in rural areas of Asia, Africa or Latin America do not agree that we study down, or that the relationship is an unequal power relationship. More often anthropologists are totally at the mercy of the communities they study, struggling to gain acceptance and coping with what goes on around them, and rarely being in a position to influence anything of importance, even if they should wish to do so. To suggest otherwise demonstrates a high degree of lack of understanding on the part of the critics. At the same time, as the people we study are being educated, they increasingly become acknowledged partners in the anthropological enterprise, thereby enhancing the understanding and knowledge of the fieldworker. Secondly, to claim, as Giddens did, that there are no more exotic places to study is equally uninformed. Anyone who has travelled in Central or Southeast Asia or Melanesia knows that there is no shortage of fascinating localities in which to settle in to conduct in-depth anthropological fieldwork.

## MORE EXTERNAL FACTORS: 'POP ETHNOGRAPHY'

Much more can be said about the writing culture movement, but I am convinced that it was in danger of throwing out the baby with the bathwater. It certainly contributed to a perceived epistemological vacuum that has been difficult to fill. It is, I think, an ironic fact that, as television documentaries about travel to distant 'exotic' places are increasing in popularity, students of anthropology are less and less interested in these places. A number of television series (often British) in which one or more individuals set out to explore places that are unfamiliar to them and to Western audiences are currently being produced. They are very popular and appear to appeal to the general public's sense of adventure. During a recent sabbatical spent in Oxford I watched with interest many such programmes, most of which, it seems, are more interested in the character of the traveller than in trying to achieve a serious understanding of the societies visited. In this respect they differ markedly from the ethnographic films that were produced during the 1970s, 1980s and 1990s, such as the "Disappearing world" and the "World about us" series, neither of which would receive funding today. Instead, we are treated to the travels of Michael Palin, who, with great charm, takes us to a range of places from the Himalayas, to South America and Eastern Europe. He presents the viewer with a number of rather strange people and quaint habits that he encounters on the way, which he valiantly tries to understand, always with a smile that can easily be construed as kindly condescending.

The series entitled "Tribe" is perhaps the one that comes closest to the anthropological endeavour in its stated aims and, as such, is the most provoking.

A former army officer, Bruce Parry, travels to extremely remote places (in Borneo, Amazonia, Siberia, Melanesia, etc), where he lives with 'tribal people'. He stays for one month, and the stated aim is 'to live like one of them' in order to experience how their society works. Parry is the main character, who bravely undergoes a range of horrific ritual practices. He grins and bears it; the people he lives amongst grin and enjoy his discomfiture. But we learn nothing of their social, political or religious organisation beyond whatever catches Parry's attention, which is then presented totally without context. Another popular series, which has also been produced in Norway and other European countries, is one in which a family is transported to a 'primitive' society somewhere, where they live 'like the natives' for three weeks. Again, the purpose is to chart how they cope, not how the 'natives' live – what makes them tick from their own point of view. These programmes could with good reason be subjected to a devastating critique of 'othering', neo-colonialism and gender blindness. This would be much more appropriate than the writing culture criticism levied at ethnographic texts.

Whatever one may say about these and similar programmes, the main characters display a terrific sense of adventure, reminiscent of former generations of anthropologists, and are willing to succumb to much physical and emotional deprivation and hardship – albeit with the presence of an invisible (to the viewers) crew of cameramen, producers and others. The pay-off, of course, is fame and, probably, in some cases fortune. There is a seemingly insatiable demand for such programmes. However, none of the central characters are anthropologists: they are celebrities, they are photogenic, and they are adventurous. So, I ask myself, where are the anthropologists? If the general public has become so interested in seeing how people live in distant exotic places, one would assume that anthropologists would also be so, that university departments would be inundated by young people wanting to rush off to carry on the tradition of their forefathers and mothers and that they would wish to do a better job than the Bruce Parrys of this world. The reality today is different. To be sardonic, few Ph.D. students in the UK and Norway seem willing to subject themselves to the challenges of living alone among people in faraway places, where discomfort must be expected, where they are far from Internet cafés and where there is no mobile telephone reception. Rather, in so far as they travel to Asia, Africa or Latin America, the vast majority settle in an urban area, studying topics such as domestic migration, syncretism of religious or healing practices, diaspora communities, urban elites, youth and pop-music, fashion and so on.

What characterised the endeavours of my generation was that, by and large, we were on our own, there was very little institutional assistance (this was not always positive), and the whole thing took on the aura of a personal quest. While it probably led to much personal distress resulting from feelings of inadequacy during fieldwork, it also resulted in much good ethnography.

I want to end on personal note, and try to draw some lessons from it. I did my obligatory eighteen months of fieldwork for my doctorate among the Chewong, a small and hitherto unstudied group of hunters, gatherers and shifting cultivators who lived deep inside the tropical rain forest of Malaysia. Thirty-one years ago I began what was to become a protracted engagement with these people. I have visited them many times since, most recently in April 2008. I have observed them having to face a number of externally initiated changes that pull them into the modern industrialised world of contemporary Malaysia. In fact, my current research project concerns precisely my involvement with them over such a long period of time. Together with a group of international colleagues with similar experiences, I am exploring the methodological and epistemological implications of what I call multi-temporal fieldwork.

However, having completed my doctoral thesis and published it and written a few articles, I felt that I did not have much more to say about the Chewong for the time being. As a student I had been particularly excited by structuralism. As typical hunter-gatherers, Chewong social organisation was extremely loosely structured and did not provide me with the kinds of 'pegs' upon which I might perform some kind of structural analysis. I turned therefore to Eastern Indonesia. From the anthropological literature, it seemed likely that the kind of social and cultural organisation to be found there – complicated kinship system, elaborate ritual life and highly structured socio-political organisation – would enable me to think in terms of more classical interpretations. I therefore started fieldwork with the Lio on the island of Flores in the mid-1980s. Although I was unable to undertake uninterrupted fieldwork with them for more than five months at a time, I returned several times and discovered that *Übung macht den Meister* (literally 'practice makes the master', or more loosely translated, practice makes perfect). I was, if not a better, at least a more efficient fieldworker the second time round, more confident about my anthropological identity, and less intimidated by the people I studied.

My third research project, begun in 2000, was a typical project of the kind that I have been criticising here, thematically delineated and based in my own country. Tired of physically difficult fieldwork, I started to investigate the recent and fast-growing practice of the transnational adoption of infants from the poor South to involuntarily childless people of the rich North mainly Norwegians. It was meant to be a short interlude, but turned out to be so interesting in anthropological terms that I continued with it until last year. However, the completion of this last project can to a large extent be brought back to the fact that I had the experience of traditional participant observation. I was used to looking for insights in unlikely places, and to follow leads as they emerged. Undoubtedly, my ability to identify and take advantage of serendipitous events was enhanced by this experience. It stood me in good stead in this latest project. Because I was able to undertake only a semblance of ethnographic fieldwork in my research on adoption, I had to compensate by exploring many less obvious paths that would enable me to achieve some kind of thick description and to give my interpretations a holistic as well as a comparative dimension. But I found it challenging to distance myself from the known social and cultural world of contemporary Norway, to look at it as if everything was unknown. In many ways this was my toughest project. For these reasons, I agree with those of my colleagues who argue that anthropology at home is best done after anthropology far away from home.

## To conclude

What is the future of anthropology in today's world? With more and more anthropological research undertaken on the anthropologist's own geographical turf and guided as much by grant-givers' needs and understandings as by the researchers' own inclinations, I have severe misgivings. Clearly, present-day external factors are not conducive to the continuation of the old Malinowskian ideals. But internal factors that have similar effects are also observable. New generations of anthropologists – whether for political, intellectual or private reasons – increasingly choose 'safe' research projects, driven as much by pragmatic reasons of future employment, family demands or financial constraints. As anthropologists increasingly involve themselves with contemporary problems, defined as much by Western values and concerns as springing out of local ones, will they cease to find the classical literature of relevance? Indications are that undergraduate students are beginning to find much of it irrelevant, a few iconic classics excepting, such as Marcel Mauss's "The gift" (1954), Mary Douglas's "Purity and danger" (1960) and Edward E. Evans-Pritchard's "Oracles, witchcraft and magic among the Azande" (1937). Increasingly, they demand 'up-to-date' literature, what in their view is relevant for the contemporary world. They certainly try to avoid reading whole ethnographic monographs, especially if they are from parts of the world that they are not interested in. I ask myself to what extent today's students are driven by a spirit of adventure, and whether they have a commitment to the holistic ambition and to the rigorous ethnographic fieldwork that this necessitates. If not, then I fear for the future.

If I am right in positing that there is a trend towards thematically deliminated and narrowly focused studies – in the sense that broad and deep knowledge about social intuitions, values and practices anchored in one particular social world are not produced – then what can anthropologists contribute to an enhanced understanding of the complexities of human life? With narrowly problem-focused fieldwork carried out with the help of interpreters, what insights can anthropologists produce that a clever journalist cannot, or someone from cultural studies armed with exciting theoretical concepts (Howell 1997)? I think this is becoming an increasingly relevant question. As far as I am concerned, anthropology is empirical philosophy. This suggests that we can only provide a unique contribution to knowledge about other life-worlds and our own by insisting on long-term participant observation carried out in fieldwork. By all means let us acknowledge that many myths have grown up around this disciplinary holy cow, but, at the same time let us seek to improve upon the practice and openly acknowledge the many pitfalls and the ultimately very personal nature of such a scientific enterprise. Cultural relativism is not a philosophical stance, but a methodological one necessary for exploring the deeper meanings of practices and for drawing comparisons. Moreover, we must retain our broad interest within the discipline. I for one am an enemy of hyphenated anthropology. We are social anthropologists, first and foremost, whose research interests may range at different times in our career from, *inter alia*, indigenous medical systems, to mythology, to power relations and socio-political change, to principles of classification, to development aid, to new kinds of human reproduction, to the morality of trade and barter. But in order to say anything interesting about these and all the other topics that anthropologists have written about, our information and our interpretations must spring out of solid, rigorous fieldwork, the ultimate aim of which continues to be to interpret the natives' point of view, and to relate this to human social life generally and to overarching theoretical debates.

*References*

AHMED, Akbar S. and Cris SHORE (eds.)
1995    *The future of anthropology: its relevance to the contemporary world*. London: Athlone

BORNEMAN, John and Abedellah HAMMOUDI (eds.)
2009    *Being there: the fieldwork encounter and the making of truth*. Berkeley: University of California Press

CLIFFORD, James and George E. MARCUS (eds.)
1986    *Writing culture: the poetics and politics of ethnography*. Berkeley: University of California Press

DOUGLAS, Mary
1960    *Purity and danger: an analysis of concepts of pollution and taboo*. London: Routledge & Kegan Paul

ECONOMIC AND SOCIAL RESEARCH COUNCIL (UK)
2006    *International benchmarking review of UK social anthropology*. London: ESRC

ERIKSEN, Thomas Hylland
1995    *Small places, large issues: an introduction to social and cultural anthropology*. London:
        Pluto Press

EVANS-PRITCHARD, Edward E.
1937    *Witchcraft, oracles and magic among the Azande*. Oxford: Clarendon
1940    *The Nuer: a description of the modes of livelihood and political institutions of a Nilotic
        people*. Oxford: Clarendon.

GIDDENS, Anthony
1995    "Epilogue: notes on the future of anthropology", in: Akbar S. Ahmed and Cris
        Shore (eds.), *The future of anthropology: its relevance to the contemporary world*,
        272–277. London: Athlone

HOWELL, Signe
1997    "Cultural studies and anthropology: contesting or complementary discourses?", in:
        Stephen Nugent and Cris Shore (eds.), *Anthropology and cultural studies*, 103–125.
        London: Pluto Press

MARCUS, George E. and Michael M.J. FISCHER
1986    *Anthropology as cultural critique: an experimental moment in the human sciences*.
        Chicago: The University of Chicago Press

MAUSS, Marcel
1954    *The gift: forms and functions of exchange in archaic societies*. London: Cohen & West

SPENCER, Jonathan
1989    "Anthropology as a kind of writing", *Man* (N.S.) 24:145–164

STRATHERN, Marlyn
2000    *Audit cultures: anthropological studies in accountability, ethics and the academy*.
        London: Routledge

# 7

# TRANSITIONS
Notes on sociocultural anthropology's present and its transnational potential[*]

Andre Gingrich

Two major academic events in international anthropology recently raised a very similar topic: the 108th Annual Meeting of the American Anthropological Association in 2009 in Philadelphia addressed "The end/s of anthropology"; and, less than a year earlier, the Jensen Memorial Lecture Series in Frankfurt (Germany) asked about "The end of anthropology?" In their invitations, the respective organisers of these events carefully avoided any pessimistic emphasis on anthropology's future, while acknowledging that recent changes in our field had also resulted in increased doubt and uncertainty about where anthropology now stands and what comes next. As a participant in, and contributor to, both the AAA 2009 meeting and the Jensen lectures, many of the presentations made me wonder if sociocultural anthropology has perhaps been so richly creative during the recent past that to an increasing extent it has come to play a vanguard role among today's humanities and social sciences at large. If this were indeed the case, then the growth of uncertainty and doubt as reflected in those two academic events and the similarity in their overall themes would be a healthy sign: a relatively small field is shouldering responsibilities not only for itself but also for others, and those responsibilities indeed include strategic and programmatic questions about the field's current and next phases.

In this article, I hope to contribute to some of these strategic and programmatic questions by focusing on the main argument that sociocultural anthropology is undergoing a long process of transition into a transnational and global phase of critical research. Transitions are always accompanied by uncertainty and doubt about the exact outcome as well as about what is left behind. I shall discuss three main dimensions of sociocultural anthropology's present transition: the historical, institutional, and epistemological.

In the first section, I will show that while our field's present transition is not entirely unprecedented in its history, sociocultural anthropology is far better equipped

[*]    I wish to thank Don Brenneis (University of California, Santa Cruz), John Comaroff (University of Chicago), and Karl-Heinz Kohl (Johann Wolfgang Goethe University Frankfurt am Main) for their comments on several aspects of this text; Olga Sicilia (Vienna) for her help in the manuscript's production; and Julene Knox (London) and Mayumi Shimose for their generous assistance in editing the final draft of this article. I also gratefully acknowledge the helpful comments by AA anonymous reviewers and Editor-in-Chief Tom Boellstorff.

than ever before to cope with these major transitional challenges. Responding
to these challenges requires, however, the simultaneous observance of some very
practical and some highly theoretical tasks: I suggest that some key institutional and
epistemological advances are essential to move onto a transnational phase, while
maintaining and improving the distinctiveness of the anthropological enterprise and
of sociocultural anthropology's role within it. In the second section, assessing the
more practical institutional aspects of sociocultural anthropology's transition, I will
then focus on global minimal standards for doctoral degrees in anthropology, on
'transnationalising' research-funding opportunities, and on transnational criteria
in employment policies. Although the pragmatic priorities of institutional criteria
will be central to sociocultural anthropology's ability to maintain and develop its
distinctiveness and its vanguard role in everyday academic life, in the long run it will
be the status of our critical academic knowledge that counts most. This is why in the
third section I argue for a strategic approach throughout sociocultural anthropology's
transition that combines an expanded, global framework for institutional concerns
with a new emphasis on the transnational status of anthropological knowledge
– that is, a reinvigoration of our epistemological foundations. Institutional and
epistemological advances that connect us as researchers across national boundaries
with each other, with other academic fields, and with a changing world will thus be
indispensable for maintaining and enhancing the distinctive role of sociocultural
anthropology in a new transnational and global phase.

## HISTORICAL DIMENSIONS: A LONG TRANSITION?

Are we experiencing the end of sociocultural anthropology as we knew it? Many
aspects of an earlier anthropology are disappearing, while new currents emerge.[1] I
suggest interpreting our field's present as one of simultaneous disappearance and
emergence (Rabinow and Marcus with Faubion and Rees 2008). An older phase
persists but is gradually fading out. At the same time, new currents have already
emerged and are gradually getting stronger.

Like all formal academic research, sociocultural anthropology represents a
complex web of intellectual and social processes that interact with their respective
contexts of political economy and society. Our understanding of sociocultural
anthropology's present may thus benefit, as is suggested in this first section, from a

---

[1]   This article's title explicitly indicates that the present text primarily addresses sociocultural anthropology. I shall therefore sometimes use anthropology and anthropological as synonymous
terms for this particular subfield among the four fields and shall only be explicit about the other
subfields when they are directly referred to in this text. For the early periods of anthropology's
history outside the United States (e.g., British or German anthropology before World War I),
however, I use the term 'anthropology' in the inclusive sense that is appropriate for that era.

medium- and long-term perspective on the main movements and directions of these complex processes. From such a perspective, it would not be sufficient, however, to identify sociocultural anthropology's present as just another routine and relatively short transitional phase, connecting a narrowly defined recent past with a loosely defined emerging future. Several of the effects and implications of the major waves of sociocultural anthropology's critical self-examination throughout past decades have been far too profound for that. Framing the current processes of change as normal or routine is therefore not appropriate for such a profound transition. One after the other, these various sequences and movements of critical anthropological self-examination – neo-Marxist, feminist, postmodern, and post-colonial – assessed the prevailing hegemonic forms of sociocultural anthropology in their time. Each of these critiques identified its own priorities regarding epistemologies, concepts, content, and methods. These intellectual movements usually related to each other only in indirect ways – that is, mostly without directly targeting one another. The primary foci of those respective critiques were various epistemological, conceptual, thematic, and methodological key dimensions in contemporaneous hegemonic sociocultural anthropology.

The content and direction of sociocultural anthropology's recent processes of self-examination therefore indicate a profound and sustained transition of almost unprecedented historical significance. I suggest conceptualising anthropology's present as a moment in the long and complicated transition from a past that, while we have successfully started to leave it behind, remains powerful and strong among us, and a future that we have begun to envision and to enact, although we may still have a long way to go – not to mention our uncertainty regarding which path to choose. That past in our present refers to the era of anthropology's national and quasi-national traditions, whereas the future in our present refers to anthropology's emerging era of transnational and global activity in research, teaching, and public engagement (Hannerz 2007).

Starting from this premise, the current transition processes indeed seem to be unique in anthropology's history. In one way or the other, such a transition would transform this academic discipline, leading it away from its hitherto established architecture of national traditions – which is, in its own right, a historically situated, multifaceted, and flexible structural arrangement. We can compare a shift of such significance to other transitions encountered during earlier phases of the discipline's history only to a very limited extent. In particular, those earlier transitions come to mind that established this structural arrangement in the first place. During the initial two decades of the twentieth century, anthropology was transformed from a late imperial field of research into a set of early national traditions with continuing, strong colonial legacies (Barth *et al.* 2005). Less than a century later, anthropology is well on its way to leaving behind these national traditions, with their enduring remnants of neo-colonial legacies: in this sense, the current transition attains truly historical significance, although its outcome is still anything but certain.

Relatively uncertain prospects, however, are nothing exceptional in the current era of neoliberal, world-capitalist globalisation. Rather, such uncertainty is a familiar by-product of this era and a normal condition of life for everyone. Acknowledging the uncertainty of a relatively small academic discipline's future in the present world therefore represents a realist approach, while predicting an end to any kind of anthropology as an almost inevitable worst-case scenario would represent the very different approach of pessimistic fatalism. I therefore tend to interpret the concerns and worries of some among us about our discipline's future as the anxieties and pains of a field in transition. Not every transition need turn into a crisis, nor is every crisis in itself a catastrophe. Neither an alarmist attitude nor a position of denial are, however, very helpful in such a transition. Instead, both positions might work in their different ways to turn a transition into a crisis that could otherwise be avoided.

In fact, a number of good reasons for cautious and realistic optimism emerge if we briefly contrast some features of the current transition 'out of' national traditions with those of the historical transition 'into' the era of national traditions. In the early twentieth century, World War I saw the end of a previous (hegemonic, imperial, and colonial) period, which had also been marked by what some historians of science call 'scientific internationalism' (Manias 2009). Anthropology's subsequent post- and late-imperial transitions 'into' the era of national orientations and traditions actually concerned only the very limited number of scholars and institutions that existed at that time in the field. The main centres of the discipline were situated in those countries that had turned out post-1918 to be the key powers of the late colonial era (i.e., in Western Europe, Japan, and the United States) and several subcentres of the colonial realm (e.g., Australia, Canada, South Africa). In addition, anthropology took a postimperial turn or was newly introduced in countries such as the Soviet Union or the new national states of northern, central, and south-eastern Europe. The very few other anthropological institutions that existed in Asia, Africa, or the Americas were heavily influenced by those in the discipline's centres in western Europe and the United States.

Under its different local and regional names, sociocultural anthropology basically entered its era of national traditions in two different, albeit intersecting, forms. Because of the hegemonic late colonial contexts, anthropologists studied societies and cultures, first, in exoticising ways either in colonies overseas or among local and indigenous groups at home. Second, in the less influential but at times more common early national contexts, anthropology was established primarily as folklore studies to research 'one's own' national culture. By necessity, these political and institutional conditions also shaped some of the content of that transition into anthropology's era of national or quasi-national traditions. The main national traditions had gradually emerged under these conditions and interacted with them,

---

2      Barth *et al.* (2005), Kuklick (2008), Kuper (1996), Stocking (1996)

being promoted by influential 'founding fathers' in the respective centres of cultural relativism in the United States, of the Durkheimian School in France, of British functionalism, of Soviet 'ethnography', of German diffusionism, and so forth.[2]

It could be argued that anthropology's era of national traditions peaked in several ways in the contexts of World War II and its aftermath, which led into the Cold War (Price 2008). These contexts permanently discredited those among the national and quasi-national traditions that had directly served murderous dictatorships and systems of mass persecution. At the same time, these experiences permanently discredited the national and quasi-national restrictions, bias, and distortions that these regimes had imposed. In the end, the Nazis, for instance, entirely failed in their vicious efforts toward establishing 'German mathematics', 'German physics', but also 'German folklore studies' and 'German anthropology' in any enduring sense as respected academic fields. This was a consequence of not only their murderous and reactionary cause but also the outcome of World War II. In addition, this also was caused by the fact that, in the long run, serious academic research cannot flourish under conditions of rigid national limitations (Cornwell 2003). This experience also made the field in general much more sensitive toward the potential abuses by anthropologists and by political powers and more self-aware about the discipline's future after a colonial era that was clearly coming to an end. It is out of these contexts, and despite the inherent asymmetries and contradictions, that the best of anthropology's national legacies became part of international anthropology and will remain a defining and inspiring part of the discipline's record for the future.

Compared with the first transition in the early twentieth century, anthropology today in fact turns out to be in a far better position to come to terms with its second historical transition. By contrast to a few hundred professionals in a very limited number of countries then, anthropology today comprises thousands and tens of thousands of professionals with institutional affiliations in the majority of countries around this globe. In contrast to the relative political naiveté and the positivist belief in 'pure science' as represented by a few schools of thought of the early twentieth century, today's anthropology by and large has learned from some of its major disasters, and it has matured and advanced. Today the discipline has become more multicentred than ever before, and the majority of professionals share a sceptical or cautious attitude with regard to the field's political instrumentalisation by hegemonic powers. In contrast to the two mutually exclusive forms of either studying exoticised cultures elsewhere or one's own glorified national culture in the early twentieth century, anthropology today comprises research at home as much as elsewhere under unified humanistic premises. Anthropology's opportunities and potential to cope with the transition into a new and emerging era of transnational research are therefore rather good.

As is evident from above, this new era represents more than the mere continuation of sociocultural anthropology's internationalisation, which has in fact been going on for some time: it emerged together with the introduction of U.S. and European academic institutions into the late colonial and early post-colonial worlds, and continued with the globalisation of English as an academic lingua franca in the Cold War era. The concept of 'internationalisation' implies cooperation on the basis of entities whose priorities nevertheless continue to be defined within national limits. In that sense, the present is to a significant extent characterised by a continuation of dominant Anglo-American visions in and for sociocultural anthropology, or by what Bernard De L'Éstoile calls 'hegemonic internationalism' in our and other parts of academia (2008). At the same time, that hegemony in many ways and to an increasing extent has become a contested one: for example, by the regional priorities of other important national clusters of anthropology, whether Brazilian, Indian, east-central European, South African, or other (Ribeiro 2006). Moreover, a growing number of anthropologists around the globe refuse to consider any strictly national priorities whatsoever; rather, they define their research interests from the outset across national boundaries and in view of those interactive processes among local, regional, and global factors that have become too important to be ignored today. Sociocultural anthropology's new and emerging transnational phase therefore is the initial era of an increasingly contested Anglo-American hegemony in our field and of dissolving national metanarratives (Restrepo and Escobar 2005).

Two important additional factors further improve anthropology's potential for moving ahead through the second transition: namely, (1) the discipline's long-established emphasis on addressing macrotopics through microanalysis and (2) the past decades' series of critical self-examinations about the best ways in which this should be pursued. As outlined above, these major waves of anthropology's critical self-examination were the neo-Marxist, feminist, postmodern, and post-colonial autocritiques between roughly the late 1960s and the end of the twentieth century. Drawing on significant predecessors such as the Manchester School, the neo-Marxist critique in French and U.S. anthropology, for instance, introduced political economy and the critique of colonialism into anthropology. In turn, the feminist critique built on the work of the likes of Audrey Richards or Hortense Powdermaker to expose male biases in anthropology so as to give female perspectives in local societies and in anthropology their legitimate position. The postmodern critique further radicalised these profound challenges to the established orthodoxy of objectivist representations by questioning the methods of written analysis as narrative displays of ideological power. In turn, the post-colonial and transnational critique demonstrated how global transformations have redefined the conditions of subjectivity to an extent that makes subaltern and hegemonic claims on reality a matter of permanent contest and conflict.

---

3    See, e.g., Marcus (1999), Ortner (1984), and Sahlins (1976) as some among the major turning points and defining texts in those successive debates.

To an extent, these autocritiques gradually moved from critical objectivism to critical subjectivism, with cumulative but also noncompatible elements connecting them.[3] A careful and balanced history of those sequences of anthropological autocritique still remains to be written, but to my mind, one may argue with some justification that each of these critiques in some ways went too far and that none of them fully achieved what its main advocates originally had in mind. In spite of these failures and shortcomings, and to an extent also because of them, the impact of these critical movements has changed anthropology in enduring ways. In sum, these movements have decisively generated anthropology's inner dynamics of moving away from, and beyond the limits of, the discipline's era of national metanarratives.

Some of the questions raised and addressed by these critical intellectual movements were clarified in consensual ways; others remain open for current and future debates. Many of these open questions focus on anthropology's methodologies and epistemologies in the current era of increasingly globalised transformations and crises (Hastrup 2005). Although this indicates some of the important terrain that still needs consolidation, the answers and new orientations that have already been provided by these movements of anthropological autocritique demonstrate that anthropology is in fact quite advanced in the transition toward an era of transnational and global research.

In fact, anthropology was much better equipped from the outset for coping with this transition, as mentioned above, and it embarked on it more speedily than many of the much larger, neighbouring disciplines in the humanities and social sciences. Among some of these such as sociology (Beck 2008, Wimmer and Glick Schiller 2002) or philosophy (Mbembe and Roitman 1995), instances of 'methodological nationalism' and of implicit 'national container' paradigms seem to have represented much heavier legacies and thereby constituted much more stubborn obstacles than in anthropology. By contrast, anthropology's established priority of addressing large-scale human topics through small-scale analysis (Eriksen 2001) made it much easier for the discipline to deal with the new round of globalisation as soon as it set in after the end of the Cold War. On the conceptual level, anthropologists were among the first to deliver substantial contributions in this regard, and on a methodological level, there is a greater demand than ever before for the meticulous precision of ethnographic field studies, which quantitative analysis alone could not deliver.

For all these reasons, the prospects for anthropology's transition into its transnational and global era look reasonably good. That transition, however, is not only possible but also actually an urgent requirement in terms of anthropology's own research logic as much as in terms of political context.

Regarding research logic, the various movements of self-examination in anthropology's recent past call for outcomes that address challenges and arguments rather than merely respond to fashion and star cult. I identify one major common denominator in the broadening and reinforcement of anthropology's transnational, pluralist foundations in theory, methodology, and epistemology. I shall return to this issue in the concluding section by discussing what I regard as the field's urgent transnational challenges in methodology and epistemology. In terms of political context, this first section's historical reflections point in exactly the same direction. It is high time to press onward with sociocultural anthropology's further transnationalisation, not only for reasons of research logic but also because of political, professional, and normative factors. No serious academic enterprise in the twenty-first century will be able to survive if it allows national compartmentalisations of knowledge that simply ignore what is going on elsewhere in the world in its own field to linger. That would result in ignorant provincialism. Other neighbouring disciplines among the 'four fields' – for instance, archaeology or physical anthropology – could not survive if such attitudes were to prevail among their main cohorts of scholars and students. Any research group from the United States – for example, in archaeology or physical anthropology – that would dare to remain ignorant of important findings in, say, Flores (e.g., the 'Flores man') or in the Alps (e.g., the 'Man in the ice') would have to answer serious questions about their professional skills and to justify the funding they receive. If academic curiosity alone does not provide enough reasons to continuously cross national barriers, then questions of professional ethics, standing, and reputation should contribute in this regard.

In this ethical, normative, and professional sense, sociocultural anthropology's reasoning at the very least includes an inherent transnational potential to cross national boundaries by intellectual means. That potential invites us to ask how our particular case might relate to, or differ from, comparable cases elsewhere in the world as well as in the field's record. It is that inherent transnational potential that often drives us to formulate our research questions: if I want to explore some aspect of indigenous rights in, say, North America or Siberia, then the generic concept of 'indigenous rights' has already helped me to understand that these issues cross-cut many national boundaries and occur in diverse forms in several national contexts around the globe. If during my research in, for instance, a European country, I encounter several cases of discrimination against gay or Jewish people, then the concepts of 'homophobia' and of 'anti-Semitism' hopefully will guide me to the insight that these are perhaps not entirely unique cases in a global context. Only a small minority of orthodox empiricists would deny that each particular case also deserves to be assessed, sooner or later, in terms of its wider relevance beyond local settings and across national boundaries and legacies – that is, for the benefit of sociocultural anthropology's record at large.

Thus, sociocultural anthropology will thrive if we continue to further develop this transnational potential along pluralist lines of knowledge, debate, and expertise by tearing down the barriers of national compartmentalisation wherever appropriate. These national barriers have significant epistemological dimensions to which I shall return in my third section, but they also include a number of important and seemingly profane institutional dimensions, which are the topic of my second section.

I have argued in the first section that anthropology's present can be characterised as a moment in the long transition process from an enduring past marked by national traditions into an emerging future of transnational and global research. In this sense, the 'end of anthropology' in the form of its hitherto established national legacies has already set in or is about to happen. I have made the case that this does not, however, imply the dissolution of anthropology altogether but, instead, its continuing elaboration as a transnational field of research. Internal academic and wider political, normative, and ethical factors provide good reasons to pursue the anthropological project along these lines.

In fact, this is what the majority of anthropologists are actually doing most of the time. The Brazilian medical anthropologist who presents her research results at a conference in Lisbon where she absorbs additional inspiration for her forthcoming publication from the comments of a Californian colleague, for instance: both scholars are involved in doing just that – elaborating their transnational field of research. The Danish expert on shamanism who gives a lecture series in Seoul benefits from comments by colleagues in his audience who draw his attention to recent Korean and Japanese research of which he was unaware. They too are actively involved in elaborating the kind of transnational anthropological record that characterises the future in our present: polycentric, transnational pools of research results, concepts, theories, and methods. In spite of existing hierarchies and barriers of language, anthropological knowledge by most of its orientations in contents has already become transnational today.

The pursuit of anthropological knowledge, however, confronts many of us on a daily basis with fundamental contradictions. As I have just argued, anthropological knowledge tends inherently and dynamically to become transnational and global if the relevant normative, ethical, and professional potential is activated – because our curiosity and our professional ethics always encourage us to cross national boundaries by intellectual means. The financial and legal conditions under which anthropological knowledge is being produced and circulated, however, are usually not transnational and global; instead, they are determined by local, national, and regional factors (Shore and Wright 1999). This leads us to a short discussion of some of the main institutional factors in sociocultural anthropology's continuing national compartmentalisation.

The conditions under which our students receive their training and counselling and the conditions under which we carry out fieldwork and write up, present, and discuss our results are strongly shaped by financial means and institutional or legal rules that we may influence but are essentially imposed by others. These legal and financial conditions regulating fundamental aspects of the production and circulation of anthropological knowledge, in fact, are 'relations of production', or at least belong to some of the core elements of these relations of anthropological-knowledge production. Many of us therefore are constantly facing a fundamental contradiction between the inherently transnational and global potential of anthropological knowledge and the inherently local, national, or regional character of the relations of production of that knowledge.

As themes and topics of reflection and dialogue, the regulations and laws under which we teach and research and the financial means that may or may not be allocated to us for these purposes lead a bizarre double life in our professional worlds. They tend to occupy a significant share of informal conversation, but they hardly figure at all in our professional analyses. In the middle of a historical transition process, it could become important to give that topic a somewhat higher profile in our formal academic communication. The relations of anthropological-knowledge production deserve to be more explicitly addressed while we pursue our transitional processes, precisely because some local and national features in these relations of production actually function as obstacles to the transition toward a transnational era. The inherent contradictions between the transnational potential in anthropological knowledge and the national and regional forms of its relations of production simultaneously impose the necessity for transnational professional communication about these national forms.

A number of these localised features of course need not be changed – or cannot be changed for anthropology alone. For instance, we usually work and teach at academic institutions that are either privately or publicly funded within market contexts. As long as they prevail, we have to adapt our BA and MA programs to a certain degree to this fact as well as, to an extent, to local or national conditions of the respective job markets and the opportunities they offer to practicing and applied anthropologists (Dracklé et al. 2003). It is a feature of anthropology's present that many of our university departments are training large portions of their student body up to graduate level only, after which students enter the job market. I regard this as a good sign of a field's mature professionalization. Not everybody who studies medicine is a researcher or professor in the medical sciences; many others are practicing MDs. In similar ways, the BA and MA levels in anthropology should also continue to contain stronger local and national elements, while preparing some for Ph.D. programs along internationally and transnationally valid lines. In that regard, however, a small field like ours needs to reach some minimum consensus about transnational quality standards.

For my part, I would have great difficulties envisioning future postdocs in anthropology who have never done any fieldwork whatsoever, who speak no other language than their own, and who have never heard or read anything about Franz Boas, Bronislaw Malinowski, or Marcel Mauss. I therefore suggest that at least three components should be considered as indispensable basic elements in sociocultural anthropology's transnational minimal quality standards of Ph.D. education and training.

First, one needs a creative and critical appreciation of this field's relevant record of concepts and theories, which, in addition to recent and diverse choices, should always include a body of basic texts by classic authors. Second, one requires a substantial component of methodological and practical orientation toward long-term ethnographic fieldwork in its multiple facets and evolving forms, which nevertheless conveys the specific qualities of fieldwork as one of our distinctive methodological and, in fact, epistemological tools that sets the stage for mastering participant-observation and what Michael Herzfeld (2004) aptly calls the fieldworker's critical 'cultural intimacy' penetrating the nation state's culturally hegemonic intimacy. And third, bilingual skills should be a basic precondition of admission to Ph.D. studies in sociocultural anthropology anywhere in the world – that is, English in countries where English is not commonly understood and another language than English in all English-speaking countries. As part of this field's minimal quality standards, this version of required bilingualism could promote a basic qualification to carry out fieldwork both 'at home' and 'elsewhere'; it would facilitate access to anthropological knowledge as published in one other major language than one's own; and last but not least, it would ensure practical usage of the one global academic lingua franca that we have.

Research funding and its modes of allocation are another key dimension in the production relations of anthropological knowledge and a field in which strong national limitations often continue to make the future elaboration of transnational research and cooperation more than difficult for anthropologists (Knorr-Cetina 1981). It is a fact that on a global scale, the financial means for any research in the social sciences and humanities remain unevenly distributed, and this enduring inequality in many ways continues to correspond to divisions created by colonialism and the results of World War II. Far-reaching expectations about fundamental changes in this uneven global distribution of research funds would be unrealistic as long as the global political and economic inequalities continue. Hopes to the contrary would represent naive reformism.

Still, anthropologists should not make peace with the status quo. If anthropology is more advanced in its transition to a transnational era than are many other fields in the humanities and social sciences, this is the case because, as a cross-cultural research discipline, anthropology is more directly and more regularly confronted with these global inequalities, which are most heavily imposed on many of our partners and hosts in the postcolonies. This is why anthropologists in the more affluent parts of the world face the task of making some of the unevenly distributed research funding for the humanities and the social sciences more accessible and more available for their research and cooperation partners who operate under the much more difficult funding conditions of marginalised or post-colonial contexts (Brenneis 2004).

This requires more comprehensive and energetic strategies of noncompliance with the prevailing pattern of overfunding the 'haves' and of underfunding the 'have nots' in global anthropology. Sceptical arguments against the elaboration and implementation of such strategies often refer to existing funding shortages for anthropology even within the more affluent parts of the world and to the overwhelming competition for the same funds from larger and stronger fields.

It cannot be denied that these competitive, neoliberal pressures are part and parcel of our research-funding conditions (Strathern 2000). But as a general argument, one's own funding shortages are not always a valid reason for opposing research proposals that include funding for partners in post-colonial or other marginalised contexts. On the contrary, my own experience as reviewer or panel member in various European and U.S. funding institutions and especially in the European Research Council indicates at least four factors that should encourage anthropologists in the more affluent countries either to try harder or more often to obtain funding for partners in marginalised or post-colonial contexts – or, in some cases, to start trying period.

First, anthropologists by definition are usually much more favourably situated to argue why their project proposals require international cooperation, and this argument is better understood in today's world than it was only a short while ago. Second, several national and regional funding institutions provide extra funding budgets for international cooperation in such ways that applying for these budgets does not directly compete with simultaneously applying to the same institution for other projects. For instance, within the European Union's 7th Frame Program, the "Tempus" program was a case in point that helped social scientists and anthropologists from Europe and Bir Zeit (Palestine) to cooperate, and several private foundations have sponsored cooperation between anthropologists from eastern Europe or Asia and North America or western Europe. Our main journals could and should assess, disseminate, and discuss the experience gained through these cooperation projects with regard to empowering the underprivileged and opening up access to funding for those who need it most. Third, some European national funding agencies (e.g., in Germany and Scandinavia) already implement the rule that their funding for projects relating to Africa, South America, Asia, parts of eastern Europe, and Oceania is only possible if these projects also include substantial research benefit for institutions in those countries. Anthropologists could use these instances as best-case examples for developing AAA and EASA funding policies in this regard. Fourth, compared to some of the larger fields in the humanities and social sciences, anthropology has been doing fairly well in some of the major international research-funding institutions, such as the EU's key research-funding programs like "Ideas" and "Peoples", and especially those with new funding options for basic and collaborative research.

Strategies of noncompliance with the existing global status quo in research-funding inequalities thus are less difficult to pursue than it appears at first sight. My general impression is that anthropologists in the more affluent countries may not even have fully approached and accessed those means that are currently already available in this regard, nor have their professional calls for improved funding opportunities to benefit their research partners been raised and heard.

In addition to striving for transnational instead of national standards for anthropology's doctoral degrees and 'transnationalising' research-funding options, a third element concludes this list. Academic employment policies, to my mind, represent that third key dimension where national biases continue to dominate the relations of production of anthropological knowledge to the extent that these are often obstacles to our transition into a transnational era. Basically, these obstacles comprise 'national' regimes of recruitment. A whole range of academic search committees in anthropology operate under these regimes as if the domestic job market counted much more than transnational qualifications and skills in the field. It is interesting to note that these national regimes of recruitment do not, however, apply to many of the world's best departments, which for good reasons tend primarily to hire the best available candidates from all over the world. The biographical backgrounds of academic staff members at anthropology departments at, say, the Universities of Chicago, Cambridge, or Berkeley are good examples in this regard. It is a welcome development that several key departments in South Asia, southern Africa, and South America have begun to orient their recruitment policies along similar transnational lines. By contrast, continental Europe and Japan in fact stand out as those regions where many anthropology departments so far have done the least in this regard. Instead, most of them continue modes of reproducing national legacies in employment policies. A truly transnational orientation will no longer ignore this key question or cover it up with references to visiting scholars and international conference participation. Employment is the field in which anthropologists can bring about most change within the shortest period of time.

In most of our departments, some of our staff members do 'anthropology at home' mostly, while others at the same departments do 'anthropology abroad' most of the time: so, in sum, the overall staff of most departments does both. It could be useful to approach questions of recruitment: that is, of newly recruited staff members and their respective institutional backgrounds in degrees and training, in similar ways. Some could have a training background from the same department where they are now being hired. Others should not but should by all means have backgrounds from different departments, including such departments that are situated not in the same language zone but elsewhere. Similar practices are already operating in some important branches of anthropology but not yet where this would be needed most. Transnationalisation of employment practices, of course, would have to be combined with corresponding moves toward transnationalising staff members' language skills, preferably toward bi- or trilingualism that includes active English writing. The active and passive circulation of anthropological knowledge will be impossible in a transnational era without our global academic lingua franca.

In the short as well as in the medium term, our discipline's future will be decided not only by the kind of anthropological knowledge we produce and communicate but also by the changing conditions under which we do this, including those aspects discussed here. Our transition toward a transnational era for anthropology also requires strategies for transnational relations of production that actually promote that transition. Opponents will not remain inactive. In times of crisis, it is not difficult to predict that some forces will emerge that will argue either for an intensification of anthropology's applied subordination and instrumentalisation at the service of other needs and fields or for anthropology's radical downsizing – or for both, as one step toward its dissolution. By contrast, an attitude of realistic optimism requires that we prepare ourselves for these potential risks and threats. We can do so first by pursuing and communicating the kind of good and diverse research that is already being carried out in our field today. Second and simultaneously, we need to communicate among ourselves and to society at large what kinds of relations of production we need for the future and to engage in struggling for those we do need as well as against those we do not.

## Epistemological dimensions: their relevance for the status of knowledge in anthropology

At the end of this article's first, mainly historical part, I raised an epistemological argument that we may now continue. I pointed out that sociocultural anthropology's recent development requires attention to some of its current main epistemological and methodological foundations, which should be addressed from transnational perspectives. I have argued that sociocultural anthropology is moving through a unique and complicated process of transition, for which it is well equipped but the outcome of which is still uncertain. As a result of the field's past self-examination, such a new transnational focus on sociocultural anthropology's epistemological and methodological foundations could provide important orientations throughout the next phases in this transitional process.

For all these reasons, I wholeheartedly support the realistic avenues for perseverance that are outlined and argued by the other contributors to this volume. Without reference to some key messages such as sociocultural diversity, Ulf Hannerz quite rightly suggests, anthropology would not be able to regain the kind of public respect and support it deserves. In particular, however, I wish to continue an argument introduced by John Comaroff through his notion of indiscipline. By this notion, he refers to a discourse that redefines the scale, the conceptual foundations, and the techniques of knowledge production in our field. Out of my own contributions to the topic of comparison in anthropology (Gingrich and Fox 2002), I would want to add to Comaroff's good argument that comparative analyses are at the core of the redefinition of scale that he is addressing here and that in this sense they are part and parcel of what he calls 'techniques of knowledge production' and what I would call our methodological toolkit. In turn, our large methodological toolkit is not the same as, but closely related to, 'the conceptual foundations of knowledge production' in Comaroff's words or to what I would want to refer to as new transnational debates on epistemology in anthropology. In short, our discipline's future can only benefit from a new, continuous, and self-reflexive discourse on methodology and epistemology.

Two main factors stand out with regard to why, to my mind, such debates could in fact represent one of the main steps during the next phase of our field's further development. One of these factors is interdisciplinary competition along neoliberal lines; the other is an intradisciplinary factor – in other words, competition internal to anthropology.

The interdisciplinary factor of neoliberal competition among academic fields relates to what I am tempted to call unfavourable interdisciplinary exchange rates for a small discipline like ours, wherever capitalism imposes increased academic regimes of competition on us. Under these conditions, a comparatively small field has greater problems in thoroughly absorbing and digesting its intellectual imports within temporal cycles that tend to become shorter and shorter. Simultaneously, the same academic field also has greater problems in successfully putting its disciplinary trademark and branding on its own intellectual export goods. It is a good sign for anthropology's overall development during the past couple of decades that a great deal of intellectual imports from other fields have occurred, and it is an even better sign for our field's attractiveness to others that we have also exported much to them. Cases in point of significant imports were the strong influence of literary criticism on our postmodern debates or of historians' work on our post-colonial debates. Examples of significant exports were the widespread 'sale' of 'ethnographic fieldwork' to sociology or of anthropological insights into nationalism, ethnicity, or tribalism to political science and history. Continuing the market metaphors, my point is, however, that our imports were somewhat too expensive and our exports were far too cheap. We therefore need to improve our checks and balances, so to speak. Because anthropology will hopefully never become a transnational company and instead will remain a transnational web of networks among professionals, students, and their institutions, improving our checks and balances is not a simple matter of counting. Instead, for our intellectual imports, we need improved disciplinary tools of quality control before we import too much for too high an effort, only perhaps to find out that three-fourths of our newest acquisitions were useless.

Simultaneously, as for our intellectual exports, it certainly represents a wonderful success story that today the large social sciences teach their own students courses in ethnography after decades of ridiculing its allegedly useless imprecision. It is equally satisfying to see that law schools today teach their own students courses in mediation and segmentation after decades of denying any of anthropology's competencies in this field. Something similar could be said about the introduction of concepts and theories on colonialism or tribalism into the repertoire of political scientists and historians: in all these cases of 'cheap exports', my metaphoric allusion to invisible trademarks and absent branding refers to our weak insistence that these concepts actually include important elements from anthropology that we are happy to export if they are applied in an appropriate way. In short, we have not always engaged actively enough in communicating our understanding of an appropriate usage of these concepts, and we need to improve that. It is good if the rest of the world in the social sciences and the humanities enthusiastically rushes into our supermarket of concepts, theories, and methods to shop for tools for understanding and explaining nationalism, ritual, ethnography, mediation, or ethnicity, but maybe it was not such a good idea to receive these customers in the past while, in the metaphorical roles of shopkeepers and salespersons, we were often busy doing other things. This might have encouraged our customers to help themselves to whatever they wanted, while we were often discussing the status of our work and of our products among ourselves. Instead, our supermarkets and shops today should advise customers that the good products we have are valuable objects of interest and that their users should carefully read the anthropologist's instructions and then pay the asking price.

Summing up this first factor, there is a need for improved disciplinary quality assessment of intellectual imports, while, for intellectual exports, improved communication of disciplinary basics is required. Both of these elements can only be addressed if through good, focused debates we refine and sophisticate our skills and expertise in basic, internal anthropological epistemology and methodology (Csordas 2004). Because these 'unequal interdisciplinary exchange rates' require a more solid and epistemologically well-founded resistance by sociocultural anthropologists across national boundaries, this first factor comprises an important element of transnational collaboration and mutual support among sociocultural anthropologists around the globe. The second factor and reason why transnational debates on anthropology's epistemologies and methodologies could become central for the discipline's next phase of development has to do with internal constellations of our field and how these relate to the world at large.

In today's world, any specialised academic field needs key competencies and defining skills that are less of an interdisciplinary kind but, rather, are specific to that specialised field. These key competencies and defining skills would include main research questions and themes, methods, concepts, and, last but not least, insights and research results that are widely acknowledged internally. It remains relatively difficult, however, to identify anthropology's widely acknowledged research results from any given present perspective. One reason for that is epistemological or, rather, the underdeveloped state of epistemological debates about what actually constitutes our knowledge. This deficiency puts us in a complicated position in relation to funding institutions, academic boards, politics, the media, and society at large (Strathern 2006). A field that cannot clearly answer questions about the status of its knowledge will gradually manoeuvre itself into an extremely high-risk, precarious position – particularly so under increasing pressure for 'evidence-based' research, which requires more than merely negative or defensive coping on our part (Engelke 2008). The epistemological status of our knowledge production deserves communication, clarification, and consolidation. In the realm of intellectual contents and concepts, this is therefore the area where sooner or later, through debates and practices, we need new discourses that clarify anthropology's main epistemologies in its transnational era (Das 1998, Rabinow 1997).

As a result of our past self-examination and of 'high-cost imports and low-cost exports' of intellectual goods, anthropology's epistemological landscape today looks to me like a fertile Yemeni *wadi* after a season that has seen too many floods: it is potentially rich and fertile, but there is some work to be done before it can yield a new harvest. Chunks of classical positivism sit around here and there, pieces of exhausted constructivism mingle with elements of phenomenology in one part, with pragmatism in a second, and with Wittgensteinian approaches in a third. As I have recently argued elsewhere, each of these epistemological approaches offers specific advantages and disadvantages for the pursuit of sociocultural anthropology moving into its new transnational and postnational eras (Gingrich 2009).

At the same time, philosophy has lost its former hegemony as a metascience of sciences. There is no need for anthropologists to go shopping in the next philosophical supermarket. Instead, we could continue to try out these fragments of philosophical epistemologies that we have already acquired, after putting them into shape for own purposes, to see how they work in our anthropological practice. We might improve them accordingly while communicating this among ourselves (Duranti 2006).

In the process, we will sooner or later notice that all these diverse philosophical fragments in anthropology's current epistemological activities have one common denominator: they are all derived from a common Euro-American epistemological legacy, as several authors have pointed out (see, e.g., Godelier 2009, Jain 1977). It will also be important to move beyond that legacy as an exclusive source of epistemological inspiration, while anthropology develops further into its transnational era. We all know that there are also other epistemological legacies, whether they are Indian, African, Buddhist, or indigenous (Gingrich 2009).

So, in addition to reinforcing our epistemological and practical resistance against 'unequal interdisciplinary exchange relations' across national boundaries, moving beyond the narrow boundaries of Euro-American epistemological legacies represents a second major task for the next phases of sociocultural anthropology's complicated transition process. Breaking up and leaving behind the enduring Euro-American epistemological monopoly in our field certainly is a task of transnational and global dimensions – and perhaps the most important one of all. Among other exciting sources of inspiration, such as the philosophical legacies of Asia or Africa, this may in fact also imply a thorough reconsideration of sociocultural anthropology's own, vastly rich fieldwork records. They certainly include a multitude of contextualised popular epistemologies that emerged outside of, and against, the monopoly of Euro-American reasoning.

This concludes the present argument for actively furthering sociocultural anthropology's transition into its transnational phase. I have shown that current concerns about an 'end of anthropology' have to be unpacked: to some extent, they represent the difficulties, concerns, and problems of a major historical transition marked by the simultaneity of disappearing national traditions and the emergence of transnational and global approaches. That transition is contested, its outcome is uncertain, but there are several ways to promote it so as to ensure sociocultural anthropology's prosperity, distinctiveness, and vanguard role among the social sciences and humanities. Institutional efforts for ensuring global and transnational minimum-quality standards represent a main pragmatic element in these efforts. At the same time, epistemological concerns should focus on consolidating and communicating the status and content of anthropological knowledge, while breaking down the epistemological monopoly by Euro-American legacies. Ethnographic fieldwork continues to play a central role both in the pragmatic as well as in the epistemological aspects of these efforts: as our central research and training methodology in the next transnational era and as a resourceful and inspiring research record for reassessing anthropology's epistemological foundations beyond Euro-American limits.

REFERENCES


BARTH, Fredrik, Andre GINGRICH, Robert PARKIN, and Sydel SILVERMAN
2005     *One discipline, four ways: British, German, French, and American anthropology.*
         Chicago: University of Chicago Press

BECK, Ulrich
2008    *Die Neuvermessung der Ungleichheit unter den Menschen.* Soziologische Aufklärung im 21. Jahrhundert (The new measuring of human inequality: sociological enlightenment in the twenty-first century). Frankfurt: Suhrkamp

BRENNEIS, Don
2004    "A partial view of contemporary anthropology", *American Anthropologist* 106(3):580–588

CORNWELL, John
2003    *Hitler's scientists: science, war and the devil's pact.* London: Penguin

CSORDAS, Thomas
2004    "Evidence of and for what?", *Anthropological Theory* 4(4):473–480

DAS, Veena
1998    "Wittgenstein and anthropology", *Annual Review of Anthropology* 27:171–195

DE L'ÉSTOILE, Bernard
2008    "Hegemonic gravity and pluralistic utopia: a comparative approach to internationalization in anthropology", *Journal of the World Anthropologies Network* 3:109–126

DRACKLÉ, Dorle, Iain R. EDGAR, and Thomas K. SCHIPPERS (eds.)
2003    *Educational histories of European social anthropology.* Oxford: Berghahn

DURANTI, Alessandro
2006    "The social ontology of intentions", *Discourse Studies* 8(1):31–40

ENGELKE, Matthew (ed.)
2008    *The objects of evidence: anthropological approaches to the production of knowledge.* London: Royal Anthropological Institute

ERIKSEN, Thomas H.
2001²   *Small places, large issues: an introduction to social and cultural anthropology.* London: Pluto

GINGRICH, Andre
2009    "Evidence in socio-cultural anthropology: limits and options for epistemological orientations", in: João De Pina-Cabral and Christina Toren (eds.), "What's happening to epistemology?", 177–190. *Social Analysis* 53(2)

GINGRICH, Andre and Richard G. FOX (eds.)
2002    *Anthropology, by comparison.* London: Routledge

GODELIER, Maurice
2009    *In and out of the West: reconstructing anthropology.* London: Verso

174 Andre Gingrich

HANNERZ, Ulf
2007    "The neo-liberal culture complex and universities: a case for urgent anthropology?",
        *Anthropology Today* 23(5):1–2

HASTRUP, Kirsten
2005    "Social anthropology: towards a pragmatic enlightenment?", *Social Anthropology/
        Anthropologie Sociale* 13(2):133–149

HERZFELD, Michael
2004²   *Cultural intimacy: social poetics in the nation-state.* New York: Routledge

JAIN, Ravindra K. (ed.)
1977    *Text and context: the social anthropology of tradition.* Philadelphia: Institute for the
        Study of Human Issues (A.S.A. Essays in Social Anthropology 2.)

KNORR-CETINA, Karin
1981    *The manufacture of knowledge: an essay on the constructivist and contextual nature of
        science.* Oxford: Pergamon

KUKLICK, Henrika (ed.)
2008    *A new history of anthropology.* Oxford: Blackwell

KUPER, Adam
1996³   *Anthropology and anthropologists: the modern British school.* London: Routledge

MANIAS, Chris
2009    "The race prussienne controversy: scientific internationalism and the nation", *Isis*
        100(4):733–757

MARCUS, George E. (ed.)
1999    *Critical anthropology now: unexpected contexts, shifting constituencies, changing
        agendas.* Santa Fe, NM: School of American Research Press

MBEMBE, Achille and Janet ROITMAN
1995    "Figures of the subject in times of crisis", *Public Culture* 7(2):323–352

ORTNER, Sherry B.
1984    "Theory in anthropology since the sixties", *Comparative Studies in Society and
        History* 26(1):126–166

PRICE, David H.
2008    *Anthropological intelligence: the deployment and neglect of American anthropology
        in the second world war.* Durham, NC: Duke University Press

RABINOW, Paul
1997    *Essays in the anthropology of reason.* Princeton: Princeton University Press

RABINOW, Paul and George E. MARCUS, with James FAUBION and Tobias REES
2008     *Designs for an anthropology of the contemporary*. Durham, NC: Duke University Press

RESTREPO, Eduardo and Arturo ESCOBAR
2005     "Other anthropologies and anthropology otherwise: steps to a world anthropology framework", *Critique of Anthropology* 25(2):99–128

RIBEIRO, Gustavo L.
2006     "World anthropologies: cosmopolitics, power and theory in anthropology", *Critique of Anthropology* 26(4):363–386

SAHLINS, Marshall D.
1976     *Culture and practical reason*. Chicago: University of Chicago Press

SHORE, Chris and Susan WRIGHT
1999     "Audit culture and anthropology: neo-liberalism in British higher education", *Journal of the Royal Anthropological Institute* 5:557–575

STOCKING, George W. Jr. (ed.)
1996     *Volksgeist as method and ethic: essays on Boasian ethnography and the German anthropological tradition*. Madison: University of Wisconsin Press

STRATHERN, Marilyn
2006     "A community of critics? Thoughts on new knowledge", *Journal of the Royal Anthropological Institute* 12(1):191–209

STRATHERN, Marilyn (ed.)
2000     *Audit cultures: anthropological studies in accountability, ethics and the academy*. London: Routledge

WIMMER, Andreas and Nina GLICK SCHILLER
2002     "Methodological nationalism and beyond: nation-state building, migration and the social sciences", *Global Networks* 2(4):301–334

# 8

## DIVERSITY IS OUR BUSINESS[*]

### Ulf Hannerz

*1.*

Almost since the beginnings of anthropology as an organised endeavour, its practitioners – some of them at least – seem to have had a morbid tendency to dwell on the likelihood of the impending demise of the discipline. In "Argonauts of the Western Pacific", perhaps the earliest field-based ethnography still reasonably widely read, Bronislaw Malinowski started his foreword by proposing that his discipline was 'in the sadly ludicrous, not to say tragic, position, that at the very moment when it begins to put its workshop in order, to forge its proper tools, to start ready for work on its appointed task, the material of its study melts away with hopeless rapidity' (1922). In the 1960s, as he had just moved on to a chair in sociology, Peter Worsley warned in an oft-cited conference paper with the title "The end of anthropology?" that the discipline might disappear, or survive only as a particular form of history, if it continued specialising in isolated 'primitive societies' (1966).[1] Not so many years later, Rodney Needham, a very different British professor, could foresee that aspects of anthropology would be assimilated into other disciplines, so that future anthropologists might be orientalists, art historians, depth psychologists, political scientists, or whatever – in each case bringing with them an ethnographic knowledge of other cultures (1970). More recently, George Marcus, beginning to respond to a question of whether the discipline might be falling apart, suggested that 'anthropology is not on the verge of disintegration. Institutional inertia alone will keep it going for some time' (Rabinow and Marcus with Faubion and Rees 2008:45). That is hardly a very comforting answer: these days, inertia seems like a

---

[*]  I presented the first draft of this article for the Jensen Memorial Lecture Series, "The end of anthropology?" at the Frobenius Institute, Johann Wolfgang Goethe University Frankfurt am Main, on April 21, 2008. I am grateful to Karl-Heinz Kohl for the invitation to participate in the series and to the audience on that occasion for a fruitful discussion. I express my thanks also for the valuable comments by the anonymous reviewers for the American Anthropologist and by the editor, Tom Boellstorff. An extended version of this article can be found as a chapter in my book "Anthropology's world: life in a twenty-first-century discipline" (Hannerz 2010).

[1]  In his lively autobiography, "An academic skating on thin ice", Worsley notes about this paper that 'I was wrong – it didn't die at all' (2008:154).

[2]  As Marcus continued his argument, he made it clear that he did not see it as a complete answer either.

rather less reliable feature of academic organisation than it may have been in the past.[2]

What follows here also first took form in an international lecture series with the overall title "The end of anthropology?" Although I take on the question mostly by trying to deal at some length with one more specific kind of threat to the discipline, I address it briefly in a more general way first, noting that it reminded me of a very well-known and controversial journal article published about twenty years ago: Francis Fukuyama's "The end of history?" (1989). Fukuyama was of course not concerned with the possible demise of the academic discipline of history but, rather, envisioned the completion of large-scale world historical process, with the end of the Cold War, the decline of state socialism, and the absolutely final triumph of liberal democracy. Although it appeared in a somewhat obscure publication, the article nonetheless drew a great deal of attention worldwide, yet when Fukuyama reviewed its reception some years after its publication, it turned out he was not altogether pleased (1995). He complained that he had very often been misunderstood. He could list Margaret Thatcher, Mikhail Gorbachev, the first President Bush, and Hosni Mubarak among the people who, noting in their speeches that history still goes on, had rejected what they had thought was his thesis. But probably they had not read the article – and perhaps neither had their speech writers. Moreover, Fukuyama also found that many of his commentators had failed to note that his original article title had ended with a question mark.

This kind of formulation, then, is a bit risky. Some people might mistake a rhetorical question, or a titillating courtship with imagined danger, for a prognosis or a statement of fact. And in these times of information or disinformation overload, they may not remain around, with undistracted attention, to hear the elaborated and possibly obscure answer. In fact, all they remember might be that first catchy string of words.

I see some number of reasons why the answer to the question of whether we've come to 'the end of anthropology?' should be 'no'. The number of practitioners and students of anthropology has grown greatly over the past half-century; the scope of the discipline has kept widening. In the early twentieth century, there were few anthropologists outside the countries that had overseas empires or those where dominant white settlers had indigenous populations within the national borders. Now just about all countries have their own anthropologists (even if it is true that numbers and working conditions vary considerably), so anthropology is now as close as it has ever been to realising its potential as a truly global endeavour. Additionally, as far as intellectual vitality is concerned, anyone who wanders through the book exhibits at major national or international anthropology meetings, or just skims through the catalogues of the relevant publishing houses, can hardly fail to marvel at the many books continuously produced within the discipline (in times when 'the future of the book' also seems to be in question).

In fact, the number of journals devoted wholly or in large part to anthropology seems also to have grown substantially in the latter decades of the twentieth century.[3] This seems not to be a time to suggest that the last anthropologist to leave the building should turn off the light.

How are we doing with regard to our scholarly interests? In his major overview of contemporary anthropology, Michael Herzfeld concludes that 'it is abundantly clear that the vast increase in available topics, scale of perception, and sheer complexity of subject matter do not seem to be compelling the discipline to early retirement' (2001a:19). Probably most of us simply want to get on with our work, which by now does not appear to be inevitably shaped by any of the more dramatic theoretical divides or confrontations of the later decades of the past century. In a wide-ranging survey, aptly titled "Anthropology in the middle", Bruce Knauft has argued that recent thought within the discipline has tended to move away from grand theory into a fertile middle ground where new connections cross-cut such divides as those among global, regional, and local scales; between structures and events; between ethnography and history; between objectivism and experimental genres of writing; and between theory and practical concerns (2006). In a postparadigmatic period, anthropologists tend to be reasonably comfortable with, and stimulated by, bricolages that allow them to combine different intellectual strands in new ways and take them to new materials. And Knauft sees such tendencies as characteristic not only of anthropology's present but also of its continued renewal and future promise. Although his survey focused on sociocultural anthropology in the United States, I am inclined to believe that we can discern the same tendencies elsewhere in the anthropological world. No real state of crisis here either, then.

More dramatically, one might imagine that the end of anthropology could come about as a part of a more general dissolution of the entities called disciplines, a very large-scale change in the scholarly landscape. As we move in on many current issues, tendencies, and phenomena, discipline boundaries tend to get blurred. We also now encounter sophisticated and interesting analyses of changes in the mode of production of knowledge, toward more interdisciplinary and transdisciplinary styles of organisation (Gibbons *et al.* 1994, Nowotny *et al.* 2001).

Now it is not that during my years as an inhabitant of that landscape, mostly in my European corner of it, I have always been entirely pleased with its existing shape. In the humanities and social sciences, it may rather often have been an obstacle to vitality and creativity that discipline boundaries have been too sharply demarcated, intellectually and organisationally. Yet I do not think the best solution is to abolish disciplines, as bodies of knowledge and as intellectual communities. Occasionally I hear colleagues declaring that they would not be so concerned if the discipline

---

[3]    In 1970, e.g., there was as yet no *American Ethnologist, Cultural Anthropology, Social Anthropology, Anthropology Today, Critique of Anthropology, Anthropological Theory, Focaal, Ethnography, Identities,* or *Public Culture.*

of anthropology disappears from the organisational chart of universities, as long as the ideas of anthropology continue to be propagated there, some place, in some form. That may sound admirably broadminded – and rather in line with Needham's prognosis – but it still leaves me worried. As a matter of academic Realpolitik, I believe the survival and continued development of this kind of cluster of ideas and practices are best served by an institutional power base of their own. Meanwhile, in that same period when U.S. universities tend to be overwhelmingly dominant in the global ranking lists of academic excellence, one might keep in mind that these institutions have mostly not seemed inclined to close down discipline departments in favour of alternative modes of organisation. As I understand it, they continue to be much more likely to support both discipline departments and various cross-cutting formats for interdisciplinary encounters. So if these institutions are to stand as models for a successful, intellectually productive organisation of academic life everywhere, disciplines would not seem likely to go away soon.

After such mostly optimistic remarks about the prospects for anthropology, however, let me point to some circumstances that I find rather more disturbing. If what I have said mostly relates to a fairly healthy situation within the discipline, in its internal activities, I think we ought to be more concerned with the present relationship of anthropology to the surrounding society and its public life.

## ANTHROPOLOGY BASHING

It seems long ago that a well-known cultural critic would celebrate an anthropologist as a hero, the way Susan Sontag did with Claude Lévi-Strauss in 1966, in her book of essays, "Against interpretation".[4] We now draw less honourable mention.

An example that I wish I did not have: one of the critical moments, more precisely low points, of Barack Obama's campaign in the presidential primaries in the spring of 2008 was when he spoke – privately, or so he thought – to a gathering of San Francisco Bay Area supporters about how small-town people in 'middle America' had grown 'bitter' over lost jobs, which made them 'cling to guns or religion or antipathy toward people who aren't like them' (Bai 2008). The statement was reported and commented on widely, and it was for a while seen as a threat to his candidacy. Commenting self-critically later on, Obama described this as his 'biggest boneheaded move' and told his New York Times interviewer that it had sounded as if he was 'talking to a bunch of wine-sipping San Francisco liberals with an anthropological view toward white working-class voters' (Bai 2008). What he really meant, he told the interviewer, was that

---

[4]     Although there were reminders of such times more or less worldwide in the obituaries for Lévi-Strauss after he died in 2009.

these voters have a right to be frustrated because they've been ignored [...] in fact, if you've grown up and your dad went out and took you hunting, and that is part of your self-identity and provides you a sense of continuity and stability that is unavailable in your economic life, then that's going to be pretty important, and rightfully so. And if you're watching your community lose population and collapse but your church is still strong and the life of the community is centred around that, well then, you know, we'd better pay attention to that (Bai 2008).

Here it seems to me, then, that the candidate Obama assigns a stereotypically distant view, lacking in empathy, to anthropology – and then proceeds to sketch, as its opposite, precisely the sort of close, contextualising understanding that we as anthropologists are much more likely to claim for ourselves. And from this particular source, we may find the stereotype so much more surprising because we might have thought this candidate should have got his anthropology right – but more about that later. In any case, here is an instance of a recurrent phenomenon that we might call 'anthropology bashing'.

Surveying a range of mostly Anglophone literary portrayals, Jeremy MacClancy concludes that, while there is a great deal of variety, as individuals anthropologists come across more often as pathetic than as heroic (2005). My own overall impression from popular culture, journalism, and other sources is that there are times when the anthropologist is portrayed as reasonably likeable but somewhat unreliable and unpredictable – more trickster than hero. Very occasionally, this professional stranger is seen as somebody with a special, dispassionate ability to discern what is hidden to everyone else, but this alternative seems to show up less frequently. In another mode, the anthropologist is seen as someone distant and cold-hearted – and, at worst, as someone who uses his skills to manipulate situations in ways which are detrimental to the human beings about which he has built up an expertise.[5] If the main thrust of the imagery of cold-heartedness is precisely one of suggesting a faulty emotional makeup, however, it often goes with an implication that the anthropologist is a bumbling, incompetent observer who does not get even obvious realities right – not only less skilled in understanding than the natives who are at home in the place (that may often be fair enough) but also sometimes even less perceptive than any untrained amateur. This scholar, then, probably hurt his head when he fell into the field from the heights of the ivory tower.

In another variety of anthropology bashing, the discipline is an easy target for a kind of populism that proclaims that research in and about far-away places is useless and that money devoted to it is therefore not well-spent. The most widely known example may be U.S. Senator William Proxmire's Golden Fleece Awards, announced regularly over an extended period in the late twentieth century. Senator

---

5      This may have been the main tendency in the public commentary around the 'Yanomami affair', occasioned by the journalist Patrick Tierney's book "Darkness in El Dorado" (2002).

Proxmire, in many ways apparently an honourable man making his satirical awards
to publicise striking waste of taxpayers' money, at times makes a good point: one of
his more celebrated prizes was to the Department of the Army for a study on how
to buy a bottle of Worcestershire sauce. But in a number of instances, the recipients
were prominent anthropologists with somewhat esoteric projects in faraway fields.

Yet another kind of anthropology bashing may often be gentler. This involves
the place of the discipline in time, describing it in one way or other as an anachronism,
an activity out of the past. Thus, when an electronic journal named Inside Higher
Ed, devoted to news of higher education, reported on what had been noteworthy
at a recent annual meeting of the American Anthropological Association, the
introductory line in the correspondent's report read: 'Evoking associations with
musty, forgotten archives and spiral notebooks in the field, anthropology doesn't
immediately come to mind as a discipline fully situated in the modern, wired world'
(Guess 2007). Yet the writer went on to affirm that in fact, 'anthropologists have
been tackling the implications of technologies on ethnography with each new
innovation, from handheld 16-millimeter film cameras and cassette tapes several
decades ago to Internet and digital video in more recent times' (Guess 2007).

A second example is from a couple of years earlier. The journal Fortune Small
Business devoted an article discussing the fact that to understand the software needs
of entrepreneurs, Microsoft had hired anthropologists to undertake field studies of
small firms all over the United States (Murphy 2005). This was indeed the cover story
of the issue: on the cover, under the rubric "Pygmy hunters", was a cartoon of Bill
Gates, Microsoft's founder, wearing a pith helmet. Gates's surprising involvement
with a supposedly exotic line of scholarship, then, would be shown by a rather
antiquated tropical headgear, nowadays hardly worn either by anthropologists or
by anybody else, whether in the villages of whatever may be darkest Africa or in the
small-business offices of North America.

## A STRONG BRAND

The trouble, in other words, does not seem to be that anthropology is unknown to
the outside world. We are perhaps actually more part of a popular imagination than
most other disciplines. The problem is, rather, that what people think they know for
a fact is wrong. For a long time, we maybe have thought of this as mildly irritating
but not terribly important. I would argue that we may now be in turbulent times
when we can ill afford to not take the matter seriously. We may not be able to put an
end to all anthropology bashing, but we can try harder to be clear, and consistent,
about how we want to be understood.

My concerns here are undoubtedly influenced by the fact that I have spent
a fair amount of time, on and off over several decades, as a ground-level academic

administrator, chairing my department (and also a couple of years running a small institute of advanced study). Academic organisations have their peculiarities, but in some ways a department head is much like a small business owner: trying to make ends meet, keeping the staff reasonably happy, attracting a flow of customers, and turning out a reasonably satisfactory line of products. That role is not always easy to combine with that of a scholar (although one had better try), but it may breed a certain sensitivity to what goes on at the interfaces between a discipline and at least some segments of the external environment.

In recent times, in large parts of the world, that environment has been importantly affected by the spread of the neoliberal culture complex. When it makes its way across continents, like other such complexes in history, it takes somewhat different shapes in different settings, as it interacts with what is already in place. The complex may acquire national characteristics, and in academia, its encounters with different disciplines work out in varied ways. It is a central assumption of neoliberalism, obviously, that 'the market' generally offers a superior model for organising activities and social relationships. Yet in Europe at least, where universities tend to be in one way or another closely tied to the state apparatus, it is conspicuously present in the reshaping of state management. Some of its manifestations actually seem less in evidence in North American universities, more pluralistic, under rather less-centralised control. Yet here, too, we find recent critical, and more or less pessimistic, assessments of what is happening to universities, under titles such as "The last professors" (Donoghue 2008) and "Wannabe u" (Tuchman 2009). And I hear the rumours of the effects of this culture complex on universities and the scholarly life in other regions of the world as well.[6]

Often it seems there is little insight, in whatever may be higher-level political decision making, into the varied modes of knowledge production in different scholarly fields as well as little curiosity about the unanticipated consequences of decisions. Generally, the politicians of neoliberal academia would not appear to attach any particular importance to the reproduction of disciplines or to the survival of departments. In these times, I would be worried that arguments for a decline of disciplines and for the superiority of transdisciplinarity can turn into clichés that are made to serve as opportune alibis for politicians and administrators to do away with the autonomy of those clusters of intellectual activity that seem least profitable.

Perhaps it will eventually – I would hope sooner rather than later – be understood that universities cannot be run quite like businesses, that their multifaceted cultural roles demand some particular care, and that different disciplines may work according to different logics. Meanwhile, it seems particularly important that we

---

[6]    The growing body of anthropological commentary on neoliberalism in universities, and the related notion of audit culture, includes, for example, Brenneis (2009), Strathern (2000), and Wright and Rabo (2010).

take some care to cultivate an understanding of what anthropologists do that is readily understandable within the wider society and also acceptable to ourselves.

João de Pina-Cabral, the Portuguese anthropologist, prominent on the European anthropological scene, has written about the problem at hand, provoked by one particular incident: the danger, at one time imminent although in the end not materialising, that anthropology in France, one of the old heartlands of the discipline, would be downgraded to a status as a subdiscipline of history in the national structure of research funding (2006). Pina-Cabral's conclusion was that the public image of the discipline is seriously out of date and does not serve it well. But this is not just a challenge to various European national anthropologies. In yet another recent book scrutinising the U.S. university, Louis Menand, a regular contributor to the New Yorker and a Harvard professor of English, notes that if today one asks anthropologists what their discipline is about 'you would be likely to get two types of answer. One answer is: Anthropology is the study of its own assumptions. The other answer is: Anthropology is whatever people in anthropology departments do' (2010:118).

I do not think this is good enough. Anthropology may have its more or less well-informed friends, even admirers, in some number of adjacent fields – science studies, law, medieval history, or wherever – each with their own notions of the peculiar character and value of the discipline. There may even be enthusiasts scattered far outside academia. But under the present circumstances, we may do well to offer a message that can also reach circles in which there may be no strong curiosity about what we do but that can still affect the circumstances of our lives: journalists, politicians, academic administrators ... even school teachers, parents, voters. As I dwell on this issue here, I will perhaps at times be in danger of stating the obvious, but then it happens that I find what anthropologists say on such matters a little thoughtless and at worst counterproductive. Sometimes the obvious requires restating.

Perhaps provocatively, in drawing on a characteristic current vocabulary, I would argue that anthropology needs to cultivate a strong brand. Those who feel ill at ease with that term, thinking that in its crassness it sullies their noble scholarly pursuits, can perhaps just as well continue to call it 'public image' or even just 'identity', but in times of not just neoliberal thought but also of media saturation and short attention spans, it may be that 'brand' is a useful root metaphor, a word to think with in the world we live in.[7] Brands should attract outsiders: customers, visitors, members of the public. At the same time, they should preferably offer a fully acceptable identity for whoever may count as insiders to reflect on and be inspired by.

---

[7]    These days, too, not only corporations or consumer goods are linked to brands but also for example cities and countries. I have also seen a book review by the Archbishop of Canterbury with a title describing Virgin Mary as 'a global brand' (Williams 2009).

It does not seem difficult to identify some criteria for a successful brand that could apply to the brand of an academic discipline as well. Preferably it should be quickly grasped and clearly understood. Academics, given to precise but not necessarily snappy definitions of their terms, may need to take note here. It is no good to formulate a brand in such a way that any innocent inquirer will lose interest and be halfway down the stairs before the reply is complete. The few words it needs to put together should be simple ones, understood by everybody. And the formulation, again, should not lend itself too easily to misinterpretation: remember again that striking catch phrase 'the end of history?' and then Fukuyama's later complaint about the world leaders who had failed to understand it.

Getting closer to specifics, I take it that one would be better off with a brand that is consistent and more or less equally acceptable, even attractive, to all the varied others one hopes to reach with it – insiders as well as outsiders. Consider some examples from the way we talk about anthropology. Menand, above, offers a version of our occasional, somewhat flippant conclusion that 'anthropology is whatever anthropologists do'. In times when a number of disciplines may well be characterised by a great deal of internal variation and fuzzy boundaries, there could seem to be something to this, just as 'history is whatever historians do' and 'economics is whatever economists do'. Nevertheless, it is an insider joke, and it may be a little risky to take it outside our own circle. I do not think I would expose students to it (at least not immediately) for fear of confusing them further. Moreover, I would suspect that faculty deans, university rectors (or call them presidents, or vice-chancellors, in different national contexts), and ministers of higher education would neither feel well-instructed nor be terribly amused. Perhaps we had better get used to looking for what makes anthropology a reasonably coherent endeavour rather than emphasising apparent incoherence.

There is also a certain intellectually rebellious streak in our discipline, which we may cherish and may well want to emphasise at times. This is an idea of anthropology as cultural critique, which certainly goes back at least to Malinowski and Margaret Mead and made a prominent comeback in the twentieth century. More recently yet, at a conference on teaching, I heard it affirmed that anthropology is a 'subversive discipline'. Again, that may appeal to many of us and may attract some of the more independent thinkers among students. But I would not have recommended it, in the past or at present, as the best brand to take into negotiations with academic administrators or ministry officials who may nervously maximise order and predictability in their domains.

---

8      But note here also Marshall Sahlins' comment: 'Some Cultural Studies types seem to think that anthropology is nothing but ethnography. Better the other way around: ethnography is anthropology, or it is nothing' (1993:9).

Rather more substantively, there has been some tendency to define anthropology centrally in terms of how we work: that is, in terms of field research or ethnography. Certainly there is something attractively concrete about this, yet we may feel that in the end it is not satisfactory as a central image of the discipline. Indeed, in the very title of his Radcliffe-Brown Lecture to the British Academy, Tim Ingold (2007) has asserted that "Anthropology is not ethnography".[8] In passing, Ingold notes the extreme case of the lowly 'ethnographic researcher',

> tasked with undertaking structured and semi-structured interviews with a selected sample of informants and analysing their contents with an appropriate software package, who is convinced that the data he collects are ethnographic simply because they are qualitative (2007).

This is surely not a particularly representative instance of what we usually take ethnography to be, but in any case Ingold shares with many other anthropologists a dislike of the inclination, in adjacent disciplines and disciplinoids (such as cultural studies), to assume that ethnography is all there is to anthropology. As an evolving body of thought and knowledge, anthropology cannot be reduced to a method – some sort of qualitative counterpart to statistics.

All the same, it is hardly helpful in the long run to come up only with brand formulations that suit some audiences but not at all others or formulations that most strongly emphasise what anthropology is not. This is certainly also still the problem with that widely accepted but outdated image that we took note of before: portraying the anthropologist either in 'musty, forgotten archives' or in the jungle, wearing his pith helmet. We may reject that – but then when the Royal Anthropological Institute of Great Britain and Ireland commissions a volume to present a more current understanding of the discipline, it gets the title "Exotic no more" (MacClancy 2002). So, again, there is above all a negative statement, which could at worst be taken to mean that anthropology has given up its attempt to understand human lives across boundaries and is now all 'anthropology at home'. The wide-ranging contents of the book in question show that this is not the case, but I would have preferred a more positive formulation up front.

*A FOCUS ON DIVERSITY*

What would I then offer as a viable brand for anthropology, at present and for any future that is at all foreseeable? It is here I come to this article's title: "Diversity is our business". I will admit that this phrase is inspired by another one: a long time ago, the large U.S. corporation for which my brother-in-law worked as a young engineer used the slogan "Quality is our business – our only business". I remember that my brother-in-law used to quote it with a wry detachment, as one may be wise to do with any slogan. Yet it may still have served the corporation reasonably well, for internal as well as external uses.

I want to work through some of the implications of pushing the scholarly and practical understanding of human diversity as anthropology's brand. First of all, I think it is a valid claim that this is what the discipline is primarily about. Since the beginnings of the discipline, with its connections to natural history, we have indeed sought to document the variety of human life, even if for some time we applied this preoccupation more exclusively to what was geographically distant or 'exotic'. It is a shared stance toward what is 'out there', not so affected by variations in theoretical orientations. Secondly, I think it identifies an important contribution to knowledge. Even if 'diversity' could sound a little like 'everything', which might be a rather questionable specialty – and even comes uncomfortably close to 'whatever anthropologists do' – the value of understanding diversity should very soon become clear when one contrasts it with that still-strong inclination to assume that what is familiar is universal or that modernity necessarily breeds uniformity. A study of diversity remains the best antidote to unthinking ethnocentrism.

With this, I believe, follows the opening of anthropology to the development of cultural critique, even to identifying as a 'subversive discipline'. This line of effort may appeal more to some of us than to others, and I think the pursuit of it may well be left to individual choice. We should recognise, however, that although a primary identification with the study of diversity may sound less heroic, even a little bland, just about any claim that anthropology can have to unusual critical insight is in fact based on its special relationship to diversity, to the knowledge that other ways of thinking and acting are possible. It may be that, in the line of critical anthropology that developed in the later decades of the twentieth century, especially in the United States, such specific inspiration was more mixed with critical theory from other sources and that one had become a bit more sceptical about the immediate usefulness of contrasts with the Samoans, the Kwakiutl, or other faraway people (Marcus and Fischer 1986). Yet there was still a sense that anthropology as cultural critique should be grounded in an ethnographic understanding of alternatives.

To what extent are we as individual scholars ready to identify the study of human diversity as our major concern? Possibly each one of us, when asked about our research interest, will spontaneously come up with some rather more specific answer: 'Micronesian kinship', 'Latin American squatter settlements', 'software needs of small enterprises', 'Hausa praise singing', or perhaps 'the transnational impact of the Bollywood movie industry'. The problem of diversity as such, however we understand it, may not figure that prominently in our personal scholarly preoccupations. But what we should be aware of is that what all these remarkably different specialties add up to, in a collective intellectual enterprise, is that ever more encompassing, yet never ever complete, knowledge of human diversity. We all add our pieces to the very large jigsaw puzzle. And in that way, the understanding of the shared enterprise also offers us an umbrella for all our individual diversity, an umbrella that on the whole should allow us to get on with things.

Our inclination to think of ethnography, fieldwork, participant-observation, and qualitative analysis as central to the identity of the discipline can also, I believe, be seen as following from a primary concern with diversity. It is because the varied forms of thought and action cannot be assumed to be known, and because we do not take for granted that we know what we do not know, that we are ready to immerse ourselves, intensively and extensively, in ways of life and in documentary materials that are initially far from transparent. We do not fully trust methodologies that limit alternatives and obstruct our exploration of whatever may be unknown.

When the services of anthropologists are sought outside academia – be it by Microsoft, development NGOs, or the Pentagon – it also appears that it is mostly understandings of diversity that are in demand, whatever they are called; for example, 'local knowledge' is a notion that in large part stands for this.

## DIVERSITY UNDER SCRUTINY

Proclaiming diversity to be our business may thus allow us mostly to get on with what we do, while under an umbrella recognisable and not too puzzling to the world outside. It may provide enough room, too, for internal distinctions and cleavages – philosophical, social, political, stylistic – which may be of intense interest to members of the anthropological community but of little significance to others. Yet the brand is also likely to raise certain kinds of questions concerning our assumptions about diversity and our values, and even if not each one of us will be equally engaged in thinking about answers to these in some more organised manner, we can hardly all disregard them.

Probably we can agree that diversity is a notion that now figures much more prominently in public discourse than it did, say, a couple of decades ago. The fact that there is such a wider resonance is on the whole, I would think, one reason for pushing it as a brand key word. Clearly we cannot pretend to be the only people with an interest, even expertise, in diversity. I would not think, however, that within the division of organised scholarly knowledge, any other field can make an equally strong claim to it as a specialty. Yet if diversity has on the one hand turned somewhat fashionable, and is on the other hand not entirely uncontroversial, there are also certain risks involved. We should try and stabilise and institutionalise our own understanding of it, hoping to avoid being dishearteningly stuck any time soon with the favourite flavour of yesteryear. Also we should have a sense of where there are grounds for contention. We may aim at mapping diversity and understanding it, but are we also inclined to celebrate it and to assume that it is limitless?

I like to think of anthropology as a cosmopolitan discipline – in the way I understand cosmopolitanism.[9] I see the latter as a two-faced concept. On the one hand, there is a concern with humanity as a whole and its condition – a moral and at times political engagement with community, society, and citizenship at a more or less global level. On the other hand, cosmopolitanism involves an awareness, and often an appreciation, of diversity in meanings and meaningful forms. These two faces may appear separately from one another: one may often be a cosmopolitanism with a worried face, trying to come to grips with very large problems, while the other is perhaps more often a cosmopolitanism with a happy face, enjoying new sights, sounds, tastes, people. At best, however, I think there is an affinity between them, and it should not be hard to find this kind of double cosmopolitanism among anthropologists.[10]

Between the two faces of cosmopolitanism there may also be a certain tension, however, so a cosmopolitan stance should not entail an unconditional commitment to diversity as either pleasure or possibility. There is that engagement with shared humanity as well. I do not think we should just accept the fairly strong tendency in some contexts of public discourse, not least in recent times, to leave diversity unexamined as something self-evidently good and valuable. Let us, rather, draw on whatever expertise we have to be a bit more intellectually hard-nosed, a little less soft-hearted. We should try to clarify the issues surrounding diversity as we have a chance, publicly or among ourselves, to elaborate on our brand.

On the one hand, it seems to me that the most basic argument for diversity, or one that tends at least on a preliminary basis to work out as such, is a kind of human rights argument: a respect for people's rights to be who they are, and think and do as they choose, within some limits of social justice and concern for the corresponding rights of others. This is an argument that gets complicated by a conflation of individual rights with collective rights; without going into that issue now, I will just say that I have primarily individual rights in mind. Beyond that, I have attempted elsewhere to bring together and make explicit other more tangible arguments for diversity that one can find. I will not repeat them here, only note that I came up with seven, all of which, I believe, are in some need of further discussion and qualification (Hannerz 1996:56–64). On the other hand, I think it is as obvious to anthropologists as to most other people that diversity, in the sense of difference,

---

[9]  The literature on cosmopolitanism has grown enormously, in anthropology and adjacent fields, especially since the 1990s; for my own point of view toward the recognition and appreciation of diversity, see Hannerz (1990), and toward the interrelations of cultural and political dimensions, see Hannerz (2004).

[10]  But then I doubt it would be a good idea to try and bring the word 'cosmopolitanism' into the formulation of an effective public brand of the discipline, as it is so strikingly variable in its connotations – to exemplify, for some people it smells of Western elitism, to others cosmopolitanism is again something subversive, disloyal.

is sometimes a nuisance, involving misunderstanding and conflict. If diversity is our business, this part of it is also included.

In this context, I would like to note that while anthropologists have gone about studying diversity in their way, since the latter decades of the twentieth century there has also been a growth of fields that specialise precisely in dealing with diversity as something concretely problematic, fields of 'intercultural communication' and 'diversity management'. I once referred to the former somewhat facetiously as 'the culture shock prevention industry' (Hannerz 1990:245). That may suggest the rather sceptical, and even ironic, stance of academic anthropologists to this mostly applied field of consultancy and training: to the extent that we pay attention to it at all, we have our doubts about both its theories and its practices.[11] Nonetheless, it may be that if we do make diversity our business, we should take the public demand for knowledge and insight in this area seriously and consider further how we can meet that demand in our way.

There is also that other very big question about how far human diversity stretches. Indeed, the suggestion that anthropology is the study of human diversity is not quite the entire story. At the level of ethnographic work, the preoccupation with diversity may be most noticeable. Yet from early in its intellectual history, anthropology has also had a marked interest in the limits of diversity: in human nature, in 'the psychic unity of mankind', or whatever the formulations may have been. Such concerns have been stronger in some periods than others. Almost half a century ago, in his brief but elegant overview of what was then recent (mostly U.S.) anthropology, Eric Wolf referred to 'a pendulum swing in anthropological thinking' between 'an interest in the gamut of human variability as expressed in the multiplicity of human cultures' and the attempt to define 'some underlying reality beneath the ever changing surface of human phenomena [...] the common blueprint of the human animal' (1964:33–34). That pendulum continues to swing, kept in motion by shifting theoretical and practical stimuli, although it would still seem that in anthropology (mostly unlike other fields of knowledge) the search for unity or uniformity is fundamentally an endeavour carried out in recognition of diversity rather than in disregard of it – a search, rather than a facile assumption.

At present, too, it seems to me necessary that our claim to expertise on diversity also includes an interest in the limits of diversity. Understandings of these limits must continue to be taken as tentative and subject to change, not least in a dialogue with those scholars who study human beings primarily as biological beings. Clearly there has been a great deal of activity in this field recently. As social and cultural anthropologists, we may not always have been very impressed by the proposals of early sociobiologists or later evolutionary psychologists, but let us not

---

[11]    I believe the dissertation by Tommy Dahlén (1997) remains one of the most illuminating over-
         views of the field of 'intercultural communication' from an anthropological perspective.

respond to arguments in this area only with a dogmatism of our own. Generally, the credibility of our claim to expertise in the field of diversity should rest not on premature attempts to establish a consensual party line on critical issues but, rather, on providing an arena for the best-informed discussion of them (Bloch 2005:1–19; Eriksen 2007).

## CULTURE: A CONTESTED CONCEPT

I have waited until this point to explicitly bring the concept of culture into my argument. It is probably clear that just about every time that I have referred to diversity, I might as well have said 'cultural diversity'. But then culture is a contested concept, forever in the public arena, and for the last twenty years or so inside anthropology. Consequently, opinions may differ on whether it should be up front in a presentation of our brand. The debate on the topic may no longer be so intensive within anthropology, and it may have come more or less to an end without being resolved one way or other.[12]

I can see the reasons why some colleagues may feel ill at ease with some of the uses of the culture concept, especially in the essentialist, not to say fundamentalist, varieties employed by political extremists in public life. My own view, however, which I have already elaborated more fully in other contexts, is reformist, rather than abolitionist, and fairly pragmatic (Hannerz 1996:30–43, 1999). Undoubtedly we can manage to find ways of avoiding just about any concept if we try hard enough, but for my own purposes I do find it practical to use 'culture' and 'cultural' to refer to the fact that human beings are learning animals, using meanings to which they have access through their interactions with other humans. Such a usage can be processual in its attention to stability as well as change and does not assume internal uniformity or sharply bounded units. It does not have to succumb to 'culturalism' either, in the sense of exaggerating the importance of beliefs, values, or habits at the expense of factors of power or material circumstances. The goal must certainly be to analyse the relationships among culture, power, and materialities – and this should not be an impossible task. As I remember an old psychological finding, human beings are supposed to be able to keep as many as seven different things in mind at the same time, so it would not seem unreasonable to ask of anthropologists that they try to handle two or three simultaneously.

---

[12]    Among the enduring references in a more critical vein here are Abu-Lughod (1991) and Fox and King (2002); Brumann (1999) takes a more culture-friendly view. For a thorough overview of the uses of the culture concept through the history of anthropology until the present, see Fischer (2007); and for useful discussion of the spread of culture concepts in academic as well as popular contexts, see Breidenbach and Nyíri (2009).

Then, obviously, the question of what we do with the culture concept has a particular connection to our concern with our brand, our public image. It seems to me that at least in some circles within the wider public, 'culture' has been understood as an area in which anthropologists have some expertise and can thus speak with a certain intellectual authority. If we stop using the concept, I doubt that this will have any particular effect outside the discipline. Probably very few people will notice, and we may simply leave more room for uses that we find unacceptable. It may just turn into yet another case of anthropologists trying to define themselves by telling the world what they are not, what they do not do. I think whistle-blowing, and trying to propagate our own view of culture, is a better strategy. We may remember from fairly long ago the line 'whenever I hear the word "culture", I reach for my revolver'. Precisely which leading figure in Nazi Germany used it first, and exactly what the original word formulation was, may be somewhat hazy. But I am afraid if this speaker had been a certain kind of present-day anthropologist, he may have picked up his gun only to shoot himself in the foot.

It should follow from what I have said that I do not believe that a claim to a special concern with diversity necessarily implies any single stand with regard to what in public life in large parts of the world has in recent decades been labelled as 'multiculturalism', whether as a politics of identity or as government policy. Such multiculturalism involves one kind of claim or other of taking diversity into account, but it can be critically examined with varied results. There is certainly some tendency to confuse cultural diversity with multiculturalism, but it is important to distinguish between diversity as a fact and multiculturalism, as an '-ism', as a policy, program, or ideology for the organisation of diversity.[13] And again, it would appear useful if anthropology could provide a scholarly arena, accessible to the interested public, for debate over relevant concepts and realities. Rather unfortunately, such debate, particularly at a theoretical level, has mostly been carried out within the confines of political philosophy.[14]

[13]   For one case where diversity as a political term is largely identified with late-twentieth-century North American expressions of multiculturalism, see Wood (2003). This author, identified on the back cover as a professor of anthropology at Boston University, recognizes that 'diversity' can be understood in other ways as well, but the book is largely devoted to connecting it to identity politics, political correctness, and so forth.

[14]   See, e.g., Barry (2001), Benhabib (2002), Kelly (2002), Kymlicka (1995), Parekh (2000), Taylor (1992).

Here is another consideration: Does a branding of anthropology as a discipline specialising in diversity really take us safely away from the public image that we reject, that of being a discipline only of the past, antiquarian and itself antiquated? There is the possibility that diversity itself is seen as something mostly declining, even vanishing. Fukuyama's 'end of history', with its global triumph of liberal democracy and whatever supposedly would belong in the same package, could perhaps equally well be read as an end of diversity. Over the years illustrious anthropologists have come up with formulations that point more or less in that direction. Again, there are those lines of Malinowski's with which this article began. Nearly eighty years later, Clifford Geertz suggested that 'we may be faced with a world in which there simply aren't any more headhunters, matrilinealists, or people who predict the weather from the entrails of a pig' (2000:68).

It is very likely that the range of cultural variation in the world is no longer what it has been. Insofar as anthropology has an interest in keeping a record of all the kinds of more or less patterned thoughts, activities, and relationships that have at one time or other occurred in some corner of humanity, we may indeed take an interest in the past and in documenting now what may soon disappear as a part of ongoing human life. Not so long ago, this was what the notion of 'urgent anthropology' usually referred to, and for some of us it may still be a priority.

We may remember, too, that long-established tendency in anthropology to place the Other somehow in another time, which Johannes Fabian (1983) criticised in what has become one of the discipline's more recent classics. In any case, we must now insist that our business is diversity in the past, present, and future. And our present present, of course, is not that timeless 'ethnographic present' of the past but indeed this particular period in the flow of history that does not end. That means we must resist those simplistic narratives of global homogenisation that keep showing up in new versions and attend to the sources of resilience in human modes of thought and practice that keep much diversity rather stable. To use the plural form 'modernities' is to insist that there is diversity in modernity.

I can have much respect and even intellectual affection for those colleagues who devote their labours to ever closer views of the cultural minutiae of the longue durée, or of vanishing tradition. Yet I think we should also take some special interest in the way that new cultural forms keep developing, bringing about new diversity. I see a growing interest in anthropology in the future, and in ideas about the future.[15] No doubt it is wise to abstain from claims to predictive powers; the anthropology of

---

[15]   For some examples of anthropological interest in the emergent and the future, see the early volume by Wallman (1992), and more recently Malkki (2001), Hannerz (2003a, 2008), Miyazaki (2003), Appadurai (2004), Guyer (2007) and the responses published with it, and Rabinow (2008).

the future can only be a subjunctive genre. Yet I would propose – as do, for example, Michael Fischer (2003:37–38) and Bill Maurer (2005) – that our methodological inclination toward ethnography, toward open-ended encounters with a potential for serendipitous discoveries, should be of particular value in studying what is emergent. Rather than engaging with diversity mostly by looking backward, anthropology can be in the avant-garde of describing what is growing and what may be coming. Does not the recent interest in such different areas as cultural blending (hybridity, creolisation), the varieties of virtuality, and science studies all demonstrate that much diversity is alive and well around us and ahead of us?

Making diversity the keyword of our brand could also have implications for the kind of writing we do. There has been much debate over writing in anthropology recently, but in large part, recent critiques, and resulting experiments, have been aimed at an internal audience made up of colleagues and forever intellectually news-hungry graduate students. Certainly this has been one of the sources of vitality in the discipline, but mostly such efforts do not reach out. It may be that in a very large national academic system – notably the U.S. one – with a considerable degree of autonomy, in which the attention and esteem of colleagues are what matters most in continued career mobility, there is a particular logic to the concentration on internalist writing. Generally, with a concern for the public image of anthropology, we should think of other styles of writing as well (Eriksen 2006, Waterston and Vesperi 2009). Surely there is still room for much experimentation here. In the context of a foregrounding of diversity, however, I would like to put in a word for the possibilities of comparison.

It has been one of the recurrent ways of describing anthropology to say that it is comparative, which in fact is mostly another way of saying that it is concerned with diversity, but the fact is that not very much anthropology in recent times has been explicitly comparative – which ends up being merely another variety of saying what anthropology is not, or not quite, or no longer. Perhaps for a generation or two now, it seems to me, whether they know it or not, anthropologists have been in a silent battle with the ghost of George Peter Murdock (e.g., 1949) and the style of comparison connected with cross-cultural surveys and the Human Relations Area Files. That kind of comparative work rather soon turned out to involve serious epistemological problems, and it was probably just as important that its dry abstractedness had very little general intellectual and aesthetic appeal to most anthropologists. But then comparisons can be done in a great many ways, and I sense that there is again a wider growing interest in their potential, not least for portraying diversity, explaining it, and discussing its implications as well as for identifying whatever unity or order may underlie diversity (Fox and Gingrich 2002, Moore 2005).

A more widespread use of comparison might have one particular consequence for our work. As I said before, in building our overall picture of human diversity, as a collective enterprise, we tend to add to it our own individual pieces without necessarily having so much of an immediate concern with the whole. Now there are ways of being just as individually engaged in comparative work, if we can draw on varied research experiences of our own, perhaps in different groups, in different places. Michael Herzfeld, for example, has offered an account of his own reflexive globetrotting between the Mediterranean and Thailand.[16] Further back, there is the well-known instance of Geertz's "Islam observed" (1968), set in Indonesia and Morocco. Often, however, we may need to draw on the work of other anthropologists, other ethnographers, to accomplish comparisons. If we think of ethnography as a highly personal expression – much more like art than science – or if we somehow see it as intellectual property where the rights of use cannot be transferred, comparison may be in trouble. No doubt there will be varied preferences within the community of anthropologists here as well, but on the whole I do not think the obstacles to a more effective sharing of our ethnographic resources must remain insurmountable. What of the writings of our colleagues can be used in comparisons, and how, is more likely something that we can decide on after close critical reading rather than on the basis of overall assumptions or proclamations.

*Conclusion: friends in high places*

Finally, then, what might be the future for diversity as our business, what kind of receptivity can we hope to cultivate for this brand? Again, we may not be in the forecasting business, and one should not underestimate the ability of various segments of the public to stick to old, established, and undesirable stereotypes: the colonialist in the pith helmet, the arrogant bumbler, the profligate spender of ordinary people's tax money.

Let us also note the signs of success, however, which do show up in varied places. I return one more time to Fukuyama, who is still a globally prominent public intellectual. As I have said, one might suspect that his 'end of history' scenario could also be understood to entail an end of diversity. But no, that seems no longer, or not entirely, to be the way Fukuyama has it. On the website of the School of Advanced International Studies of Johns Hopkins University, where he has recently had a leading role, I find him making the point that 'most of what is truly useful for policy is context-specific, culture bound and non-generalizable' (Fukuyama 2003). He complains that the typical article now appearing in the American Political Science Review contains much complex-looking mathematics, the sole function of which is often to formalise a behavioural rule that everyone with common sense understands must be true. 'What is missing', argues Fukuyama, 'is any deep knowledge about

---

16    Herzfeld (2001b). This kind of work by scholars working alone has recently found new expression in multisite research projects, which usually have a comparative dimension (Hannerz (2003b)).

the subtleties and nuances of how foreign societies work, knowledge that would help us better predict the behaviour of political actors, friendly and hostile, in the broader world'.

As I followed the 2008 U.S. presidential campaign, too, I perused the statements that candidates were making about their foreign policy views and plans. 'Today, understanding foreign cultures is not a luxury but a strategic necessity', argued Senator John McCain (2007:24); more concretely, he proposed setting up a new agency patterned after the World War II-era Office of Strategic Services (OSS), which could draw together 'specialists in unconventional warfare, civil affairs, and psychological warfare; covert-action operators; and experts in anthropology, advertising, and other relevant disciplines from inside and outside government'. That old Office of Strategic Services, we may remember from the history of anthropology, was where Ruth Benedict, Margaret Mead, Gregory Bateson, and others were active in World War II. Of course, we may worry about the suggested company.

And then again, there was Senator Obama. At a public meeting during the primary campaign in New Hampshire, according to one news website, a questioner made passing mention of a famous anthropologist, and Obama's response was that 'the Margaret Mead reference I am always hip to' (Shapiro 2007). The senator went on to say that his country's policy makers had a problem with understanding non-Western cultures:

> This is a chronic problem in Washington. It has to do with our 30-second attention span. You want to get to know a country and figure out what are the interests and who are the players. You can't parachute in. We don't have good intelligence on them. And we're basically making a series of decisions in the blind. And that is dangerous for us (Shapiro 2007).

Since then, we all have become aware that Obama's late mother had actually earned a doctorate in anthropology at the University of Hawai'i.[17] In the recently published version of her dissertation, which is in large part about Javanese blacksmiths, we can learn that these, like their colleagues here and there in the world, are understood to have certain mystical powers; the master smith's role 'overlaps with that of the magician, ritual specialist, puppet master, poet, priest, and even musician' (Dunham 2009:43). We can perhaps wish that some of these unusual powers have rubbed off on the ethnographer's son. He needs them in the office into which he has moved, and even if he does not he takes up his competitor's suggestion of a new-style OSS, we must also hope that he uses his powers with good intelligence.[18]

---

[17] For some very appreciative reminiscences of anthropologist and mother Stanley Ann Dunham by a colleague who knew her well, see Dove (2009).

[18] New York Times columnist Maureen Dowd sees it as something like 'diversity management': 'Barack Obama grew up learning how to slip in and out of different worlds – black and white,

Meanwhile, as the Fortune Small Business story on Bill Gates and his pygmy hunters concludes, 'anthropology marches on'.

## REFERENCES

ABU-LUGHOD, Lila
1991    "Writing against culture", in: Richard G. Fox (ed.), *Recapturing anthropology*, 137–162. Santa Fe, NM: School of American Research Press

APPADURAI, Arjun
2004    "The capacity to aspire: culture and the terms of recognition", in: Vijayendra Rao and Michael Walton (eds.), *Culture and public action*, 59–84. Stanford: Stanford University Press

BAI, Matt
2008    "Working for the working-class vote", *New York Times Magazine*, October 19. http://www.nytimes.com/2008/10/19/magazine/19obama-t.html (accessed July 16, 2010)

BARRY, Brian
2001    *Culture and equality*. Cambridge, MA: Harvard University Press

BENHABIB, Seyla
2002    *The claims of culture: equality and diversity in the global era*. Princeton: Princeton University Press

BLOCH, Maurice
2005    *Essays on cultural transmission*. Oxford: Berg

BREIDENBACH, Joana and Pál NYÍRI
2009    *Seeing culture everywhere: from genocide to consumer habits*. Seattle: University of Washington Press

BRENNEIS, Don
2009    "Anthropology in and of the academy: assessment, and our field's future", *Social Anthropology* 17:261–275

BRUMANN, Christoph
1999    "Writing for culture: why a successful concept should not be discarded", *Current Anthropology* 40:S1–S13

foreign and American, rich and poor. The son of an anthropologist, he developed a lot of "tricks", as he put it, training himself to be a close observer of human nature, figuring out what others needed so he could get where he wanted to go' (2009).

DAHLÉN, Tommy
1997    *Among the interculturalists.* Stockholm: Almqvist and Wiksell (Stockholm Studies in Social Anthropology 38.)

DONOGHUE, Frank
2008    *The last professors: the corporate university and the fate of the humanities.* New York: Fordham University Press

DOVE, Michael R.
2009    "Dreams from his mother", *New York Times*, August 10. http://www.nytimes.com/2009/08/11/opinion/11dove.html (accessed July 16, 2010)

DOWD, Maureen
2009    "Op-ed columnist: the first shrink", *New York Times*, April 5. http://www.nytimes.com/2009/04/05/opinion/05dowd.html (accessed July 16, 2010)

DUNHAM, S. Ann
2009    *Surviving against the odds: village industry in Indonesia.* Durham, NC: Duke University Press

ERIKSEN, Thomas Hylland
2006    *Engaging anthropology: the case for a public presence.* Oxford: Berg
2007    "Tunnel vision", *Social Anthropology* 15(2):237–243

FABIAN, Johannes
1983    *Time and the other: how anthropology makes its object.* New York: Columbia University Press

FISCHER, Michael M.J.
2003    *Emergent forms of life and the anthropological voice.* Durham, NC: Duke University Press
2007    "Culture and cultural analysis as experimental systems", *Cultural Anthropology* 22(1):1–65

FOX, Richard G. and Andre GINGRICH (eds.)
2002    *Anthropology, by comparison.* London: Routledge

FOX, Richard G. and Barbara J. KING (eds.)
2002    *Anthropology beyond culture.* Oxford: Berg

FUKUYAMA, Francis
1989    "The end of history?", *The National Interest* Summer
1995    "Reflections on *The end of history*, five years later", *History and Theory* 34(2):27–43
2003    "How academia failed the nation: the decline of regional studies", *SAISphere* 2003. http://www.campus-watch.org/article/id/1507 (accessed July 16, 2010)

GEERTZ, Clifford
1968     *Islam observed: religious development in Morocco and Indonesia.* Chicago: University
         of Chicago Press
2000     *Available light: anthropological reflections on philosophical topics.* Princeton:
         Princeton University Press

GIBBONS, Michael, Camille LIMOGES, Helga NOWOTNY, Simon SCHWARTZMAN,
         Peter SCOTT, and Martin TROW
1994     *The new production of knowledge: the dynamics of science and research in
         contemporary societies.* London: Sage

GUESS, Andy
2007     "Downloading cultures", *InsideHigher Ed*, December 3.
         http://www.insidehighered.com/news/2007/12/03/newmedia (accessed July 12,
         2010)

GUYER, Jane I.
2007     "Prophecy and the near future: thoughts on macroeconomic, evangelical, and
         punctuated time", *American Ethnologist* 34(3):409–421

HANNERZ, Ulf
1990     "Cosmopolitans and locals in world culture", in: Mike Featherstone (ed.), *Global
         culture: nationalism, globalization, and modernity*, 237–252. London: Sage
1996     *Transnational connections: culture, people, places.* London: Routledge
1999     "Reflections on varieties of culturespeak", *European Journal of Cultural Studies*
         2(3):393–407
2003a    "Macro-scenarios: anthropology and the debate over contemporary and future
         worlds", *Social Anthropology* 11(2):169–187
2003b    "Being there ... and there ... and there! Reflections on multi-sited ethnography",
         *Ethnography* 4(2):201–216
2004     "Cosmopolitanism", in: David Nugent and Joan Vincent (eds.), *Companion to the
         anthropology of politics*, 69–85. Oxford: Blackwell
2008     "Scenarios for the twenty-first century world", *Asian Anthropology* 7:1–23
2010     *Anthropology's world: life in a twenty-first century discipline.* London: Pluto

HERZFELD, Michael
2001a    *Anthropology: theoretical practice in culture and society.* Malden, MA: Blackwell
2001b    "Performing comparisons: ethnography, globetrotting, and the spaces of social
         knowledge", *Journal of Anthropological Research* 57(3):259–276

INGOLD, Tim
2007     *Anthropology is not ethnography.* 2007 Radcliffe-Brown Lecture to the British
         Academy, London, March 14.

KELLY, Paul (ed.)
2002     *Multiculturalism reconsidered: "culture and equality" and its critics.* Cambridge:
         Polity

KNAUFT, Bruce K.
2006     "Anthropology in the middle", *Anthropological Theory* 6(4):407–430

KYMLICKA, Will
1995     *Multicultural citizenship: a liberal theory of minority rights*. Oxford: Clarendon

MACCLANCY, Jeremy
2005     "The literary image of anthropologists", *Journal of the Royal Anthropological Institute* 11(3):549–575

MACCLANCY, Jeremy (ed.)
2002     *Exotic no more: anthropology on the front lines*. Chicago: University of Chicago Press

MALINOWSKI, Bronislaw
1922     *Argonauts of the Western Pacific*. London: Routledge

MALKKI, Liisa H.
2001     "Figures of the future: dystopia and subjectivity in the social imagination of the future", in: Dorothy Holland and Jean Lave (eds.), *History in person: enduring struggles, contentious practice, intimate identities*, 325–348. Santa Fe, NM: School of American Research Press

MARCUS, George E. and Michael M. J. FISCHER
1986     *Anthropology as cultural critique: an experimental moment in the human sciences*. Chicago: University of Chicago Press

MAURER, Bill
2005     "Introduction to 'Ethnographic emergences'", *American Anthropologist* 107(1):1–4

MCCAIN, John
2007     "An enduring peace built on freedom: securing America's future", *Foreign Affairs* 86(6):19–34

MENAND, Louis
2010     *The marketplace of ideas: reform and resistance in the American university*. New York: Norton

MIYAZAKI, Hirokazu
2003     "The temporalities of the market", *American Anthropologist* 105(2):255–265

MOORE, Sally F.
2005     "Comparisons: possible and impossible", *Annual Review of Anthropology* 34:1–11

MURDOCK, George Peter
1949     *Social structure*. New York: Macmillan

MURPHY, Richard McG.
2005    "Pygmy hunters: why Microsoft (and others) are hiring anthropologists to study
        fast-growing little companies", *Fortune Small Business* 15(5):40–46

NEEDHAM, Rodney
1970    "The future of social anthropology: disintegration or metamorphosis?", in:
        *Anniversary contributions to anthropology: twelve essays*. Leiden: Brill

NOWOTNY, Helga, Peter SCOTT, and Michael GIBBONS
2001    *Re-thinking science: knowledge and the public in an age of uncertainty*. Cambridge:
        Polity

PAREKH, Bhikhu
2000    *Rethinking multiculturalism: cultural diversity and political theory*. London:
        Macmillan

PINA-CABRAL, João de
2006    "'Anthropology' challenged: notes for a debate", *Journal of the Royal Anthropological
        Institute* 12(3):663–673

RABINOW, Paul
2008    *Marking time: on the anthropology of the contemporary*. Princeton: Princeton
        University Press

RABINOW, Paul and George E. MARCUS, with James D. FAUBION and Tobias REES
2008    *Designs for an anthropology of the contemporary*. Durham, NC: Duke University
        Press

SAHLINS, Marshall
1993    *Waiting for Foucault*. Cambridge: Prickly Pear

SHAPIRO, Walter
2007    "Barack Obama is hip to Margaret Mead", *Salon.com*, November 28. http://www.
        salon.com/news/politics/roadies/2007/11/28/obama_vignette (accessed July 13,
        2010)

SONTAG, Susan
1966    *Against interpretation and other essays*. New York: Farrar, Straus and Giroux

STRATHERN, Marilyn (ed.)
2000    *Audit cultures: anthropological studies in accountability, ethics and the academy*.
        London: Routledge

TAYLOR, Charles
1992    *Multiculturalism and "the politics of recognition"*. Princeton: Princeton University
        Press

TIERNEY, Patrick
2002    *Darkness in El Dorado: how scientists and journalists devastated the Amazon.* New York: Norton

TUCHMAN, Gaye
2009    *Wannabe u: inside the corporate university.* Chicago: University of Chicago Press

WALLMAN, Sandra (ed.)
1992    *Contemporary futures: perspectives from social anthropology.* London: Routledge

WATERSTON, Alisse and Maria D. VESPERI (eds.)
2009    *Anthropology off the shelf: anthropologists on writing.* Malden, MA: Wiley-Blackwell

WILLIAMS, Rowan
2009    "Hail Mary: Rowan Williams on how the mother of Jesus became a global brand", *Financial Times*, February 15

WOLF, Eric R.
1964    *Anthropology.* Englewood Cliffs, NJ: Prentice-Hall

WOOD, Peter
2003    *Diversity: the invention of a concept.* San Francisco: Encounter Books

WORSLEY, Peter
1970    "The end of anthropology?", *Transactions of the sixth world congress of sociology.* Volume 3, 121–129. Louvain: International Sociological Association
2008    *An academic skating on thin ice.* Oxford: Berghahn

WRIGHT, Susan and Annika RABO
2010    "Introduction: anthropologies of university reform", *Social Anthropology* 18(1):1–82

# 9

# IN TODAY'S WORLD, ANTHROPOLOGY IS MORE IMPORTANT THAN EVER[*]

## Maurice Godelier

"The end of anthropology?" – This theme inspires a certain fear for some of our colleagues, for others, on the contrary, it expresses a hope. For me – and I am not alone – the problem is already behind us.

But whatever our reaction, the question itself grew out of the fact that, for a number of years, beginning somewhere in the 1980s in anthropology and slightly earlier in the literary disciplines, the social sciences and the humanities entered a period of crisis which called into question their concepts, methods and, more fundamentally, their legitimacy. Some of our colleagues denied that the work of the anthropologists who had gone before lacked any scientific authority, as did their own work before they became aware of the fictitious and ideological character of the 'narrations' constructed by Western anthropologists to disseminate what they claimed to have understood about other forms of culture and society.[1]

For the crucial question that anthropology, history, archaeology and other social sciences have struggled to answer since the beginning is: How can we come to understand and explain the existence of facts, attitudes and representations that have never been part of our own ways of living and thinking?

Obviously this question is not restricted to scientific knowledge alone: it arises every time that, for various reasons, human individuals or groups are brought to interact with other individuals or groups from different social classes within their own society or from societies that are profoundly different from their own.[2] Understanding the otherness of others means discovering the meanings and the reasons behind the forms of thought and lifestyles of those who are different from you. It means discovering what relations these others have among themselves, what positions they occupy in them and how they represent them. But understanding is not explaining. To explain means seeking to discover how the different social ways of existing we have managed to understand appeared here and there over time and were reproduced – sometimes over several centuries, and sometimes over several

---

[*]  Translated from the French by Nora Scott.

[1]  The so-called 'writing culture debate' is also referred to by Crapanzano, Kohl, Jebens and Münzel in the present collection.

[2]  On cultural difference and critique, see also the contributions by Crapanzano, Kohl, and Jebens in the present collection.

millennia – even as they changed, sometimes profoundly, for example, the world's great religions, Buddhism, Christianity, Islam.

From Lewis Henry Morgan to Claude Lévi-Strauss, from Bronislaw Malinowski to Marshall Sahlins, anthropologists believed that, with the help of their concepts and methods, it was possible to gain knowledge of the social and cultural otherness of others at a distance, which would therefore be relatively objective. And each believed he was contributing to this in his own way. But it was precisely this claim to knowledge and this faith in the methods, concepts and theories that were developed to achieve it that some of us began to contest in the 1980s, thus setting off a crisis that was far from being wholly negative, as we shall see. Why this challenge and the resulting crisis? A look at the context of the 1980s may help us answer this question.

In 1945, Europe emerged victorious from a war with Nazi Germany, fascist Italy and imperialist Japan that had bled it white and made the United States the first world power, ahead of Soviet Russia. It was in this new balance of power that, between 1955 and 1970, the last European colonial empires disappeared one by one, either in the wake of bloody wars of liberation or more peacefully. From then on it was no longer possible to say that colonising meant civilising and that civilising meant helping other people advance more quickly on the path towards the progress already achieved by the West. Liberated from direct domination by the European powers, the former colonies, now independent nations, took a different path to development. Between 1980 and 1990 another global upheaval occurred in the form of the accelerated disintegration and then long-awaited collapse of the communist regimes that had been set up after World War II in Central and Eastern Europe, as well as in Asia, the Far East, Africa and Cuba. Today, only a few shreds of that experience remain. These two upheavals profoundly modified the West's relations with the rest of the world, but also with itself, and they would go on to shake the intellectual world that grew up in Europe and the United States after the Second World War.

In effect, after the First World War, the Russian Revolution represented to many intellectuals – and not only to intellectuals – the birth of a new world and a new kind of man, the next stage in the progress of humanity. This progress was to consist in doing away with the capitalist economic market, the exploitation of human labour and the wasting of the natural resources that underpinned this system. But it also meant replacing the so-called 'bourgeois' forms of democracy serving the propertied classes with a higher form of democracy that would serve the people. In short, once again the West – but another West – held itself up as the measure and mirror of human progress.

It must be recalled here that the West is not singular, but plural, and that it was the West itself that spawned the critique of the economic and political systems that gave it its strength. It is therefore understandable that, at the end of the Second World War – in which Stalin's Russia fought on the side of the Allies and greatly contributed to their victory, before the socialist regimes showed themselves for what they were, dictatorships that exploited the masses – the dominant intellectual trends in the social sciences and philosophy, at least in France, were Marxism (as in the work of Althusser), structuralism (as in the work of Lévi-Strauss) and existentialism (as in the work of Sartre). Sartre's position on the inalienable liberty of the individual opposed him to the Marxists and to Lévi-Strauss's structuralism, which argued for the existence of impersonal structures – whether conscious or unconscious – and their structural consequences. In the political arena, however, Sartre rapidly rallied to the partisans of revolution to bring down the bourgeois order.

The successive disappearance of the colonial empires and the socialist regimes shook the European intelligentsia and sparked a crisis that brought us into – to use the term coined by Jean-François Lyotard (1979) – the 'postmodern condition'. For Lyotard, this new condition meant two things for thinkers. First it meant the death of all 'meta-narratives', in other words, of explanations of history and of the complex diversity of societies in terms of a first cause that was effective in the last analysis, such as the Marxist notion of 'modes of production' or the Lévi-Straussian 'unconscious structures of the mind'. And second, the postmodern condition necessarily meant a return to the subject as an agent of history. This was illustrated in France by the second part of Michel Foucault's work, which, having joined Althusser and Lévi-Strauss in proclaiming the 'death of the subject', he devoted to analyzing the subjectification of individuals in various institutions structured by relations of power (Foucault 2001, 2008, 2009). Having come this far, it seemed clear that the next urgent task of theory was to 'deconstruct' – to quote Jacques Derrida (1991) – all of the former discourses found in philosophy and the social and human sciences.

There is in itself nothing surprising about deconstructing a discipline. It is a necessary and normal moment in the development of all sciences, natural as well as social. It is something that has to be done following the appearance of new ways of interpreting well-known facts, or in the face of new facts. But there are two ways to deconstruct a discipline. One leads to its dissolution and eventual disappearance; the other – based on the positive critiques produced during the deconstruction process – paves the way for the reconstruction of this same discipline on new foundations which are more rigorous, more critical and therefore analytically more effective than they were before.

It is therefore indispensable to point out a few of these positive criticisms of anthropology, since they already enable us to begin rebuilding. Furthermore, the very existence of these critiques shows that we must not confuse all of the publications and authors that fly the postmodernist flag. George Marcus is not Paul Rabinow, James Clifford is not Vincent Crapanzano, and Stephen Tyler is not Michael Fischer. And none of them were Clifford Geertz, who inspired them. Each is only himself. But before listing some of these results, I feel it is important to show that the theme of "The end of anthropology" itself falls into the first way of deconstructing a discipline, that which leads to its disappearance.

How, in effect, can a scientific discipline disappear? In two ways. A discipline can disappear because its very 'object' ceases to exist; or because, although its object still exists, the discipline that claimed to bring us to know it proved incapable of doing so. Let us consider the first possibility. Has the object of anthropology disappeared? The Nuer, the Kachin, the Tikiopia and the Baruya have not disappeared. They exist. But their societies and their ways of living and thinking changed under colonial rule and are still changing. But does a science disappear merely because its objects evolve? If this were so, the discipline of history would have ceased to exist long ago, since all the past societies it studies have either disappeared or still exist but in completely different forms. Should anthropology disappear simply because, for instance, a large portion of Trobriand Islanders now live in New Zealand or in Los Angeles? This would implicitly presuppose that anthropology has no object other than so-called 'primitive', 'traditional', 'pre-industrial', 'non-urban' or 'non-Western' societies. In effect, this presupposition is an ideological a priori that anthropology was already forced to combat at the time of the publication of Lewis Henry Morgan's "Ancient society" (1985), in which the author divided all known societies into three stages located along a scale of human progress that went from 'savage' to 'barbaric' to 'civilised'. The latter, of course, was represented in Morgan's eyes by European and North American societies, at last liberated from the feudal regimes of the Middle Ages and borne up by the forces of modern market, industrial civilisation and democracy. The development of urban anthropology, gender studies and medical anthropology show that this is far from being the case.

Let us now look at the second reason that might cause the disappearance of our discipline. As I have already noted, the question asked by anthropology, history and other social sciences is the same: how can we come to understand and explain the existence of what has never been part of our own way of living and thinking? The argument no longer concerns the disappearance of the object of anthropology but the inability of anthropology to exist as a science. Proponents of this criticism argue that, since it came into being, anthropology has done nothing but produce ethnographic accounts that are no more than the projections of the ideologies of Western observers onto the societies they study. Two critical positions can be found in this line of thought. The first is that held by George Marcus, who nonetheless tendered the hope of a 'new ethnography';[3] the second is the radically critical position of Stephen Tyler (1986), who disputes that a new ethnography is even possible. For

---

[3]     On 'multi-sited ethnography', see also the contributions by Crapanzano, Jebens and Kohl in the present collection.

Marcus and Clifford, the ethnographies written by Malinowski, Edmund Leach, Edward E. Evans-Pritchard and the like were above all 'narrative fictions' (Clifford 1984) written with the complicity of the two parties engaged in getting to know another society – the ethnologist and his informant – and in producing 'fictions that each side accepts' (Marcus 1998:110). Marcus, however, believes that we can do otherwise and better. For Stephen Tyler, on the other hand, all ethnographic accounts are fated to be merely a 'reality fantasy of a fantasy reality' (1986:139). In his opinion, anthropology as a science was still-born, for any ethnographic account is 'neither an object to be represented nor the representation of an object [...] no object of any kind precedes and constrains ethnography. Ethnography creates its own objects in its unfolding and the reader supplies the rest' (Tyler 1986:131). Here we recognise the theoretical position of Derrida and Paul de Man, for whom it was mandatory to 'deconstruct the illusion of reference, the possibility that a text could refer to a non-textual reality' (de Man 1986:19–20). Yet it is difficult to believe that the events and practices of other societies reported by anthropologists were all hallucinations (a fantasy reality) and that, for example, the attacks of 11 September 2001, claimed by Bin Laden and al-Qa'ida, were no more than a TV show (a reality fantasy).

I suggest that most of these criticisms bear on a single aspect of the anthropologist's trade, on the moment the anthropologist attempts to give a written account of his fieldwork and subsequent analyses. Clifford's criticism of ethnological monographs is at odds with reality. Indeed, an ethnographic monograph is not a literary work (though it may have literary qualities), and there are two reasons for this. Unlike Macbeth, a character sprung from the mind of Shakespeare, the *kula* existed before Malinowski landed in Kiriwina and continued to exist after he left. The second reason is that no one can complete or refute Shakespeare's work, whereas the studies carried out by Fred Damon, Nancy Munn, Annette Weiner and others, fifty years after Malinowski, completed, enriched and corrected his analysis of the *kula*. By contrast, curiously enough, there are two essential moments in the anthropologist's trade that have not been the object of fundamental criticism: the period in the field known as 'participant observation', and the moment when the anthropologist sits down to work out the interpretation of his or her field-notes, a time that begins in the field but continues beyond it. Perhaps these omissions can be attributed to the fact that Clifford, who was so critical of the ways others had of 'writing culture', never conducted fieldwork himself. But let us leave Tyler's provocations and Marcus's exaggerations to consider a few positive consequences yielded by the critiques of our 'postmodern' colleagues.

One very important result is to have pointed out the absence – or near absence – in the publications of numerous anthropologists of any analysis of the colonial relations being inflicted on indigenous populations even as they were carrying out their fieldwork with them. Evans-Pritchard, for example, hardly alludes to the arrival of British troops to subdue the tribes near where he was working. That does not necessarily mean that Evans-Pritchard was an agent of colonialism, nor that what he wrote about Nuer kinship and the political structures was false. Nor have all anthropologists passed over the colonial context of their work in silence. Take, for example, Raymond Firth (1967), who is clear about what was happening in Tikopia, or Germaine Tillion (1957, 2007), who worked in Algeria at the height of the colonial war, which she criticised publicly in France. Anthropologists were also right to point to the presuppositions underlying the notions of 'progress' and 'civilisation', especially since the Western ideology of progress is not dead. This ideology has simply mutated into the ideology of human rights, which provides Westerners and their allies with new reasons to judge other societies and to interfere in their own way of life. On all these points, subaltern and post-colonial studies have picked up where the first critiques left off, and they have made considerable contributions.[4]

Another important point was the appeal launched by George Marcus and others that anthropological texts speak with a plurality of voices, not only that of the anthropologist. Of course there was a risk that all these voices would then claim to be equally valid and the anthropologist would have nothing specific to add that would give him any particular weight in this concert. Other critiques arose not from the changing balance of power and interests between the West and the Rest, but from the struggles occurring within Western countries themselves, which also contributed to showing the work of our forbears in another light. I am talking about the criticisms – which developed first in the United States and the other Anglo-Saxon countries – of all the forms of discrimination, segregation and exclusion found in our societies, and also in the rest of the world for reasons of sex, skin colour, religion, etc. These forms of discrimination are not necessarily perceived as such in other societies, as for example in Islamic societies, where the fact that women are subordinated to men is considered to be grounded in religious principles. In the West, such views are now criticised in the name of the equality of all human beings before the law. This idea was certainly not present at the beginning of social life in caste-based India, in the Islamic world or in Baruya society,[5] and it is still not accepted in many aspects of European social life. Clifford made a useful contribution on this point when he showed that, in the otherwise remarkable book by Godfrey Lienhardt, "Divinity and experience: the religion of the Dinka" (1961), women did not appear except for one occasion when a woman explained to the

---

[4]    See Ludden (2001) and, for a critical overview, Pouchepadass (2004).

[5]    'Baruya' is the name of a tribe living in the highlands of Papua New Guinea. 'Discovered' in 1951 by James Sinclair, they were known as famous salt makers. The group was divided into 15 patrilineal clans, eight of them being descendents of Yoyué people, who took refuge among the Andje and lately conquered the territory of their hosts. The Baruya are known for their male initiation rituals. I have done fieldwork among them during seven years between 1967 and 1981 (cf. Godelier 1982).

anthropologist what cattle meant to men. This is probably a case of *androcentrisme*, but it is also notoriously difficult in certain societies for a male anthropologist to enter into contact with women.

A final point in this retrospective of positive contributions made by postmodern criticism: postmodernists have strongly contributed to the rejection of any essentialist interpretation of the otherness of others. This is not a new criticism. In the first decade of the twentieth century, Franz Boas (1920) had already shown that Northwest American Indian societies were open to and borrowed from each other: they were by no means totalities closed in around their essence. This is not to say that there are not dominant aspects of culture and organisation in all societies that are borne by their members as chief components of their identity and experienced as such. And it is easily understood that these dominant aspects do not vanish in a day, since they are largely responsible for the very reproduction of these societies.

In short, there is nothing in all of these criticisms to indicate that we are going through what Sahlins calls the 'the twilight of anthropology'.[6] The conclusion is clear: we must keep on deconstructing, but so as to reconstruct the discipline on foundations that are better equipped to meet the challenges of the globalised world in which we will live and work in the twenty-first century.

I would like finally to return to the question I raised at the outset – How can we come to understand the otherness of others? – and to show how and why I believe anthropology is now better able to provide an answer than it was in the past, but on certain conditions. First, the social and historical otherness of others must be relative and not absolute. Next, others must be capable of understanding what humans invented for the purpose of interpreting the world around them and themselves within this world, and therefore for the purpose of acting on the world as well as on themselves – whether this cultural invention be the Aboriginal 'Dreamtime', Mahayana Buddhism or Marxism. It is also essential to stress that, while humans can understand the social otherness of other humans, they are not obliged to espouse the principles and values that produced this otherness, nor are they obliged to practice them themselves. Anyone can verify in his own experience of others that these two conditions exist in a very real way and that they invalidate the theses of those who argue for a fundamental incommunicability between cultures. To be an anthropologist is to exercise a profession that entails the production of verifiable and therefore refutable knowledge; the anthropologist's aim and methods are not those of the missionary, the soldier or the merchant, who intervene in societies that are not theirs. And to exercise his profession, it is not enough that the otherness of others be knowable – the anthropologist has to acquire the means to learn about this otherness.

---

6 Anthropologists' ideas about the imminent decline of their discipline are also referred to by Crapanzano, Jebens, Kohl and Münzel in the present collection.

To do so, he must begin by constructing his own cognitive ego, which is different from his social ego and his intimate ego. The social ego can be inherited from birth – one is the son or daughter of a Brahmin, for example – or constructed over the course of a lifetime. The intimate ego is fashioned from birth by pleasant or painful encounters with others. This is the ego of desires, pleasures and sufferings, the ego that fashions a sensibility; it is also a way of being with others. Of course the social ego and the intimate ego are inextricably intertwined, and in this the anthropologist is no different from other people. What distinguishes the anthropologist is the fact that he must construct yet another ego, the cognitive ego just mentioned.

The cognitive ego is first of all an intellectual ego that is put together before leaving for the field from mental components – concepts, theories, discussions, controversies – acquired at the university or elsewhere and bearing the mark of their time. At one time one is readily a structuralist, at another a post-structuralist. But whatever the epoch, the cognitive ego is an ego which must learn to decentre itself with respect to the other egos. Yet at the same time the cognitive ego is also an ethical and political ego that must maintain a state of critical vigilance against the ever-possible intrusion of the judgments that the anthropologist's own society has already formulated about other societies. To decentre oneself is also to suspend one's own judgment, to push back to the very horizon of consciousness the presuppositions of one's own culture and society, including those of one's own life story.

But the cognitive ego is not made up of ideas alone. The anthropologist must engage in a practice called participant observation, in the course of which he immerses himself in another society or another social milieu so as to study and understand them. But this raises a formidable problem that has remained unspoken in the criticisms addressed to anthropology: what does it mean to 'observe' and to observe while 'participating', and what is one supposed to participate in and to what extent? Participating in the life of others is not at all the same thing as going hunting a few times with a group of Inuit and helping to feed oneself and others on those days. To claim to be really 'participating' in the life of others, the anthropologist would have to 'behave like the others', to marry into the society, to have children and raise them, to take part in their rites. The great majority of anthropologists do not do these things, and it is not necessary for them to do so in order to understand the ways those with whom they live think and act. There is a fundamental difference between the anthropologist and those with whom he lives when it comes to how he uses what he gradually learns about the principles guiding their thinking and acting. For the members of the surrounding society, the knowledge they have of their myths, their rites, their kinship rules, the habits of the game they hunt, etc. serves to produce their concrete conditions of existence and thereby to reproduce – up to a certain point – their society. This goes on day in and day out. For the anthropologist conversely, the knowledge he has worked so hard to acquire and which is never complete almost never serves to produce the concrete conditions of his own existence in the society in which he has immersed himself. To be sure it serves to understand others, but not to act and interact as they do on all occasions. For as he accumulates this knowledge, at the same time the anthropologist produces himself as an anthropologist, a status that endows him with a position in his own society. This sheds some light on the nature of the place the anthropologist occupies when he is in the field. It is a place that he must construct, and this is difficult: it is a place that puts him at the same time outside and inside his own society, but also inside and at the same time outside the society in which he has chosen to live.[7] This place is thus at once concrete and abstract, which makes the presence and the work of the anthropologist an original experience of the relationship a man or a woman can have with others and with him- or herself.

Whatever the limits of his participation in the life of others may be, it is in this context that the anthropologist observes them. But just what does he observe? In principle all of the interactions that go on around him, in the most diverse concrete situations, between the individuals and groups that make up the society in which he has chosen to live and work. To be sure, he does not observe the whole society, but his field of observation is structured by several kinds of events which are most enlightening. Certain recurring and predictable events are continually offered to his observing gaze: people get up, eat, go hunting or into the fields, come home, go to bed, and so on. Other events occur that are not repetitive, but which are up to a certain point predictable, such as a hunting accident or a murder and its aftermath. Last of all, there are cyclical events that come around again after several years and which concern all members of the society: the Baruya's male and female initiations, for instance. And yet, alongside these events – which in a sense are offered up for observation – the anthropologist also has to make use of observations that he has prompted by launching systematic large-scale studies and surveys, which can last for months and bear on different aspects of the social life of others, such as their agricultural practices, their initiation rites, forms of land-holding, land use and use of territory. When the field data are cross-checked, they produce results and discoveries that often surprise the anthropologist and contribute to giving him an even better understanding of the logic behind the ways the people around him think and act.

When these observations have been gathered – something that can take years – they must be interpreted and then disseminated. The anthropologist must then move on to other forms and levels of work. He must, for example, compare his data with those gathered by anthropologists in other societies. For instance, when I realised that the Baruya used an Iroquois-type kinship terminology – and since I knew that the same type of terminology in Iroquois society was associated with a

---

7       On the 'in-betweenness' of the anthropologist, see also the contributions by Crapanzano, Kohl and Jebens in the present collection.

matrilineal descent rule, whereas in Baruya society it is associated with a patrilineal descent rule – I was led to ask myself some theoretical questions concerning the conditions in which Iroquois-type kinship systems appeared and how they came to be distributed over several continents (Godelier 2004). These theoretical questions came to me, but they were of no interest to the Baruya. Of what practical use would it be to the Baruya to know that they have the same kinship terminology as certain Indians in North America? It might have interested some of the Baruya who had already been to university, or were interested in European or other societies. But aside from a very limited impact, this anthropological concern – entirely legitimate from the standpoint of the effort to learn about human modes of existence – does not mesh with any of the Baruya's existential problems.

This analysis of the difference between the knowledge shared by the actors themselves and that possessed by the anthropologist makes it clear that, for the actors, this concrete knowledge is an existential truth, whereas for the anthropologist it is abstract knowledge that will become the material he will use to try to construct some scientific truths. The discovery that the Baruya have a patrilineal kinship system which uses an Iroquois-type terminology allows us to understand how and why the notions of mother, father, sister, brother or cousin are different for them than for someone from the West. In effect, if all of my father's brothers are also my fathers, and if all of my mother's sisters are my mothers, if all of their children are my brothers and sisters, then when my mother's husband dies I still have other fathers. And if I do not have a sister to give in exchange for a wife, I have the right and therefore the possibility to exchange my father's brothers' daughters, because they too are my sisters. Confronted with any number of problems, by the very nature of his kinship system a Baruya has at his disposal a network of solidarity and mutual assistance that we do not have. And that is something the anthropologist can observe and verify.

However much these essential truths may differ from one society to the next, they are nevertheless all attempts to answer existential questions, which, indeed, are present in all societies, although in specific forms. Humans, always and everywhere, have endeavoured to understand what it means to be born, to live and to die. Everywhere they have thought about the kinds of power they could legitimately wield over themselves or over others. Everywhere they have been concerned to define the relations humans are supposed to have with their ancestors, with nature spirits, with the gods or with God. Everywhere they have been concerned to give meaning to their environment: mountains, forest, sea, etc. And everywhere they have assigned a sense to the inequalities they have established between the sexes, between the castes, and so on, whether in order to legitimise them or to challenge them. In short, one of the objects of anthropology – and of history, too, in fact – is to compare these cultural and social answers and to explain, if possible, the conditions of their appearance and disappearance over space and time. These are levels of the theoretical work that go beyond the anthropologist's singular experience of a society in the field.

To conclude, I would like to use my personal experience to illustrate what I have learned from my efforts to deconstruct and reconstruct anthropology. When I undertook to deconstruct a few self-evident anthropological truths, I came to realise that some of these celebrated truths were now dead for me personally. I showed that nowhere are kinship relations, and even less the family, the basis of societies. This conclusion is valid for all societies, even those without classes or castes – which seemed to be proof to the contrary – and which the textbooks called 'kin-based societies'.

When I began researching kinship systems and their past or recent metamorphoses, I also looked at an aspect that is usually neglected: the way societies, in accordance with their kinship systems and their descent rules – unilineal, bilineal or undifferentiated – represent the way children are made, from the time of their conception. I therefore compared such representations from twenty-two societies in Oceania, Africa, Asia and North America as well as the European Christian view. To my great surprise, I found that all of these societies, despite their different kinship systems, had one point in common: all, in one form or another, maintained that sexual intercourse between a man and a woman was not enough to make a child. What they made with their semen (the Baruya) or with their menstrual blood (the Trobriand Islanders) was a foetus; but for this foetus to become a child, it always took the intervention of other invisible and more powerful agents such as ancestors who were reincarnated in the child's body (Inuit, Trobriand Islanders) or the Christian God who at a time of his choosing introduces a soul into the child's body (Godelier 2004:301).

In other circumstances I was led to re-examine Marcel Mauss's famous analysis of the gift, revisited and criticised by Lévi-Strauss (Godelier 1996). In the process, I discovered that, alongside things one sells and gives, there are also things that Mauss and Lévi-Strauss neglected to analyse, namely things that must be neither sold nor given, but must be kept and passed on to later generations. This third category of 'things' always bears a major aspect of the identity of human groups. They belong to what we call the domain of the 'sacred', but we must be careful here: the sacred extends beyond the religious domain to include the political. In our democratic societies, the constitution, which sets down the rules that enable millions of people to live together, is an object that can be neither sold nor bought; the constitution itself is not a commodity. What can be bought, however, are electoral votes. The existence of this area of life which does not fall into the categories of either commercial exchanges or exchanges of gifts and counter-gifts – equivalent or not – shows the limits of Lévi-Strauss's (and others') claims that social life rests entirely on exchange: the exchange of women, of wealth and services, of signs and of meanings – in other words, kinship, economy and culture. In fact, they had simply forgotten that, in order for things to be exchanged and to circulate, there had to be other things that did not circulate and could not be exchanged.

These analyses then led me to raise two problems, which turned out to be connected. One was the presence and the role at the heart of all social relations of imaginary cores. An example from kinship: patrilineal societies claim that the man's semen makes the body of the foetus and that the woman is a mere vessel for this semen. Conversely, Trobriand Islanders maintain that the semen does not make the body of the foetus, which is the job of the mother's menstrual blood. The Baruya claim that it was the sun that gave the ancestor of the Kwarrandiar clan the *kwaimatnie*, the sacred objects and secret formulas that allow them to initiate their boys and turn them into warriors (Godelier 2004:255–269).

Of course, all these stories refer to facts that we regard as imaginary and that are enacted in the initiation rites that constitute symbolic practices which transmute imaginary facts into real social relations in which individuals occupy distinct but interconnected positions according to sex, age, or their capacity to become great warriors or shamans. Contrary to Lévi-Strauss, but in line with Geertz, what we are looking at here is not the primacy of the symbolic but the primacy of the imaginary by means of the symbolic.

The Baruya case raised another problem, but at the same time suggested an answer. According to Baruya tradition and my own calculations, their society appeared recently, somewhere around the eighteenth century. It originated with a group of men and women from several clans of one tribe, the Yoyué, who, fleeing a massacre, found refuge and succour with the Andjé, a tribe living a few days' walk away. Several generations later, the refugees' descendants massacred their hosts and took over part of their territory, where they built their own initiation house and initiated their own boys. In this case it is clear that it was neither the kinship relations nor the economic relations between individuals and groups that made them into a society. It was what we in the West would call political-religious relations: 'religious' because, in the course of the initiations, the gods and the ancestors work together with the initiation masters to initiate the boys; 'political' because the initiations are believed to cleanse the boys of what they have received from women and to prepare them to govern their society without them. In short, it is these political-religious relations that establish and legitimise the sovereignty the Baruya exercise over their territory, the boundaries of which are known if not recognised by the neighbouring tribes.

I shall pass over the example of Tikopia. According to the traditions reported by Firth, Tikopia was invaded by groups from other islands – Ontong Java, Pukapuka, Rotuma, Anuta, etc. – which engaged in constant battles until the clan ancestor of the Kafika instituted rites in which each group had its function and place and which made them into a society. The founding ancestor having been assassinated by a rival, the gods of Polynesia changed him into an *atua*, a god of the Island of Tikopia, and his direct descendants thus came to have first place in the rites because their bodies now possessed the *mana* of a god. In Tikopia too, then, it was political-religious relations that welded the various non-related human groups into a society (Firth 1967:15–30).

A last example will bring us up to the present century and to the globalised world in which we are now practising our trade. Saudi Arabia is a state that did not exist at the beginning of the eighteenth century. It arose between 1740 and 1742 from the joint ambitions of two men: Muhammad 'Abd al-Wahhab and Muhammad Ibn as-Sa'ud. The first was a religious reformer and member of a tribal confederation that had expelled him when he called for a *jihad* against what he considered to be the bad Muslims who populated the holy places of Islam, Mecca and Medina. In the same vein as Hanbalism, one of the four schools of law within Sunni Islam that emerged in the ninth century, Muhammad 'Abd al-Wahhab was opposed to all innovation, all personal interpretation of the Qur'an, and wanted to force all Muslims to return to the traditions of the early believers. The other figure in this story, Muhammad Ibn as-Sa'ud, an ambitious tribal chief and ruler of the small Nadj city of al-Dir'iya in central Arabia, aspired to bring all of the surrounding tribes under his rule. But in the Muslim world this also required religious legitimacy. This was provided by the preacher Muhammad 'Abd al-Wahhab and his call to *jihad*, for which he needed the support of a political and military power. The meeting between the two men resulted in the alliance of two types of social power – the religious and the political – and in the birth of the first Saudi state and the taking of Mecca and Medina in 1802–1804. Wahhabism became the state religion at that time (al-Rasheed 2002, Vassiliev 2002).

Now let us fast-forward a century and a half. In 1938 oil was discovered in Saudi Arabia, which found itself in possession of a quarter of the world's reserves. In 1945, Franklin Roosevelt signed a treaty with the Saudi king in which the United States promised to defend the kingdom against neighbouring Iraq and Iran in exchange for its oil. In 1979, under Ayatollah Khomeini, Iran, with Shi'a Islam as its official religion, became the first Islamic republic, and the Russians invaded Afghanistan. Thousands of Muslim volunteers, among them Osama Bin Laden, armed by the Americans and funded by Saudi Arabia, spent a decade battling the Russian army, forcing them to withdraw from Afghanistan in 1989. After the Russian departure came the Taliban and al-Qa'ida ('the Base'), which was created to launch *jihad* no longer just against bad Muslims, as in the eighteenth century, but against Jews, Christians and the materialistic West in general that had been humiliating and exploiting Arabs and Muslims since the nineteenth century.

Once again, neither kinship relations nor economic relations explain the formation of this new society. The economy of the eighteenth-century central Arabian tribes did not in itself drive the formation of a state, no more than did the kinship relations found in the tribes or tribal confederations – although once the state began to take shape, marriages and alliances between the great 'houses' and tribes bolstered the power of the as-Sa'ud dynasty (Godelier 2007:221–248).

This is where we stand today. After 9/11, which once again upset the balance of power in the world, we saw the U.S. fail in its intervention in Iraq and lose its global political hegemony. Other peoples and other nations – China, India, Russia – are now bringing their own influence to bear on relations between the West and the Rest, though this may not mean the death of capitalism, but rather a new opportunity for a multitude of local societies to re-affirm or re-invent their cultural and political identities. As economies find themselves ever more closely integrated into the capitalist market system, an opposite trend is prompting the segmentation of political regimes and resistance from local identities.

Nothing in this process seems to predict the approaching death of anthropology. On the contrary, anthropology – together with history – is one of the social science disciplines that is best able to help us understand the complexity of our now globalised world and the nature of the conflicts and the crisis we are experiencing. In such a world, it would be irresponsible and indecent for anthropologists to stop trying to understand others – and themselves at the same time – and making their results known. After all, that is our job.

## References

AL-RASHEED, Madawi
2002    *A history of Saudi Arabia.* Cambridge: Cambridge University Press

BOAS, Franz
1920    "The method of anthropology", *American Anthropologist* 22:311–321

CLIFFORD, James
1984    "De l'ethnographie comme fiction. Conrad et Malinowski", *Etudes rurales* 97/98
1986    "Partial truths", in: James Clifford and George Marcus (eds.), *Writing culture: the poetics and politics of ethnography*, 1–26. Berkeley: University of California Press

CLIFFORD, James and George E. Marcus (eds.)
1986    *Writing culture: the poetics and politics of ethnography.* Berkeley: University of California Press

CUSSET, François
2003    *French theory.* Foucault, Derrida, Deleuze & Cie et les mutations de la vie intellectuelle aux Etats-Unis. Paris: Editions La Découverte

DERRIDA, Jacques
1991    *Donner le temps.* Paris: Gallilée

FIRTH, Raymond
1967    *Tikopia ritual and belief*. Boston: Beacon Press

FOUCAULT, Michel
2001    *L'Herméneutique du sujet*. Paris: Gallimard
2008    *Le Gouvernement de soi et des autres*. Volume 1. Paris: Gallimard
2009    *Le Gouvernement de soi et des autres*. Volume 2: Le Courage de la vérité. Paris: Gallimard

GEERTZ, Clifford
1973    *The interpretation of cultures*. New York: Basic Books
1988    *Works and lives: the anthropologist as author*. Stanford: Stanford University Press.

GODELIER, Maurice
1982    *La Production des Grands Hommes*. Pouvoir et domination masculine chez les Baruya de Nouvelle Guinée. Paris: Fayard
1996    *L'Enigme du Don*. Paris: Fayard
2004    *Métamorphoses de la Parenté*. Paris: Fayard
2007    *Au Fondement des Sociétés Humaines*. Ce que nous apprend l'anthropologie. Paris: Albin Michel
2009    *In and out of the West: reconstructing anthropology*. Charlottesville: University of Virginia Press

GODELIER, Maurice and Marilyn STRATHERN
1991    *Big man and great man: personifications of power in Melanesia*. Cambridge: Cambridge University Press

LIENHARDT, Godfrey
1961    *Divinity and experience: the religion of the Dinka*. Oxford: Oxford University Press

LUDDEN, David (ed.)
2001    *Reading subaltern studies: critical history, contested meaning and the globalization of South Asia*. New Delhi: Permanent Black

LYOTARD, J.F.
1979    *La condition post-moderne*. Paris: Editions de Minuit

MALINOWSKI, Bronislaw
1927    *The father in primitive psychology*. New York: Norton

MAN, Paul de
1979    *Deconstruction and criticism*. New York: Seabury Press
1986    *The resistance to theory*. Minneapolis: University of Minnesota Press

MARCUS, George E.
1998    *Ethnography through thick and thin*. Princeton: Princeton University Press

MARCUS, George and Michael FISCHER

1986    *Anthropology as cultural critique: an experimental moment in the human sciences.*
        Chicago. University of Chicago Press

MORGAN, Henry Lewis

1871    *Systems of consanguinity and affinity of the human family.* Washington D.C.:
        Smithsonian Institution (Smithsonian Contributions to Knowledge 218.)

1985    *Ancient society, or researches in the lines of human progress from savagery through
        barbarism to civilization.* Reprint with a foreword by Elisabeth Tooker. Tucson:
        University of Arizona Press ([1]1877)

POUCHEPADASS, Jacques

2004    "Que reste-t-il des Subaltern Studies?", *Critique internationale* 24:67–79

SAHLINS, Marshall

1999a   "Two or three things that I know about culture", *The Journal of the Royal
        Anthropological Institute* 3:399–421

1999b   "What is anthropological enlightenment? Some lessons of the twentieth century",
        *Annual Review of Anthropology* 28:i–xxiii

SALADIN D'ANGLURE, Bernard

1986    "Du phoetus au shamane, la construction d'un troisième sexe Inuit", *Etudes Inuit*
        10(102):25–113

1980    "'Petit-ventre', l'enfant géant du cosmos Inuit", *L'Homme* 20(1):7–46

TILLION, Germaine

1957    *L'Algérie en 1957.* Paris: Editions de Minuit.

2007    *Combats de guerre et de paix.* Paris: Editions du Seuil

TYLER, Stephen

1986    "From document of the occult to occult document", in: James Clifford and George
        E. Marcus (eds.), *Writing culture: the poetics and politics of ethnography*, 122–140.
        Berkeley: University of California Press

VASSILIEV, Alexei

2002    *The history of Saudi Arabia.* London: Saqi Books

**10**

THE END[*]

Mark Münzel

> Where is the lighthearted youth,
> whose bright laughter echoed in the dense brushwoods?
> Where are the people who, adapted to these barren lands,
> enlivened the monotonous landscape?
> They are all gone, they have all been destroyed [...]
> The restless waves of Cape Horn alone
> sing the dead Indians a wailful dirge.[1]

This paper was delivered as one of the 2008 Jensen Memorial Lectures, the title of which contained a printing error: a question mark following 'the end'. It is the metaphor of the end which endows anthropology with a particular literary quality that other disciplines have lost in all their optimism. The discipline's proximity to the genre of *belles lettres* has allowed it repeatedly to revitalise this heuristically very fruitful figure of speech. Most of the contributions to this collection have not sought to declare anthropology dead, but on the contrary, to stress its merits and argue for its continued importance, even necessity. I would like to do the same. However, I do not wish to bury talk of the end. Instead, I would rather like to stress its value as a future-oriented part of the great tradition of anthropology as literature. In line with this tradition, I fear that I must soon lament an imminent end of another sort as well: that of the poetic laments of the end of anthropology.

This is also true, to some extent, for other scientific disciplines in which a certain sense of style was relevant in the past. One example of this lost utopia of good scientific writing, the end of which I bemoan, is to be found in the archives of the Königliche Preußische Akademie der Wissenschaften in Berlin and dates from 1837. It is interesting to read the criteria on the basis of which the submissions for an essay contest in the Philosophical and Historical Section, on the *mouseion* of ancient Alexandria, were to be evaluated. Besides accuracy, consistency and

---

[*]    Translated from the German by Andreas Hemming. I wish to thank the Spanish research project "Cuerpo y sentimiento. Expresiones culturales Amerindas" in the frame of which I was able to discuss and develop some of the ideas of this chapter.

[1]    Martin Gusinde: Urmenschen in Feuerland. Vom Forscher zum Stammesmitglied. Berlin, Vienna, and Leipzig 1946. Cited in Kunhenn (1952:70).

originality (standards we still value to this day), it was equally important that these be written in good literary style. One essay was rejected because the all too exacting precision of its textual criticism revealed 'a certain degree of dryness in the portrayal that confronts the reader, who expects inspired [stylistic] schemes' (Königliche Akademie 1839:v).

Another essay, although highly praised for its assiduity, was also ultimately rejected because 'its presentation, especially because of the numerous notes to which the reader is constantly referred, is cumbersome, its style rambling and its expression without eloquence' (Königliche Akademie 1839:v–vi). These footnotes were not taken as evidence of the author's scholarship but rather the reverse since they interrupted the flow of a stylistically pleasing text. The titles of these essays that the academy chose to honour are equally remarkable: no dry 'A contribution to ...', but thoughtful quotations from the genre of *belles lettres*. And knowledge of English was demonstrated not by citations from the linguistic house of horrors that is often encountered under the guise of seminars on global agency, but by a reference to Shakespeare. The winning essay on the *mouseion* of ancient Alexandria was entitled "The best of this kind are but shadows".[2] And in the Natural Sciences and Mathematics Section, which held an essay competition 'on the anatomy of tapeworms, nemerteans, gordius and other less-studied worms and their position in the system', a contribution entitled "Life is a dream" (the title of a play by Calderón) was submitted and would have won had the author not only described the tapeworm but also treated its position in the system of worms, as the invitation had indicated (Königliche Akademie 1839:i–iii).

This academy was no poets' circle, but an international assembly of demanding scholars, including Antoine-Cesar Becquerel, John Dalton (known for his research on colour-blindness), Michael Faraday (inventor of the Faraday cage), Justus Liebig (the chemist), Carl Friedrich Gauss (the mathematician and tragic hero of a novel),[3] Alexander von Humboldt (his co-hero in the same novel), Leopold von Ranke (the historian), Carl Friedrich von Savigny (the legal scholar), Franz Bopp (the Sanskrit specialist), and Joseph-Marie de Gérando (philosopher and precursor of the discussion of methodology in anthropology).[4] None of these scholars had any serious problem with an essay about tapeworms submitted under a title that cited a play by Calderón or a paper on classical Greek scholarship introduced with a Shakespeare quotation; they all agreed that dry science and too many footnotes spoke against an essay that should instead present 'inspired schemes'.

---

[2]  Quoting Theseus in "A midsummer night's dream"
[3]  For non-German readers: this is a joke reference to a well known German novel (Kehlmann 2005).
[4]  See de Gérando (1800).

Sixty-five years later, in 1902, the Nobel Prize for Literature (the second prize of its kind and the first to be awarded to a German) went to the historian Theodor Mommsen for the literary quality of his never completed "Römische Geschichte".[5] That such literary quality was central even to purely scientific literature still went without saying. Another forty-five years later, however, at the end of the 1940s, things were changing. At that time the question was whether Winston Churchill should be awarded the Nobel Prize for Literature. One faction of the Swedish Academy argued that Churchill was more a historian and politician, and therefore not qualified to receive the Prize. Ultimately, however, 'mastery of historical and biographical description as well as [...] brilliant oratory in defending exalted human values' would win one last time, and he received the Prize in 1953.[6] But the speaker of the academy already noted that 'very seldom have great statesmen and warriors also been great writers', and immediately dismissed as exceptions great examples to the contrary like Julius Caesar, Marcus Aurelius, Napoleon, or Disraeli.[7] And in fact 1953 would be the last time that the Nobel committee would blur the boundary between science, journalism and literature.

In anthropology, this narrow-minded boundary was ignored for a while longer. Anthropologists continued to strive to write in a good style, which increasingly isolated them in academic circles. At the University of Marburg in 1954 an anthropological dissertation was submitted, the style of which clearly had literary ambitions. But it was at the same time quite philosophical, reminiscent of the language Adorno used. One reviewer (no anthropologist) argued that the language was odd and surmised this was due to the fact that the doctoral candidate was from a Polish-Russian border region. The dean raised this with the candidate who adamantly pointed out that the province in which he was born and raised, Eastern Prussia, lay at that time well within the boundaries of the German-speaking world. The interesting thing about this episode is that the Ph.D. candidate in anthropology outshone his professors linguistically, perhaps precisely because he was from a historically more conservative province. He used foreign terms properly, and his language was formal. His professors, however, at least the reviewer and dean, were evidently no longer aware that a scientific text could be more than a dry collection of data rendered in a language as poor as the reconstruction architecture of the 1950s or the pseudo-positivism of the no longer hermeneutic sociology of the 1960s. They had probably never read a philosophical text in their lives either.

The proximity of anthropology to literature was a central issue in the 'writing culture debate' of the 1980s, and it was addressed even before that by Clifford Geertz (a debate several times referred to in the present collection, see Crapanzano,

---

5    The main volumes I, II and III were first published 1854, 1855, and 1856. See Mommsen (1861).
6    See the documentation in http://nobelprize.org/nobel_prizes/literature/laureates/1953/.
7    See http://nobelprize.org/nobel_prizes/literature/laureates/1953/press.html.

Godelier, Jebens, and Kohl). Admittedly, Geertz (who himself could write well) understood good writing more as a vice than a virtue. George Marcus and Michael Fischer and the other protagonists of the writing culture debate, however, also stressed the positive aspect of literary style in the anthropological tradition. But much like some indigenous cultures, anthropologists became aware of their own rich traditions just at the moment they began to throw it overboard. Still, the hope remains that the great literary tradition of anthropology has not been lost completely. Let us recall how anthropology once spoke of the end.

> But where are they [...], the stately Selk'nam that once, full of *joie de vivre*, strode across the great breadth of the Big Island? Where are the quieter Yamana and Halakwùlup, whose light bark canoes enlivened the many inlets? [...] Where have they all gone, the strong men full of fearless vigour, and where are the silent women with the courageous determination to fight for their existence? Where are the slim gazelle-like figures of the young girls, busy collecting mussels on the beaches; where the limber boys who with elegant dispatch shine in wrestling and archery? Where is the lighthearted youth, whose bright laughter echoes in the dense brushwoods? Where are the people who, adapted to these barren lands, enlivened the monotonous landscape? [...] They are all gone, they have all been destroyed by the never-ending greed of the white race and the deadly consequences of its presence. The Indians of Tierra del Fuego are irretrievably lost. The restless waves of Cape Horn alone sing the dead Indians a wailful dirge.[8]

It is its grounding in the literary tradition that makes many an anthropological utterance appear stylistically eccentric. The quotation above from Martin Gusinde reveals a turn-of-the-century exuberance (although the work was only published in 1946, the then sixty-year-old author was rooted in the tradition of a bygone style of writing), quite different from texts with no particular style, which do not become stylistically outdated as quickly, but will always remain, well, without style. The following discussion of anthropology's proximity to literature might sound somewhat ironic from time to time, but is not meant to be. That the texts I shall quote sometimes border on the ridiculous (or bravely transcend that fine line) is a result of the fact that in the past thirty years or so we have come close to losing one thing: a sense for texts that not only provide data but also have literary ambitions.

The Gusinde quotation on the natives of the Tierra del Feugo is not directly about the end of anthropology; but indirectly it is, because it describes the end of the 'object' of anthropology. The anthropological lament for what has been lost – so much admired but irretrievably lost – is often also a lament for one's own impending end. But in contrast to the writing culture debate, which focused on the act of representation – a perspective that maintains the clear distinction been subject and object and thus limits its criticism to the fact that scholars speak for their objects

---

[8]     See footnote 1.

of study – my own concern seeks to highlight the anthropologists' identification
with the end (and thus, indirectly, with the people they work with, as Jebens, in his
contribution to the present collection, remarks).

## THE END OF THE ANCIENTS

A particularly telling expression of the end in anthropology is the metaphor of the
fire that destroys ancient cultures, the object of anthropology, before they can be
fully studied. I want to linger over this metaphor for a moment. It is, of course, also
a metaphor of the end of anthropology itself, since once everything has been burnt,
there is nothing more to study. Even for Adolph Bastian in 1881, the recording of
ancient traditions was (in a play on words)

> a burning issue of time! It burns in all corners of the anthropological world, burning
> high, burning bright, it burns all around, Great Fire! And nobody does a thing [in
> view of] the frightening progression of approaching ruin [...] relics of human history of
> mankind, irretrievably lost, forever, as long as the world continues to turn.[9]

In 1893 Bastian coined his famous metaphor (later on ascribed to others) of the
aged carriers of tradition, whose deaths were much like the burning of a library. He
lamented that

> the last carriers of a [...] treasure of tradition have been condemned to extinction [...].
> With each of those who step into the grave, there perishes what lived in memory; and
> thus are we faced with a total loss (of documents vital to human history), similar to the
> tragedy of a burning library (when out of the charred books we can no longer glean
> what they would have had to say) (Bastian 1893:i).

I cite Bastian here in much abbreviated form, his long sentences exceeding the limits
of contemporary endurance. His form of expression is so foreign to us today, not
least because it has so much affinity with the *belles lettres* of his time.[10] Hölderlin is
clearly audible here, but so is especially Hugo von Hofmannsthal and his approach
to literature, the language of which, unlike forms of everyday speech, should form a
closed 'whole', a world complete in and of itself with its own rules. Art should serve
no external purposes – such as entertainment or information – nor should it refer
directly to reality.

---

[9]     Bastian (1881:180). I thank Annemarie Fiedermutz-Laun (1990:132) for bringing this quotation
        to my attention.
[10]    In fact, the English translation, in order to be intelligible at all, has to be clearer than the obscure
        original text.

This was a new approach to what constituted good literary style. Six decades previously, around the time of the decisions made by the members of the Königliche Preußische Akademie der Wissenschaften on the scientific quality of essays, simplicity and clarity were the literary ideals. Now, by the end of the nineteenth century, the issue was not one of simplicity and intelligibility. On the contrary, it became a matter of rising above concrete intelligibility to achieve abstraction, just as in the fine arts, where realism and an accessibility based in everyday experience soon gave way to a new ideal, that of the abstract. Innumerable footnotes, six decades previously a reason for rejection because they distracted the reader, were in Bastian's era a stylistic device to hold up the reader, to force him to read more slowly, and to spoil his hopes that he might grasp things too easily.

This does not mean that Bastian was influenced directly by von Hofmannsthal, whose most important works appeared after those by Bastian cited here. It does mean, however, that Bastian was open to a literary tradition to which von Hofmannsthal also belonged, which is precisely what makes him so inaccessible for anthropologists today, who prefer reading papers, or even just their abstracts, to a puzzling style in the manner of von Hofmannsthal.

Nevertheless, Bastian did write scientific literature, not poetic prose that is distinct from life, as with von Hofmannsthal, but science that sought its own forms of distinction, such as the footnote. The poet von Hofmannsthal could only establish a connection between art and life via the poetic metaphor. And it is the metaphor – such as the metaphor of fire – that Bastian uses to anchor himself to reality.

It is only a small step from 'the last carriers of a treasure of tradition', whose knowledge Bastian sees burning, to the Malian writer Amadou Hampaté Bâ's 'old traditionalists': 'In Africa, when a an old traditionalist dies, it is an unexplored library that burns', he cried out in UNESO in 1960.[11] He would have been better advised, incidentally, to have chosen a different forum for his plea. At the hands of the UNESCO, an instrument of global development policy, his words suffered a sad but revealing fate confronted with the incompatibility of development policy, literature and wise old traditionalists. In fact, Hampaté Bâ's words lamented the death of an old traditionalist with whom one should have done research so as to preserve what was at risk of being lost. But that does not fit the modernism of development policy and the focus of the argument was shifted. The wearisome work of taking traditionalists and scientists seriously was shortened to: 'When an old man dies, a library burns'.[12]

---

[11]   Cited in Heckmann (1987:10)

[12]   This is quoted and can be found as an 'African proverb' countless times. Searching it by Google, I found 80,100 hits, e.g. http://www.bookbrowse.com/quotes/detail/index.cfm?quote_number=12.

Nonetheless Hampaté Bâ came to adopt Bastian's metaphor, and however it then came to be perverted by the politicians of the countries of the North, one thing is clear: before the development education policy-makers usurped the metaphor, there was a situation of give-and-take between literature and anthropology that had existed since the *fin de siècle* despondency that bound them both. Bastian's fiery destruction, in which the wisdom of indigenous traditions burn, like the paper on which it might have been written, is mirrored by Karl May, the popular German writer of westerns, in the same year that Bastian published his lecture; only this time it is water that destroys the paper. At the end of "Winnetou III" May describes how he saves scraps of the Indian hero's will, but unfortunately only scraps. Like the scraps of charred paper that flutter away before our mind's eye in the metaphor of the burning library, the water-soaked scraps of paper in May's account drift away on the water's surface:

> [I]t shimmered [...] paper-white from the middle of the lake. I sprang immediately [...] into the water and swam over to it. True, it was a small scrap of the will. I scoured the surface of the lake in all directions and found three other scraps. These remnants of the will I laid out in the sun to dry, and then I tried to decipher the smeared, washed-out letters. I could not, of course, make any sense of them. After trying for quite some time I could read '... keep a half ... because of poverty ... bursting cliff ... Christ ... distribute ... no revenge'.
>
> That was it, meaning almost nothing at all, and yet enough to at least suggest the content of the rest. I have kept these little pieces of paper sacred. [...] Thus, the Apache's will disappeared as did its author and as the whole red race will disappear [...] Like the scraps of the will cast into the wind, so rootless and restless and scattered will the red man err across the wide plains that once belonged to him.
>
> But he who stands at the grave of the Apache in the Gros Ventre Mountains on the Metsur River will say: 'Here lies buried Winnetou, a red man, but a great man!' And when the last scraps of his will have decayed in the bush and water, then a right thinking and feeling people will stand before the savannahs and mountains of the West and say, 'Here rests the red race. It did not become great because it was not permitted to become great!' (May n.d.:397–398)

Dressed in literary terms, this quotation embodies the programme of anthropology since the discipline's earliest days. Like May scouring the water's surface for the shreds of Winnetou's will, the anthropologist searches for the scattered pieces of what was once the great cultural legacy of almost lost civilisations. He pieces together the scraps like a jigsaw puzzle of which unfortunately many pieces are missing. Bastian's key point is condensed by May into the literary image of water-soaked, scattered scraps of paper. And the decryption of individual pieces of an ingenious puzzle (scattered through time and thus incomprehensible) is an idea as central to Claude Lévi-Strauss's structuralism as it is to the cultural morphology of the Frankfurt Anthropological School of Leo Frobenius and Adolf Ellegard Jensen:

'Since we encounter most cultural phenomena today in a state that is not original and thus of limited use for hypothesising about their origins, everything depends of course on whether it is possible to reconstruct this original state' (Jensen 1991:25).

Shortly before the scraps of paper succumb to water and time, we save what can be saved. Conceived in another revealing metaphor, we see the programme of the anthropologist Bastian, who tries to save from the 'burning house' what little remains. It is also the programme of the writer Hampaté Bâ's plea to save oral traditions. And May keeps the legacy sacred, like the anthropologist and the writer, so that one day the misjudged and denigrated, whose end saw so much of value suppressed and squelched, might see justice done.

Impossible though it is to claim that von Hoffmannsthal had a direct influence on Bastian, it is also impossible to prove that Lévi-Strauss and Jensen were influenced by May (although it is unlikely that Jensen did n o t read May). But I do not want to recite here a chronology of who influenced whom. Nor do the rest of the quotations from literary works that will follow here have the weight of anthropological references. I wish only to point out certain trends in the *belle lettres* genre that echo those in anthropology. If we juxtapose texts, startling parallels appear that may well enrich our understanding of anthropological writings. This in no way suggests a direct historical relationship.

## The Grave of the Last, Culture Foreign and One's Own

In the May quotation above, we also find reference to a grave, the sight of which recalls how great the departed once was. This resonates with the 'wailful dirge' that Gusinde heard in my introductory quotation. Like May, who saw 'people stand before the savannahs and mountains of the West and say, "Here rests the red race"', the anthropologist Gusinde predicted that 'the restless waves of Cape Horn alone sing the dead Indians a wailful dirge'.

The motif of the death of one of the last, which is condensed at the sight of his grave, is, of course, older than May; we find it already in James Fenimore Cooper's "The last of the Mohicans" (2005a). The story ends with old Tamenund telling his people to go home because it is all over (in which he speaks of himself in the third person because it is all over for him as well):

> 'It is enough!' he said. 'Go, children of the Lenape, the anger of the Manitto is not done. Why should Tamenund stay? The pale-faces are masters of the earth, and the time of the red-men has not yet come again. My day has been too long. In the morning I saw the sons of Unamis happy and strong; and yet, before the night has come, have I lived to see the last warrior of the wise race of the Mohicans!' (Cooper 2005a:259–260)

We find the motif of the eulogy in Cooper, as well as the simple inscription on a gravestone that recalls the full tragedy of a whole people's fate. Cooper ends his story "The wept of Wish-ton-Wish" (2005b) with the discovery of a grave from a bygone era, the grave of the tragic hero Conanchet, chief of the Narragansett, a people who fought a courageous but futile battle against white encroachment: 'The grave was on the hill, and marked only by a stone that the grass had concealed from view. It merely bore the words – "the Narragansett"' (Cooper 2005b).

Another story of Cooper's – "The prairie" (1997) – ends with reference to a gravestone as well, in this case not that of an Indian, but of the Indians' friend Nathaniel Bumppoo. The Chief Le Balafré (himself approaching the end) announces the death of an old friend:

> The voice of the old Indian seemed a sort of echo from that invisible world, to which the meek spirit of the trapper had just departed. 'A valiant, a just and a wise warrior has gone on the path, which will lead him to the blessed grounds of his people!' he said. 'When the voice of the Wahcondah called him, he was ready to answer. Go, my children, remember the just chief of the Pale-faces!' (Cooper 1997:276)

The Pawnee Indians make a gravestone for him, and Chief Middleton writes the inscription:

> The grave was made beneath the shade of some noble oaks. It has been carefully watched to the present hour by the Pawnees of the Loup, and is often shown to the traveller and the trader as a spot where a j u s t white man just sleeps. In due time the stone was placed at its head, with the simple inscription, which the trapper himself had requested. The only liberty, taken by Middleton, was to add, – 'May no wanton hand ever disturb his remains!' (Cooper 1997:276; emphasis M.M.)

This describes the melancholy dream of the anthropologist: to be buried by one's Indians. The end of the free, indigenous lifestyle, the threat posed to the prairie by the ravages of civilisation, is echoed in the death of one who befriended the once free inhabitants of this prairie. Nathaniel Bumppoo is an anthropological ideal, his trapper's way of life the ideal of an anthropology that follows its red friends to the grave – or even leads the way to it.

May, who claimed to have travelled the open prairie himself – allegedly not simply the Indian's chronicler but also their loyal friend – could, for his part, not die in the course of the narrative, otherwise he would not have been able to record the events of the story. Thus, only his red friends die. But with them dies a part of his own heart. The first to die, in "Winnetou I" (May n.d.), is Winnetou's sister, the quiet, beautiful Nscho-tschi, who wanted to learn about the ways of the white man so that she might win his heart. With her death the story is basically over, May's heart is broken, his spirit dead. But he must live on for the reader's sake to write two more volumes before Winnetou himself dies at the end of "Winnetou III", along with him his people. After this, May cannot write any more. Again, the boundary between the white man and the indigenous inhabitants of the prairie or woodlands is blurred.

In Cooper more prominently than in May, the threat to the Indians is also a threat to a traditionalist white lifestyle, ultimately the best of white culture. Without delineating a precise history of these motifs, in what follows I shall evoke several that are familiar to everyone. Recall the movie "Dances with wolves" (1990), which follows a long-standing American tradition and also parallels European cultural criticism. Kevin Costner finds in the Indian not only a different culture (obviously threatened by imminent demise), but himself as well, his own humanity (no less threatened by the advance of an inane civilisation). Asked by a childish, senile officer early in the film whether he wants to see the West, Costner replies: 'Yes Sir, before it is gone'. Even before he gets there, he knows that it will not exist much longer, that it is coming to an end. This occurs to him when confronted with the officer's stupidity, which embodies the future of the West: stupidity and a lack of culture. Thereafter he dances with the wolves, and we know it is the final dance.

Let me to return once again to Bastian's image of the great fire that destroys the virtual paper in the minds of the wise old men. Honed into a melancholy critique of civilisation, this image is reversed and made concrete by Ray Bradbury in "Fahrenheit 451" (written sixty years after Bastian, and seven years before Hampaté Bâ), a pessimistic extrapolation of tendencies during the MacCarthy era to their terrible conclusion. Bradbury, incidentally one of the most anthropological authors of the very cultural relativist tradition of North American science fiction, writes not of a virtual library in the heads of the wise old men, but of actual books that are recited by, in this case, American wise old men. But worse than in the works of Bastian, where no firefighter lifts a finger to extinguish the fire, Bradbury's firefighters have made it their mission to burn all the books themselves. Bradbury's poetic vision describes an increasingly cultureless world in which television shows and amusing bonfires replace books. This cultural criticism formulated in the 1950s – a parable of anti-intellectualism and the persecution of the educated, who have incriminated themselves by not handing their books over to the firefighters for burning – touches us today precisely because it is rooted in the cultural pessimism of the early twentieth century to which anthropology owes so much.

And like Bastian and Hampaté Bâ, the only hope lies in unwritten memory. Before all the books were burned, a resistance group memorised as much great literature as possible, and each member of the group identifies himself with the author whose works he has learnt by heart:

> Would you like, someday, Montag, to read Plato's republic? ... I am Plato's Republic. Would you like to read Marcus Aurelius? Simmons is Marcus ... I want you to meet

Jonathan Swift, the author of that evil political book "Guilliver's travels"! And this
other fellow is Charles Darwin and this one is Schopenhauer (Bradbury 1953:151).

What in anthropology and in African literature is seen as the beginning, knowledge
that is preserved in people's minds (in our own society this is preserved in books),
returns in this North American distopia at t h e   e n d . The knowledge of society
in its entirety is again preserved in the human mind and survives the fire, only
to be threatened by the nuclear apocalypse. This threat is also a product of the
same European development, which in t h e   e n d is a threat to its own existence.
Progress consumes its own children. This metaphor can be found in Bastian's
work as well. Quite close to his image of the burning house, which foreshadows
Bradbury's firefighters fighting with instead of against fire, is Bastian's realisation that
science has come too late because, paradoxically, the evil that it has itself unleashed
undermines its own conditions of possiblity. 'In the early days of discovery there was
still too much ignorance on all sides', too much for anthropology to have been able
to penetrate further. To do so, Europe had to penetrate the other world through
civilisation: 'only gradually, as more points of contact emerged, were opened the
paths of intellectual traffic, and access was permitted' (Bastian 1986:66). But this
also came too late because the arrival of the European heralded the end of tradition.
    At this point, the South Seas specialist Bastian quotes another South Seas
scholar, one who, more a poet than a scholar, ignored this distinction: Adelbert von
Chamisso. Bastian links his concern that the end of these cultures had come before
their study ever really began to the observations of this poet, who laments having
missed the last chance to record the traditions preserved in the narratives of the
elders before they die, even if he does not use Bastian's metaphor of the burning
library. In 1837 Chamisso regretted that, while the Christian mission in Hawaii had
written much, nothing

> is devoted to the purpose of preserving the ancient and the traditional of these tribal
> people after the course of history and the coming new time seals its demise [...] all the
> keys to one of the greatest mysteries that the history of humankind's wanderings across
> the globe has offered have been sunk in the sea of oblivion just at the moment when
> they were placed into our hands.[13]

Chamisso speaks of the Christian mission, the work of which destroys the old myths
that are so important to the poet and the scholar. But he speaks in the 'we' form,
seeing the mission as part of a larger onslaught in which the scholar also plays a part.
    The progress brought on by globalisation, which robs anthropology of its object
by making others ever more like us, this kind of anthropological end has always been

---

[13]     Chamisso (1839:4), cited in part by Bastian (1986:66).

an issue in anthropology. We find it in the works of Lévi-Strauss, in literary form in the "Tristes tropiques" (1955) and in his comittment to academic politics before UNESCO in 1961, one year after Hampaté Bâ's speech. Lévi-Strauss professed to have given up trying to save ancient traditions that had remained unchanged since time immemorial but were now being lost in the onslaught of civilisation. He no longer believed in the unchanging nature of social and cultural phenomena; he was now interested in them precisely because they constantly transform themselves. But he also described the paradox that it is our very interest in the cultures of others that makes them more like ours and thus uninteresting, driving anthropology into unemployment, even if his interest is now a different one, no longer in the ancient but in change: 'precisely these transformations that awaken our theoretical interest in "primitives" are the cause of their disappearance' (Lévi-Strauss 1975:5).

In the same year, 1961, and again for UNESCO, Lévi-Strauss revised an older text in which he described the Janus-headed nature ('double sens') of progress. Progress feeds on culture just as it creates an alliance between cultures. This is a typical UNESCO phrase. And in the spirit of UNESCO (approximate in content to the political speeches of politicians in what has come to be called the North-South dialogue and what cynics like to refer to as heart-warming speeches), Lévi-Strauss in his text adds to this politically correct cultural pluralism the idea that the alliance of cultures is all the more fertile the greater the differences between the respective cultures and the more respect they have for one another. But Lévi-Strauss would not be Lévi-Strauss – the anthropologist would not be an anthropologist – if he did not let the optimism in this discussion of intercultural dialogue stand without giving it a good dose of anthropological paradox and sorrow. The paradox is that in this reconciliation of cultures their very difference is reduced, and thus they die as uniquely distinct cultures (Lévi-Strauss 1973). Their progress is their end. And that is also the impending end of anthropology (as Lévi-Strauss, too, notes, in his melancholy way). Under the multicultural rainbow that is UNESCO, which itself might last only a few precious moments, anthropology too fades from this world, yet it itself is one of the gravediggers. Although Lévi-Strauss refers to Western civilisation in general, he speaks in the 'we' form, as did Chamisso before him: 'Lorsque l'arc-en-ciel des cultures humaines aura fini de s'abîmer dans le vide creusé par notre fureur [...] – adieu sauvages! adieu voyages!' (1955:479; emphasis M.M.)

## ARE GERMAN ANTHROPOLOGISTS MORE MELANCHOLY?

I mention Lévi-Strauss here because the melancholy of the end is not particular to the German-speaking anthropological tradition. But the difference that exists between other Western European and German-speaking anthropologies in terms of the end is that, while in the rest of Western Europe the end comes from the outside, in central Europe it originates from within.

When Lévi-Strauss identifies the transformations that bring about the disappearance of other cultures – namely, the reconciliation of cultures within the fold of emerging global civilisation – as 'precisely these changes that awaken our theoretical interest in "primitives"' (Lévi-Strauss 1975:5), then he is confessing his interest in what at that time was still referred to as 'acculturation' and today figures under the term 'globalisation', that is, change introduced from outside.

When, however, Eike Haberland, in an article entitled "Lethargy in New Guinea", describes how he experienced the end of a great culture,[14] it sounds as if it died not so much by simply falling victim to colonialism and the Christian mission as by succumbing to the weariness of old age, geriatric 'lethargy'. This for Haberland is the melancholy of the inevitable end of every culture, a perspective central to the poetic, sorrowful quality of the Frankfurt Anthropological School of Cultural Morphology.

Bernhard Streck sees the source of this anguish in the fact that this school 'flourished in a milieu of extreme failure – [the failure] of German imperialism and of the First World War, of German millenarianism and of the Second World War' (2006:219).

Yet, at least in my view, it is less this sense of failure that is so typical of German anthropology, but rather its historical approach, which allows a culture to pursue its own path to the very end, from its rise to its final fall.[15] Lévi-Strauss's "Tristes tropiques" is no more cheerful, and no less an ode to failure. Nor is Bastian's resignation in face of the paradox of civilisation any more cheerful, even if it is comes from a very different time.

Certainly – and this is Streck's point – in the course of the first half of the twentieth century, there were more numerous and more horrifying grounds for melancholy. At this historical juncture, anthropology became ever more attuned to the literary zeitgeist. A child of Old Europe, Stefan Zweig, looks back at the dissolution of his world and takes up the once exclusively anthropological motif of the burning library, because it has now turned from a mere metaphor into reality:

> I was […] born into a large and mighty empire, into the Habsburg monarchy; but do not try to find it on a map, it has been washed away without a trace. I grew up in Vienna, the two thousand year old transnational metropolis, and I had to leave it like a criminal before it was demoted to a German provincial town. My literary work, in the language in which I have written it, has been burned to ashes […] Against my will

---

[14]    This is the summary of an interview with Haberland in the Wiesbadener Tagblatt, "Auf Neuguinea herrscht die Lethargie" (2 November 1963) that was intended for a popular audience.

[15]    Gibbon (1830) was as an admired prototype for many German historians well into the twentieth century.

I have become witness to the greatest failure of reason and of the most uninhibited triumph of brutality (1955:7–8.)

This text must certainly be understood in its context, both historical and in that of the particular biography of the author, who committed suicide soon afterwards. But still, it is not only a document of its time, it is also a timeless work of world literature. Similarly, it would be reductionistic, a kind of domestication via historicisation, if we were to regard the ideas of the Frankfurt Anthropological School of Cultural Morphology simply as products of their historical context, that is, as the outcome of the series of German defeats.

These ideas are both older and more recent. The image of the burning library can be found in Bastian's work in 1893 (long before books literally began burning in Germany), and it resounds or returns years later, in 1953 and 1961 in the works of Ray Bradbury and Amadou Hampaté Bâ, who were certainly not traumatised by German defeat.

## THE LITERARY PARABLE

Narratives of an end to which all cultures must yield sooner or later, like an old man who must inevitably face the same fate, are literary parables. And I think they can be better understood when one interprets them as such.

When I suggest that anthropology has literary qualities, I mean 'literary' mainly in two respects: (1) the desire to write in a good style, in which what constitutes 'good' is subject to change from literary epoch to epoch; and (2) the bundling of complex relationships into images, such as that of the burning house, and the juxtaposition of images in a narrative which does not mirror reality, but rather depicts a reality, as in a parable. A literary narrative is hardly ever reality; usually it is a parable of reality. But it remains tied to reality by depicting it, making a parable of it, a lens though which reality is refracted and through which new meaning is brought into focus.

But parables and how they are understood by scholars and scientists are rather thorny matters. In the eighteenth century, Enlightenment authors wrote parables to capture the course of world history and the history of humanity in short, succinct idioms. One such well-known tale relates the story of the first man who erected a fence, thus inventing private property and changing the course of human development from a state of peace to one of strife. Had people not listened to this man, Rousseau (2009) claimed, humanity would have been saved from a history of horrors. What Rousseau intended to express was a critique of private property as a driving force of conflict. Yet, instead of presenting a historical reconstruction to elucidate his point, he chose a more poetic means by setting it in a parable. In the nineteenth century these parables began to be confused with historical reality. Karl

Marx took the literary parable of ancient society quite literally; and his twentieth-century epigones, like e.g. Irmgard Sellnow (1961) and other German Marxist anthropologists, have attempted to reconstruct the specific stages of historical development from the first fence to capitalism in great chronologies. Of course it was child's play to unmask as historical nonsense such concretisations of poetic metaphors as historical reality. The facts simply did not 'fit'; they could not fit, since a parable is never historical reality. It is simply a parable.

Similarly, the facts could not 'fit' for the Frankfurt School of Cultural Morphology either. The situation here, however, is somewhat more complicated than with Rousseau, since the anthropologists who sought to describe the rhythms of the rise and fall of cultures did, as it happens, look for historical facts that they themselves believed to be true. However, even Jensen, who today bores us with his encyclopedic attempts to collect facts upon facts from which he seeks to reconstruct a historical reality, time and again lets comments slip that lead one to suspect that he was less concerned with historical reality than with reconstructing broad lines of development which he knew very well were ultimately unverifiable, but appeared to him to be quite plausible as a hermeneutic attempt to grasp the incomprehensible. Again and again we find sentences like: 'This train of thought [Jensen's own] could only be presented as a conjecture, derived from the ideas themselves, without attempting to verify them through material evidence' (Jensen 1991:393). Or: 'Such trains of thought [again, his own] drift into the hypothetical' (1991:257).

Jensen apparently knew very well that he was not working with facts, particularly given that his main sources were myths, the interpretation of which took place in a dialogue (anything but fact-based) between narrator and anthropologist. Jensen also distanced himself very clearly from fact-based history. He distinguishes on the one hand a 'chronology of those cultural layers that one appears to have identified using various tools [...] The attempt to find an answer [to this question] is not the subject of this investigation'. On the other hand there is the question of the 'meaning of the encountered phenomena [that is, the attempt to develop] an understanding for them. The following remarks are dedicated solely to this question'.[16]

Jensen's view of history is perhaps easier to understand if it is considered in the context of 'history as the poetry of the *Weltgeist*'. The phrase 'history as poetry' is a common phrase that recurs in the works of various twentieth-century authors. 'History as the poetry of the *Weltgeist*' is the wording of Zweig:

> History is not always a poet, it is usually only a chronicler, a recorder of facts. Only very rarely does history have such sublime moments [...] – sometimes we find in history individual episodes, people and epochs of such unparalleled suspense, in such

---

dramatic consummation that they are unsurpassable as works of art; in them history as the poetry of the *Weltgeist* shames the poetry of all poets and every earthly spirit (Zweig 1983:252–253).

Zweig saw it as the poet's task to capture these moments and render them faithfully. The basis of this approach is a perception of history in which apparently individual, confused, disjointed facts regarded from a poetic distance come together to form a meaningful whole, one with recurring rises and falls: 'History, this seemingly tideless ocean of events, obeys, in truth, an unchanging rhythmic law, an inner swell that divides its epochs into ebb and flow, into surges and backwashes'.[17]

The periodically recurring backwash – referred to as decline by the Frankfurt School of Cultural Morphology – that inevitably follows a civilisational rise always leads to a tragic end. But this historical rhythm is perceived only by the poet or inspired scholar who is capable of 'listening into the depths of the event' (Zweig 1983:263). Only then can he recognise the core meaning of a historical moment. In view of the horrors of the present, this provides solace. He can find meaning in today's crises, 'even if this meaning is as yet inscrutable'.[18]

This is not unlike the anthropologist Jensen's view of great mythical moments: myths are compact summaries of brief moments in history. Consider the killing of Hainuwele, for example: Jensen does not believe, of course, that Hainuwele was a historical person. But the shock expressed in the myth, that brief historical moment in which the people suddenly comprehended something about nature and themselves and were taken hold of by it, was a real historical moment, a moment that came to be reflected in myth. It is this myth that must be captured by the poet as a piece of the poetry of the *Weltgeist*, in Zweig's words. From this point onwards the apparent incoherence and confusion of mythical memory, contained in scattered ethnographic examples, take on coherence and meaning:

> The meaningfulness of the individual [examples] relative to the overarching whole serves as a measure [with the] result that a series of cultic acts, which we heretofore have had to regard entirely separately as independent phenomena, from this perspective merge into a single unity (Jensen 1966:123, 125).

The myths thus allow us to retreive, via a great mythic moment, history's forgotten meaning, not unlike how Zweig finds meaning in a seemingly confused and incoherent history through individual, narratively constructed, outstanding historical moments. Jensen, too, is likely to have found solace in this perspective.

---

17   Stefan Zweig: Der europäische Gedanke in seiner historischen Entwicklung (1932:185), cited in Mueller (2004:10).

18   Kittstein uses these words to summarises Zweig's philosophy of history (2006:224).

The poet Karl Krolow (1983) sees the ideal model of 'history as poetry' in Herodotus, who, with the help of myth, constructed a sense of meaning out of the cruel senselessness of history. Krolow shares with many of his contemporaries, and with many anthropologists, a sense of desperation in the face of history that ends in disaster. Thus, in 1951 he expressed his vision of the beginning and end of history in his poem "History" as follows:

> Men carried across the square a flag.
> Then centaurs broke from the undergrowth
> and trampled its cloth,
> and history could begin.
> Melancholy states
> disintegrated on street corners.
> Speakers remained
> with bulldogs at the ready,
> and the younger women
> made themselves up for the fittest.
> Voices argued unceasingly
> in the air, although
> the mythological creatures
> had long retired.
> Finally the hand remains,
> laid around a throat (Krolow 1975:51).

The end of the story is today. Krowlow's Herodotus continues: 'Genocide is a recent word/for nothing new' – 'The thugs, anonymous, now set/with delicate tools to their work' (this and the following quotation: Krowlow 1983:39–40).

All that remains for him is poetic mythologising that allows history to be understood differently. But everything seems clear only for a fleeting, poetic moment:

> One picks up the miracle. It is
> easy: a legible scrap of paper,
> that is true only the moment
> in which one bends down to it.

With this in mind, one can better understand Jensen. Streck (1989, 2006) and Karl-Heinz Kohl (1992) have described his trauma at having lived through a hopeless phase of history. And it sounds like an invocation of better times or of liberation from time itself when Jensen writes of the aberrations of killing 'during some unknown age', apparently referring to demythologised farming societies: 'The actual execution of the killing [...] has an effect similar to that of a hypertrophy, induced during some unknown age by savage religious zealots who pursued the underlying idea relentlessly and rationally to its logical conclusion' (1991:257).

Reality replaced myth, and that was the end in the horror of fanaticism: 'Zealots, whose rationalism is most often relentless, have thought the idea out to its cruel end, and, as always, the people followed these zealots as well' (Jensen 1966:149).

Jensen contrasts with his time – which could be denounced for both its fanaticism and its senseless rationalism – a return to myth, although he well knows that he has no facts, only his mythical solace. He does not try to deny the incoherent and often horrifying, but does seek to reveal a better myth. In his hopeless, unmythical time, myth is lost. One must bend down to pick it back up so that for a brief moment things cohere again; those few scraps of Winnetou's will need to be pieced back together so that things make sense in the end:

> When the light of an idea goes out, the figures originally belonging to it drift out of context, are extinguished or remain as individual, detached phenomena of human culture. [...] The result of this inquiry is to be seen primarily in the attempt, based on the examples of a few peoples, to reconstruct the unitary idea of their worldview (Jensen 1966:156).

Even if in this endeavour the facts are carefully examined, at issue in their compilation is not the presentation of proof but of 'history as poetry'. And, it should give pause for thought that up to now the study of myths has arrived at its most revealing conclusions when it has closely followed literature and the literary parable. Myth as a parable of the world, the scholarly narrative as a parable of the world and of history – both meet in the encounter between the narrator of myths and the anthropologist.

Jensen's successor in Frankfurt am Main, Eike Haberland, did away with the parable, facts in his view being more important than myths, and he replaced Jensen's mythical hermeneutics with the search for historical facts – something that did not prevent him from fearing the e n d in lethargy, except that he could find no solace in myth.

Having reached the end I wish to return to the end once again. This is a melancholy metaphor, certainly not triumphant of progress, or optimistic vis-à-vis cultural dialogue. But anthropology has (I think) no aptitude for such triumphalism or optimism anyway.

Let us leave that to those sciences that see themselves as success stories. It appears to me that – to follow the good anthropological tradition of using a metaphor – the difference between anthropology and the optimists of studies of the future is somewhat like the difference between two high school students: the one a tall, muscular football star always ready to rush to a touchdown, the other a melancholy reader of poetry and philosophy. Of course it is the football star, not the philosopher, who always gets the girls. But I prefer the role of the melancholy philosopher. In the end the girls always end up dumping the football star, the smart ones at least, because they can no longer tolerate his permanently optimistic grin.

*References*

BASTIAN, Adolph
1881    *Der Völkergedanke im Aufbau einer Wissenschaft vom Menschen und seine Begründung auf ethnologische Sammlungen.* Berlin: Ferdinand Dümmler
1893    *Vorgeschichtliche Schöpfungslieder in ihren ethnischen Elementargedanken.* Ein Vortrag mit ergänzenden Zusätzen und Erläuterungen. Berlin: Emil Felber
1986    *Die Heilige Sage der Polynesier.* Kosmogonie und Theogonie. Osnabrück: Biblio ([1]1881)

BRADBURY, Ray
1953    *Fahrenheit 451.* New York: Random House

CHAMISSO, Adelbert von
1839    "Über die Hawaiische Sprache", *Abhandlungen der Königlichen Preußischen Akademie der Wissenschaften zu Berlin: Aus dem Jahre 1837, Philosophische, Philologische und Historische Abhandlungen,* 1–79. http://bibliothek.bbaw.de/bibliothek-digital/digitalequellen/schriften/anzeige/index_html?band=07-abh/1837&aufloesung:int=2&seite:int=313 (accessed 29 July 2009)

COOPER, James Fenimore
1997    *The prairie.* Philadelphia: Carey, Lea and Carey 1827. University of Virginia facsimile. http://etext.lib.virginia.edu/etcbin/toccer-eafpublic?id=eaf057v2.xml&data=/texts/eaf&tag=public&part=17&division=div (accessed 29 July 2009) ([1]1827)
2005a   *The last of the Mohicans: a narrative of 1757.* New York: Stringer & Townsend 1854. Ann Arbor, Michigan: University of Michigan Library 2005. http://quod.lib.umich.edu/cgi/t/text/text-idx?sid=dd7144377ef011408f1e0acd1fbc956e&c=moa&idno=ABB2615.0001.001&view=toc (accessed 15 June 2008) ([1]1826)
2005b   *The wept of Wish-Ton-Wish: a tale.* Project Gutenberg EBook, EBook #8888. http://www.gutenberg.org/dirs/etext05/8wept10h.htm (accessed 29 July 2009) ([1]1829)

FIEDERMUTZ-LAUN, Annemarie
1990    "Adolf Bastian (1826–1905)", in: Wolfgang Marschall (ed.), *Klassiker der Kulturanthropologie.* Von Montaigne bis Margaret Mead, 109–136. Munich: C.H. Beck

GÉRANDO, Joseph-Marie de
1800    *Considération sur les diverses méthodes à suivre dans l'observation des peuples sauvages.* Paris: Société des observateurs de l'homme

GIBBON, Edward
1830    *History of the decline and fall of the Roman empire.* London and Liverpool: Joseph Ogle Robinson and A.C. Baynes ([1]1776–88)

HECKMANN, Hélène
1987    *Amadou Hampâte Bâ: sa vie, son oeuvre.* Communication au colloque des
        Associations halpoular de Paris, tenu à l'INALCO en Octobre 1987, texte complété
        et actualisé par la suite. Versailles: Kati-Cultures. http://www.chez.com/katicultures
        (accessed 15 June 2008)

JENSEN, Ad[olf]. E[llegard].
1966    *Die getötete Gottheit.* Weltbild einer frühen Kultur. Stuttgart *et al.*: W. Kohlhammer
        (Urban Bücher 90.)
1991    *Mythos und Kult bei Naturvölkern.* Munich: Deutscher Taschenbuch Verlag (dtv
        wissenschaft 4567.) ([1]1951)

KEHLMANN, Daniel
2005    *Die Verrmessung der Welt.* Reinbek bei Hamburg: Rowohlt

KITTSTEIN, Ulrich
2006    *'mit Geschichte will man etwas'.* Historisches Erzählen in der Weimarer Republik
        und im Exil (1918–1945). Würzburg: Königshausen & Neumann

KÖNIGLICHE AKADEMIE (ed.)
1839    "Jahr 1837", *Abhandlungen der Königlichen Preußischen Akademie der Wissen-
        schaften zu Berlin.* Aus dem Jahre 1837:i–xiv

KOHL, Karl-Heinz
1992    "Vom Mythos ergriffen … Dema-Gottheiten nach Adolf E. Jensen", in: Karl-Heinz
        Kohl (ed.), *Mythen im Kontext.* Ethnologische Perspektiven, 107–128. Frankfurt
        am Main and New York: Ed. Qmran im Campus Verlag

KROLOW, Karl
1975    *Karl Krolow.* Ein Lesebuch. Edited by Walter Helmut Fritz. Frankfurt am Main:
        Suhrkamp
1983    *Herodot oder der Beginn von Geschichte.* Gedichte. Waldbrunn: Horst Heiderhoff

KUNHENN, Paul
1952    *Pygmäen und andere Primitiv-Völker.* Stuttgart: Kosmos-Gesellschaft der
        Naturfreunde

LÉVI-STRAUSS, Claude
1955    *Tristes Tropiques.* Paris: Plon (Terre Humaine)
1973    "Le double sens du progrès", in: Claude Lévi-Strauss, *Anthropologie structurale
        deux*, 418–422. Paris: Plon ([1]1961)
1975    *Die moderne Krise der Anthropologie.* Wiesbaden: B. Heymann (Edition Ethnos)
        ([1]1961, Unesco Kurier 2[11] November:10–15)

MAY, Karl
n.d.    *Winnetou III.* Vienna: Tosa ([1]1893)

MOMMSEN, Theodor
1861 *Römische Geschichte*. Berlin: Weidmannsche Buchhandlung. 3 Vols. ([1]1854, 1855, 1856)

MUELLER, Karl
2004 "Abstoßpunkt 'Joseph Fouché': Geschichte, Individuum und Dichtung bei Stefan Zweig", *New perspectives on Stefan Zweig's literary and biographical writings June 6–9, 2004*. The Center for Austrian Studies, Hebrew University Abrahams-Curiel Department of Foreign Literatures & Linguistics, Ben-Gurion University. http://www.uni-salzburg.at/pls/portal/docs/1/550892.pdf (accessed 24 September 2008)

ROUSSEAU, Jean-Jacques
2009 *Discours sur l'origine et les fondements de l'inégalité parmi les hommes*. Paris: l'Harmattan (Commentaires philosophiques) ([1]1755)

SELLNOW, Irmgard
1961 *Grundprinzipien einer Periodisierung der Urgeschichte*. Ein Beitrag auf Grundlage ethnographischen Materials. Berlin: Akademie-Verlag (Völkerkundliche Forschungen 4.)

STRECK, Bernhard
1989 "Kultur als Mysterium: Zum Trauma der deutschen Völkerkunde", in: Helmuth Berking, and Richard Faber (eds.), *Kultursoziologie. Symptom des Zeitgeistes?*, 89–115. Würzburg: Königshausen & Neumann
2006 "Zur wissenschaftlichen Zielsetzung der ehemaligen Direktoren des Frobenius-Instituts", in: Karl-Heinz Kohl and Editha Platte (eds.), *Gestalter und Gestalten. 100 Jahre Ethnologie in Frankfurt am Main*, 215–240. Frankfurt am Main and Basel: Stroemfeld/Nexus

ZWEIG, Stefan
1955 *Die Welt von Gestern*. Erinnerungen eines Europäers. Frankfurt am Main: S. Fischer ([1]1944)
1983 "Die Geschichte als Dichterin", in: Stefan Zweig, *Die schlaflose Welt*. Aufsätze und Vorträge aus den Jahren 1909–1941, 249–270. Frankfurt am Main: S. Fischer

CONTRIBUTORS

JOHN COMAROFF is the Harold H. Swift Distinguished Professor of Anthropology at the University of Chicago and is a Fellow of the American Academy of Arts and Sciences. His research focuses on the peoples of Southern Africa, concentrating on politics, law, colonialism, post-coloniality, modernity, neoliberalism, and the history of consciousness. Among his many books, co-authored or co-edited with Jean Comaroff, are *Of revelation and revolution,* Volumes I and II (1991, 1997), *Ethnography and the historical imagination* (1992), *Modernity and its malcontents* (1993), *Civil society and the political imagination in Africa* (1994), *Millennial capitalism and the culture of neoliberalism* (2001), *Law and disorder in the postcolony* (2006) and *Ethnicity, Inc.* (2009).

VINCENT CRAPANZANO is Distinguished Professor of Anthropology and Comparative Literature at City University of New York. He has done field research with the Navajo in Arizona, the spirit-possessed in Morocco, whites in South Africa, Fundamentalist Christians and legal conservatives in the United States, and now with the Harkis (the Algerians who sided with the French during Algeria's War of Independence) in France. He is the author of numerous books and articles including, *The fifth world of Forster Bennett: a portrait of a Navaho* (1972, 2002); *The Hamadsha: an essay in Moroccan ethnopsychiatry* (1973); *Tuhami: a portrait of a Moroccan* (1980); *Waiting: the whites of South Africa* (1986); *Hermes' dilemma and Hamlet's desire: on the epistemology of interpretation* (1992), *Serving the word: from the pulpit to the bench* (2000) and *Imaginative horizons: an essay in literary-philosophical anthropology* (2004). Among his interests are theories of interpretation, literary anthropology, life histories and autobiographies, phenomenology and existentialism, psychiatric anthropology, the anthropology of religion, language and literature, and ritual, symbolism and mythology.

ANDRE GINGRICH is Full Professor for Social Anthropology at the University of Vienna, and directs the Austrian Academy of Sciences' Institute for Social Anthropology (ISA). He has carried out field work in the Arab peninsula and on European neo-nationalists, was a founding member of the European Association of Social Anthropologists and since 2008, he is a panel chair at the European Research Council. His books include *One discipline, four ways* (2005, with Fredrik Barth, Robert Parkin and Sydel Silverman) and *Neo-nationalism in Europe and beyond* (2006, co-edited with Marcus Banks).

MAURICE GODELIER is Professor of Social Anthropology at the École des Hautes Études en Sciences Sociales (EHESS), Paris, France, an honorary fellow of the Royal Anthropological Institute of Great Britain and Ireland and recipient of the Prize of the French Academy. Among his books translated into English are: *Rationality and irrationality in economics* (1972), *The making of great men: male domination and power among the New Guinea Baruya*

(1986), *The mental and the material* (1986), *Big men, great men: personification of power in Melanesia* (1991, co-edited with Marilyn Strathern), *The enigma of the gift* (1998) and *In and out of the West: reconstructing anthropology* (2008).

ULF HANNERZ is Professor of Social Anthropology at Stockholm University, Sweden and a member of the Royal Swedish Academy of Sciences and the American Academy of Arts and Sciences, as well as an honorary fellow of the Royal Anthropological Institute of Great Britain and Ireland and an honorary member and former Chair of the European Association of Social Anthropologists. His research has focused on urban anthropology, media anthropology and transnational cultural processes. Most recently, he has been engaged in a study of foreign correspondents, which involved field research in four continents, and in directing an interdisciplinary research project on cosmopolitanism. Among his books are *Soulside* (1969), *Exploring the city* (1980), *Cultural complexity* (1992), *Transnational connections* (1996) and *Foreign news* (2004).

SIGNE HOWELL is Professor of Social Anthropology at the University of Oslo. She has published widely on various aspects of social organization, religion, ritual, kinship and gender. Her books include *Society and cosmos: Chewong of Peninsular Malaysia* (1984), *Chewong myths and legends; societies at peace: anthropological perspectives* (1989, co-edited with Roy Willis); *For the sake of our future: sacrificing in Eastern Indonesia* (1996), *The house in Southeast Asia* (2003, co-edited with Stephen Sparkes), *The ethnography of moralities* (1997). More recently she has undertaken research on transnational adoption which has resulted in numerous articles and in the book *The kinning of foreigners: transnational adoption in a global perspective* (2006).

HOLGER JEBENS is Senior Research Fellow at the Frobenius Institute and Managing Editor of *Paideuma*. He was Theodor-Heuss Lecturer at the New School of Social Research and has been doing fieldwork in Highland and Seaboard Papua New Guinea since 1990. His interests include the anthropology of religion, cultural perceptions of Other and Self, methodology and museology. He is editor of *Cargo, cult and culture critique* (2004) and author of *Pathways to heaven* (2005) and *After the cult* (2009).

KARL-HEINZ KOHL holds the chair of Cultural Anthropology at the Goethe University of Frankfurt am Main and is Director of the Frobenius Institute. He is also a member of the Berlin-Brandenburg Academy of Sciences and, in 2007, was elected president of the German Anthropological Association. He has done field-research in East Indonesia, Nigeria and New Guinea. Besides his monograph on East Flores Lamaholot culture, entitled *Der Tod der Reisjungfrau. Mythen und Kulte in einer ostindonesischen Lokalkultur* (1998), he is author of the influential German textbook *Ethnologie – die Wissenschaft vom kulturell Fremden* (2000, 2nd edition) and has published four other books on the epistemology of ethnographic fieldwork (*Exotik als Beruf*, 2nd edition 1986), on the history of anthropology (*Entzauberter Blick*, 2nd edition 1986; *Abwehr und Verlangen*, 1987) and on sacred objects (*Die Macht der Dinge*, 2003). He is the author of approximately ninety articles, editor-in-chief of *Paideuma* and editor of eleven anthologies, handbooks and exhibition catalogues.

ADAM JONATHAN KUPER is Professor of Social Anthropology and head of the Anthropology Department at Brunel University, United Kingdom. Awarded the Huxley Medal of the Royal Anthropological Institute, he is also a fellow of the British Academy, member of the Academia Europaea, and recipient of the Rivers Memorial Medal of the Royal Anthropological Institute. His is author of *Wives for cattles: bridewealth and marriage in South Africa* (1982), *Anthropology and anthropologists: the modern British school* (1996), *Culture: 'the anthropologists' account* (2004) and *The reinvention of primitive society* (2005).

MARK MÜNZEL is Professor Emeritus of Anthropology at Marburg University, Germany, where he served as Department Chair from 1989 to 2008. His research has focused on mythology and art of South American Lowlands Indians. He has also been actively engaged in solidarity movements of indigenous peoples and was Member of the Board and Chairman of the International Workgroup for Indigenous Affairs (Copenhagen) from 1979 to 1982. More recently he has published on ethnopoetry and ethnoscenology. Among his books are *'Schrumpfkopfmacher'?* (1977), *Die indianische Verweigerung* (1978), *Die Aché in Ostparaguay* (1983), *Neuguinea. Nutzung und Deutung der Umwelt* (1987), *Die Mythen Sehen* (1988), *Trabajo de campo y reflexión antropológica* (2004, with Manuel Gutiérrez).

PATRICIA SPYER holds the chair of Cultural Anthropology and Development Sociology of Contemporary Indonesia at Leiden University and is Global Distinguished Visiting Professor at New York University's Center for Religion & Media and the Department of Anthropology. She is the author of *The memory of trade: modernity's entanglements on an Eastern Indonesian Island* (2000), editor of *Border fetishisms: material objects in unstable spaces* (1998), and co-editor of the *Handbook of material culture* (2006). She has published, among other topics, on violence, media and photography, historical consciousness, materiality, and religion. Her current book project *Orphaned landscapes* focuses on the mediations of violence and post-violence in the aftermath of the recent religiously-inflected conflict in the Moluccas, Indonesia. A co-edited volume *Images that move* with Mary Steedly of Harvard University is forthcoming.

# INDEX

www.ingramcontent.com/pod-product-compliance
Lightning Source LLC
Chambersburg PA
CBHW050416280326
41932CB00013BA/1885